THE PESHIṬTA OF
LEVITICUS

MONOGRAPHS
OF THE PESHIṬTA INSTITUTE LEIDEN

VOLUME 6

THE PESHIṬTA OF LEVITICUS

BY

DAVID J. LANE

E.J. BRILL
LEIDEN · NEW YORK · KÖLN
1994

The paper in this book meets the guidelines for permanence and durability of the Committee on Production Guidelines for Book Longevity of the Council on Library Resources.

Library of Congress Cataloging-in-Publication Data

Lane, David J.
    The Peshitta of Leviticus / by David J. Lane.
       p.   cm. — (Monographs of the Peshitta Institute, Leiden, ISSN 0169-9008 ; v. 6)
    Includes bibliographical references and indexes.
    ISBN 9004100202 (alk. paper)
    1. Bible. O.T. Leviticus. Syriac—Versions—Peshitta.
I. Title.   II. Series.
BS1255.2.L36   1994
222'.13043—dc20   94-569
                                         CIP

Die Deutsche Bibliothek – CIP-Einheitsaufnahme

Lane, David J.:
The Peshitta of Leviticus / by David J. Lane. – Leiden ; New York ; Köln : Brill, 1994
   (Monographs of the Peshitta Institute Leiden ; Vol. 6)
   ISBN 90–04–10020–2
NE: Peshitta Institute <Leiden>: Monographs of the ...

ISSN 0169-9008
ISBN 90 04 10020 2

PRINTED IN THE NETHERLANDS

CONTENTS

PART II
PESHIṬTA AND TRADITION

PREFACE

This monograph on the Syriac of Leviticus complements the Introduction and Apparatus to be found in *The Old Testament in Syriac According to the Peshiṭta Version*, vol 1, fasc 2, Leiden 1991, and it should therefore be read in conjunction with it. Yet at the same time it is a retrospect, and so can take into account other and related discussions and articles. It is the writer's hope that the selection of evidence and the synthesis of views given here may provide a suitable combination of detail and general impression for those who would like to have information and guidance on this instance of Peshiṭta studies without being overwhelmed.

There are several bodies and individuals whose help the writer wishes to acknowledge. The Canada Council and its successor, The Social Sciences and Humanities Research Council of Canada, gave support during the years of manuscript examination and collation. The British Academy awarded a Small Personal Research Grant, which made possible work on the Versions, the printed editions and secondary material. The Cleaver Trustees assisted with grants for accommodation and travel. The Master and Fellows of Pembroke College, Oxford, elected the writer to a Visiting Fellowship for the Trinity Term 1992; the College of the Resurrection gave leave of absence to take it up. The College and the Department of Theology and Religious Studies at the University of Leeds were generous in providing funds for the acquisition of a computer and word-processor, and the Rev'd T.R. Edgar in providing instruction in the use of it. Mr G.A. Kiraz gave help in the management

of fonts. For all this generosity the writer is grateful:
without it the completion of the Leviticus edition and this
monograph would have been impossible. In the event, the
work was not only possible but congenial.

Prefatory remarks should be brief, but the writer owes
much to individuals also, whose goodwill is valued and with
whom discussion has been a pleasure. Professor J.A.
Emerton's encouragement of the writer's work on the
Peshiṭta has extended over 25 years; Dr E.W. Nicholson's
encouragement of the present project has been welcome.
Visits to the Peshiṭta Institute, on all three of its sites in
Leiden, since the late 1960's have been a much appreciated
part of academic life, providing occasions for discussions
with Dr K.D. Jenner and Drs W.M. van Vliet as well as
with successive directors from the time of Professor P.A.H.
de Boer.

But students as well as colleagues have provided insight
and information: among students mention should be made of
the Leviticus seminars in Toronto, with the (then) Messrs
Len Gang, Larry Perkins, Claude Cox, Marty McRae and
Luigi Pautasso. The writer is grateful to have had the
chance of presenting papers to colleagues in the Department
of Near Eastern Studies and the Oriental Club in Toronto; to
senior seminars in the Faculties of Theology in Manchester
and Cambridge; to the Society for Old Testament Study and
to *II Symposium Syriacum* . These papers, as well as the
published material referred to in the bibliography, provided
opportunities for discussion and the confirmation or
modification of arguments put forward. Among colleagues,
gratitude for discussion and the exchange of material is
owed to Dr A. Gelston of the University of Durham, to Dr
M.P. Weitzman of University College, London, and to Dr
G.J. Brooke of the University of Manchester. Particular
mention must be made, too, of the encouragement and

generous support given by the Superior and Brethren of the Community of the Resurrection, Mirfield, and of the positive interest and tolerance shown by colleagues and students at their College.

In conclusion, the writer's thanks are particularly due to the Peshiṭta Institute at Leiden in considering the present work for their monograph series, for the great care taken by Dr P.B. Dirksen in bringing the volume to publication, and for the generous practical assistance as well as friendship and encouragement that has been given over many years by Dr Jenner.

College of the Resurrection   D. J. LANE
Mirfield,
July 1993.

ABBREVIATIONS

In the monograph itself the titles of books and of journal articles are given in a shortened form, with the surname only of the author. Full details are given in the Bibliography on pp 177-181.

The system of abbreviations generally followed is that of *JBL* 95, 1976, pp. 331-346.

Further abbreviations follow the conventions of the Leiden Peshiṭta, see *General Peface*, Leiden 1972, pp. 22, 23. Those most frequently used are these:

absol	absolutus
add	additus/a
c.sey	cum seyame
cf	confer
emph	emphaticus
fam	familia
homoe	homoeoteleuton
impf	imperfectum
INSCR	Inscriptio
om	omittit/unt
pt	participium
ras	rasura
rep	repetivit
s.sey	sine seyame
stat	status
SUBSCR	Subscriptio
tr	transposuit/erunt
vid	ut videtur
vs.	versum
vv.	versus
txt	reading in text
mg	reading, margin
*	reading, first hand
c	corrected reading

Abbreviations which are particular to a discussion are noted in the relevant places, e.g. on p. 145 for Chapter 8.

INTRODUCTION

1. *Purpose of the monograph*

The purpose of this monograph is to complement the Introduction to the Syriac text of Leviticus in the Leiden edition of the Peshiṭta. During the period 1977-1991, while the edition was being prepared for the press and was in the process of publication, it was possible for the writer to present papers to conferences and to engage in discussion with colleagues who are familiar with Peshiṭta studies and with textual criticism. The result of these papers and discussions has been to clarify issues that the Syriac of Leviticus presents and to identify the most significant comments of others who are working, for the most part, on Peshiṭta and other versions of the Hebrew Scriptures. The present therefore seems a good time to set out these matters and to complement the Leviticus edition with the fuller discussion and greater evidence that the form of a monograph makes possible. At the outset it should be emphasised that this work is a study of Leviticus, and that conclusions reached here may not hold good for other biblical books. Similarly, conclusions reached in discussions of other books do not necessarily apply to Leviticus. Nevertheless, the following discussion offers a further contribution to Peshiṭta studies with reference to the kind of version that the Peshiṭta is, the part which the Leiden edition plays in the history of Peshiṭta text editing, and, above all, the context in which the version is best to be studied.

2. *The theses of the monograph*

The present monograph does not intend to set out the awesome detail and masterly completeness of M.D. Koster, *The Peshiṭta of Exodus*, nor yet the shrewd judgment of A. Gelston, *The Peshiṭta of the Twelve Prophets*. It comes as a more modest companion piece to the present writer's text and introduction to the Leiden Leviticus in order to establish three arguments. First, that the Peshiṭta should be understood as a version, namely the rendering into another (albeit related) language with all the possibilities and impossibilities which the task entails. Secondly, that the Leiden edition, in common with all editions of texts which, after all, have a life and a history of their own, is a compromise between an ideal and the attainable: the judgments, indeed the prejudices, of an editor are as important as the available material. Thirdly, that the importance of the Peshiṭta lies less with textual criticism and more with church history and the use of the text as scripture: popular religion, liturgy and homiletics influenced both translators and scribes in such a way as to shape the version's character and also its transmission.

These three theses have important corollaries. The thesis that the Peshiṭta is to be regarded as a version, dependent upon conventions of translation, makes the discussions of its origins, authorship and purpose as complex as those concerning its transmission and later characteristics. To the debate on *Vorlage* there must be added a debate on canons of translation and the possibility of unconscious as well as conscious influence on those responsible for the Peshiṭta version at the outset. A translation is possessed of a life of its own: it has an inner drive, set by its basic work and purpose, so that the inherent characteristics of the rendering shape the patterns found in its later transmission.

In the second place, the thesis that the Leiden edition, like its fellow printed editions, is the result of compromise raises questions as to the purpose and presuppositions of editions and their users. To these questions must be added others concerning the chance and hazard which guided those who became editors of editions, and determined which manuscripts came to their hands. In the third place, there is the thesis that the Peshiṭta is to be regarded as a matter of church history and so of church authority. In this view the version's importance lies in the context of that self-definition of Syriac Christianity which came through the canon and exegesis of scripture, as well as through canon law; in liturgy and homiletic; through monasticism, and in historiography.

This process of self-definition, conscious or unconscious, is that of a church which lies to the east of Antioch, and which came to be as ambivalent towards Byzantium and Islam as it had been towards the Roman and the Sassanian empires. Although this church is pre-Chalcedonian in theology, it is not by virtue of that homogeneous. Its pre-Chalcedonian outlook finds more than one corporate expression, most typically in those corporate expressions which later controversialists named Nestorianism and monophysitism. So church history and church text reflect each other, in that they each have resemblances, divergences and invite judgments of authenticity.

That is not to say that doctrinal differences can be detected in the manuscripts; it is simply that the manuscripts show differences which come as much by reason of the differences of geography and culture between their places of writing, usually monastic, as by deliberate theological intent. It must not be overlooked that the Syriac world fell partly under Sassanian, and partly under Roman (Byzantine) control. This approach to the Peshiṭta of Leviticus brings together the frequently separated disciplines of text criticism and church history, and so goes beyond the appropriate, even if generous, confines of the Introduction to the Leiden edition in the course of developing some of the approaches made or referred to there. This synthesis of textual criticism, translation criticism and church history is the contribution of this monograph to Peshiṭta studies.

3. *Method of the monograph*

It remains now to indicate the method of the study. The monograph is in two parts, the first concerned with 7a1 and the manuscripts of Leviticus, and the second with more general matters of Peshiṭta and tradition. Part I, Chapters 1-4, is based on 7a1, with four discussions arising out of its readings and the use made of them in the Leiden edition. The first (Chapter 1) describes the character of 7a1 and its place among manuscripts older and younger than itself. The second discussion (Chapter 2) re-examines the 119 readings of 7a1 which the Leiden Leviticus has altered, discriminating between demonstrable errors and those which indicate difference of text tradition or handling The third discussion (Chapter 3) concentrates on readings from text traditions which can be identified in manuscripts earlier or later than 7a1, in order to suggest those readings which might be considered preferable, or "more authentically" Peshiṭta. The fourth discussion (Chapter 4) looks at manuscripts which give evidence of text traditions older than that of 7a1, and questions what such a phrase as "closer to the Hebrew" might mean.

Part II contains the rest of the monograph, addressing the nature of the Peshiṭta as a version: its origin, its guise in the printed editions, and its setting in early church life. Chapters 5 and 6 ask three questions concerning the Peshiṭta of

Leviticus and its presumed exemplar, with an emphasis on the problems and possibilities facing the translator moving from a Hebrew base to a desired Syriac. Chapter 5 is a general discussion of the *Vorlage* which may be presumed, the literary *genre* into which the Syriac translation may be placed, and the context of translation. Chapter 6 gives evidence of the exegesis and translation which suggest this context, showing a concern with syntax as well as lexicography. This approach differs from the atomistic approach traditionally appropriate to text criticism.

Chapters 7 and 8 set the Leiden Peshiṭta, as represented by Leviticus, in the context of other printed editions, showing the consequences which come from the cumulative effect of editorial judgments made necessarily *ad hoc*. Chapter 7 discusses the methods and purposes of the editors; Chapter 8 tabulates their differences from the Leiden edition. Chapter 9 asks questions about the Peshiṭta as an authoritative text, and the circumstances of its acceptance or promotion as such. Hence, at the end, the context for Peshiṭta studies is shown to be church history, or rather church life. A particular form of the Syriac Peshiṭta version was chosen on grounds of convenience, or even sentiment, rather than for textual excellence. Text and version lie within the boundaries of tradition, however much they may themselves determine those boundaries.

PART ONE

7a1 AND THE MANUSCRIPTS

CHAPTER ONE

7a1: A MEDIAN TEXT

Typologically as well as chronologically 7a1 stands between the manuscripts which are older and younger than itself. It reflects a stage of development in the Peshiṭta tradition from which conclusions may be drawn as to the kind of version it is, and so alerts to the danger of considering it only as a bare reproduction of MT.

1. *7a1: the basis of the Leiden edition*

7a1 (Milan, Ambrosian Library, B.21 Inf.) has been taken as the basis of the Leiden edition of the Peshiṭta. In retrospect there is no good ground to regret this decision: the manuscript is relatively free of errors and is a good representative of a particular kind of text tradition. Because this manuscript has the importance which comes from its being selected as the basis of the Leiden edition, it is given a large place in the discussions which follow. This is, inevitably, at the expense of its near-contemporary 8a1, with which it has much in common as the Introduction to the Leviticus edition shows. The evidence set out in Chapters 3 and 4 shows that, typologically as well as chronologically, as far as Leviticus is concerned 7a1 stands mid-way between the oldest of the known surviving manuscripts of the sixth century and the later, "normative", manuscripts of the ninth, tenth and later centuries. Much of what is at stake in the choice of this manuscript appeared at the outset of the undertaking. The 1966 General Preface to the Sample Edition of the Leiden Peshiṭta stated (pp. v,vi) the goal of

the enterprise, recognising that "In our opinion the time has
not yet come to produce a reconstruction of the 'original'
Peshiṭta Old Testament", and so   proposed to present
evidence from "a more or less representative array of
manuscripts as will illustrate the tradition of the Peshiṭta
text".   At the outset of the undertaking it was rightly
understood that questions of originality and transmission
should be distinguished: hence the evidence of manuscripts
was set out without attempts to reconstruct what lay behind
them.

For practical reasons 7a1, the Ambrosian manuscript, was
taken as the basis of the edition: serendipity brings other and
important advantages.   The practical reasons for its choice
are that it is the oldest complete manuscript of the Syriac
Peshiṭta Old Testament; it is in a good state of preservation;
is easily legible; has only the *lacunae* Num 3:23-5:10; I Chr
12:18-17:25; 2 Chr 13:11-20:3; needs supplementing only for
Canticles or Odes, Prayer of Manasseh, Apocryphal Psalms,
Psalms of Solomon, Tobit, and 1(3) Esra, where other
manuscripts have had to be established as the basis of
collation; and has the advantage of being available in
Ceriani's photo-lithographic edition.   In the case of Leviticus,
serendipity has provided a manuscript, which, because of its
character - that is, its omissions and additions, its lexical and
syntactic changes - makes it possible to see the kind of
adaptations which took place in the text tradition between
the sixth and tenth centuries. Yet despite the soundness of
reasons in its favour, two objections have been raised against
the use of 7a1: one concerning method in editorial policy,
the other concerning the manuscript's reliability.

2. *Objections to the choice of 7a1*

In the first place, concerning method, it was   argued in
discussions about the choice of 7a1 that a single manuscript

cannot properly be the basis for any edition, even if the
problem of choice between a "diplomatic" rather than a
"critical" edition were not resolved. In fact the approach of
the edition has changed over the years, and a policy of
minimal change to 7a1 has been changed to one of greater
flexibility in that more scope is allowed to the editors of the
fascicles. (See the present writer's remarks in the
Introductions to Wisdom and Qoheleth in vol. II,5).
Successive fascicles of the Leiden edition have therefore
increased the number of allowable alterations to 7a1, as
these came to be based on the reading of a majority of
ancient manuscripts rather than the elimination of *prima
facie* scribal errors, thus determining the text to be printed.
A comparison of the rules in the General Preface of 1972,
the revised (duplicated, not printed) rules of 1975, and those
of the Introductions to Genesis and Exodus (1977) and
Leviticus (1991) show this movement away from a rigorous
to a more flexible approach. As a result, in the later fascicles
7a1 is revised much more frequently than a bare alteration
of clear errors would warrant.

Two questions need to be addressed at this stage. The first
one concerns the choice of one manuscript as a base; the
second concerns the nature of the manuscript chosen. As
has been suggested above, the first question turns on the
nature of the edition, whether it should be "diplomatic" or
"critical". If the edition is "diplomatic", then it is be a
reproduction of one manuscript, with the simple noting of
variants and the minimum of editorial work. The object is
to present evidence leaving the assessment of its evidence to
others, even though some minimal guidance be given. A
"critical" edition, however, is concerned with an assessment
of readings for "originality". A concern to use the Peshiṭta
in Old Testament criticism fuelled a desire to have the
"original" Peshiṭta, but not even the production of such a

"critical" edition could result in any more than a hypothetical "original". It could only be the cumulative result of calculating whatever "original" reading was presumed to underly each variant.

The editorial policy turned out, in the event, to be a compromise, in that one manuscript was chosen as the basis of collation, but flexibility in emendation was permitted. The present writer considers that the basic choice of one manuscript clearly set out with minimal change is sound. There is too little early manuscript evidence for a reconstruction of an "original" to be possible, other than as a subjective hypothesis on the lines suggested above.

The second question can now be faced: that even if it is acceptable that one manuscript be chosen as the base for the edition, 7a1 is unsuitable to be that manuscript. This can be answered in two ways. The first is that, practically, the nature of 7a1 makes for a conveniently small critical apparatus: it lies mid-way (chronologically and typologically) in the middle of the traditions of the Peshiṭta text. That it can be emended on the general principle of the majority reading of pre-tenth-century manuscripts demonstrates how it has much in common with manuscripts earlier than itself and later than itself.   From this it is clear that its character shows both the kind of text from which it came, and also the kind of text by which it was supplanted.   7a1 is a middle term in that it has links with the older manuscripts 6b1 and 6k2, but anticipates the basis of *Textus Receptus* or the readings of the later, the majority of, manuscripts. For this reason it is here described as a median text, after the term used to describe the strip down the centre of a motorway. The median acts as a marker between the two carriageways, yet is an element common to them both: separating yet joining. 7a1 is a marker of this kind in the Peshiṭta text tradition, having elements in common with the manuscripts

older and younger than itself, and a resemblance to its near
contemporaries 8a1* and 8b1. Little is said of these two
manuscripts, as the focus of the present discussion is on 7a1,
but see below, pp. 6, 14, 37, for comments on 8a1. It is
regrettable that Leviticus is not represented in manuscripts
earlier than the sixth century.

But in spite of that lack 7a1 may be regarded as a useful
waymark in the history of the transmission of the Peshiṭta,
as well as being typologically as well as chronologically a
middle term. The discussion of emendations which the next
chapter provides makes this clear. 7a1 lacks words which
are found in earlier manuscripts, and provides words which
later manuscripts take up; there are interpolations in later
manuscripts which are not to be found in 7a1, and there are
expansions in 7a1 which are either taken up by few or by
the majority of younger manuscripts. Comparisons between
all the manuscripts provide evidence of additions and
omissions. It is useful to recognise that a manuscript may
seem to show an omission, whereas in fact it is the case that
an addition has been made to other manuscripts, but not to
it. This seeming omission is here, in a phrase borrowed from
New Testament criticism, termed a non-interpolation.

One thing in particular makes 7a1 stand out from the
manuscripts younger than itself: the homogeneity of those
which are of the ninth century and later, particularly of the
tenth century and later. In Leviticus this is clear, as the
Introduction to the edition demonstrates, because only
12a1*fam* can be clearly isolated from the younger
manuscripts. The remainder have much in common, and
divergences are individual or in small and irregular groups
of manuscripts. It is hard to avoid the conclusion that the
basic pattern of those manuscripts which survive had been
arrived at during or just before the tenth century. This
concurs with the position of Gelston, who uses the term

"standard text", *Twelve Prophets*, p. 65, meaning "the homogeneous tradition of all but the oldest Mss". Of this tradition he says on p. 87 "One of the puzzling features of the transmission of the Peshiṭta is the almost universal diffusion of the standard text from about the ninth century". So it is convenient that 7a1 is used as a basis for collation. It anticipates but does not identify completely with the majority of manuscripts which come after, and does not (at any rate in Leviticus) depart greatly from earlier manuscripts. It does not have a dependent textual tradition, and of near contemporaries only 8a1* shows clear affinities; nor is its ancestry clearly demonstrated among the surviving older manuscripts. It is its position between the earlier and the later and its possession of characteristics of them both which justify its choice as the basis of the edition and which result in a conveniently small apparatus.

The second objection to the use of 7a1, namely the possibility of its being a poor and unreliable text, must now be faced. It can be, and indeed has been, argued that 7a1 is a bad representative of its kind. This judgment had its roots in Cornill's comment in his *Das Buch des Propheten Ezechiel*, p. 145. It was brutal and memorable:

> Unter allen zugänglichen Textesgestalten S's ist (7a1) die schlechteste: sie steht an Werth sogar noch tief unter (Lee), und von diesem Gesichtspunkte aus ist das auf die Herausgabe von (7a1) verwendete Geld zum Fenster hinausgeworfen.

But it must be noted that Cornill, writing on Ezekiel only, was contrasting 7a1 with the printed editions of Le Jay, Lee, and Urmia. These present not only a text of a different character but a text which is the result of accident as much as critical scholarship. To a greater or less extent they presented an ideal rather than an actual text. In fact, as will be seen, the wrong conclusions were drawn. 7a1 is not worthless, and stands well: both in comparison with the printed editions and with their underlying text tradition. But there is an important pre-supposition which underlies Cornill's comment. His judgment was based on the assumption that 7a1 was adapted to the MT, and the comparison of these two seemed proof enough that it had indeed been adapted to MT. Rahlfs took issue with Cornill, in his article "Beiträge zur Textkritik der Peschita". Cornill subsequently changed his position, to the relief of J. Pinkerton, "The Origin and the Early History of the Syriac Pentateuch". Pinkerton's conclusion, p. 17, based on the Pentateuch, and especially on Genesis and Exodus, was that 7a1 "not seldom presents a good reading when most other manuscripts have gone astray". Barnes, in *Chronicles* pp. ix, x, xxii, xxiii, comments on the matter, noting that 7a1 could be judged on its own merits and need not be suspected of adaptation to MT. Mulder, writing on Ezekiel in the memorial volume to Diez Macho, similarly opposes the conclusions of Cornill for that book. Certainly Leviticus gives no proof of 7a1's having been adapted to MT; Cornill's theory can be firmly laid to rest and 7a1 regarded as Pinkerton regarded it. But for all that, it must be recognised that 7a1 belongs to a manuscript tradition, and that both it and its companions within that tradition may err, and have erred. It cannot be left entirely without emendation as the basis for any kind of edition.

To conclude, the choice of 7a1 is not one to regret, either from the viewpoint of editorial method, or from the inherent nature of the manuscript itself. It provides a median, in comparison with which the manuscripts older and later than itself can be assessed. As evidence given in Chapters 2 and 3 shows, findings for Leviticus concur with those set out by Koster, notably in his Leiden Symposium contribution, p. 126, where he compares the development of the Peshiṭta to

the growth of an egg which hatches and ultimately produces
"a well-feathered hen". 7a1 is within this pattern of growth.
But it is worth repeating here the comment made by De
Boer, looking back over the publication of some of the
major volumes of the Peshiṭta prepared while he was editor-
in-chief.   It was given in a lecture in Cambridge,
subsequently published as "Towards an Edition of the Syriac
Version of the Old Testament". He regretted the power of
the printed word, in that any text printed had a spurious
authority. To his mind, in any critical edition the apparatus
was more important than the text. Indeed he reported, p.
356, his "habit of reading the notes first, and then moving
from them to look at the text . . . ". It is thus important to
remember that while 7a1 is the basis of the text printed, the
text printed must not be taken to have an absolute value.
That the edition is a compromise makes it most important
that the apparatus be given great consideration

3. *Context and co-text*

But remarks concerning 7a1 must be set within the context
of three discussions. The first discussion is quite clearly that
of the manuscript itself, its errors and its characteristics. The
second discussion is that of its antecedent manuscript
tradition; the third discussion is that of its successors, or
indeed supplanters, in the text tradition which came to
displace it. As was suggested above, the tone of the
discussion, and indeed the terms of the discussion have
already been set out by Koster in his work on Exodus and
by Gelston in his study of the Twelve Prophets. 7a1 is found
in the company of the sixth-century manuscripts, and is
accompanied, sometimes by very few, sometimes by nearly
all, the later manuscripts of the *Textus Receptus* (Koster) or
standard text (Gelston). Hence to describe the manuscript as
a median text does not foreclose any debate on its role as

medium of transmission (which cannot be proved) or suggest that it is an average between two or even more distinguishable groups (in Leviticus it is not). Koster, in Exodus, had the advantage of 5b1 to set against his groupings of the ancient manuscripts of the seventh and eighth centuries and of the younger manuscripts of the ninth century and later. In Leviticus, where 5b1 is not available, only 6b1 (and the remarkably similar, even if later produced, 9a1 where extant) can be set against the groups of the ancient manuscripts of the seventh and eighth centuries and the younger ones as a third identifiable type of text.

The identification in Leviticus of these three groups (6b1*etc,* 7a1*etc,* 9b1*etc*) of manuscript tradition, noted here for their dissimilarity rather more than for their basic underlying similarity, raises the question of textual provenance. In fact the question of provenance is a double question: there is the provenance of the Peshiṭta version as a distinct entity, and the provenance of the characteristic differences between the three groups of manuscripts. Inevitably, given the traditional role of Peshiṭta in text critical studies, "closeness to the Massoretic text" becomes a criterion, whether to discriminate between manuscripts or to relate them to an "original" Peshiṭta There is no need to rehearse here the history of Peshiṭta studies: De Boer's article referred to above gives a brief summary, a magisterial account is to be found in Dirksen's "The Old Testament Peshiṭta". All that need be said here is that this debate is over the question as to whether closeness to the MT is the result of later adaptation or represents an authentic early stage in the development of the text of the Peshiṭta.

The present writer disagrees with the former view and supports the latter: the findings in Leviticus resemble those of Koster for Exodus and of Gelston for the Twelve

Prophets. Koster noted three groups of manuscripts and marked their differences, commenting that there was a continuous development in which three stages could be distinguished, namely 5b1; the remaining ancient manuscripts of the seventh and eighth centuries; and the later manuscripts. He had just earlier noted that 5b1 did not represent a deliberate revision according to the Massoretic text, but a genuinely older stage of the Peshiṭta (*Exodus*, p. 528). Gelston summarises much similar discussion in his comment in *Twelve Prophets*, p. 87:

> It is reasonable to conclude that in general terms the oldest Mss preserve a text closer to the original Peshiṭta than the standard text, and that the text of the oldest Mss is closer to the Hebrew than the standard text.

It must be noted that there follows a warning that this is a general conclusion which requires a close study of each instance. Brock's warning in "Text History and Text Division in P-Isaiah", pp. 58, 59, must also be heeded in this matter of taking closeness to the Hebrew as a criterion of originality:

> Clearly it would be foolhardy to propose a blanket rule that the original reading will always be the one closest to the Hebrew, for there are many other considerations whch we need to take into account.

4. *Median text and MT*

This monograph contends that indeed 7a1 may be taken as a median between older and younger manuscripts, related both to those older than itself and to those younger than itself. But such a term as "closeness to the Hebrew" is a term, indeed a judgment, which needs very careful consideration

indeed. Later discussion of this phrase will cite Brock's
arguments and then arguments of others on translation
purpose and method with just this in mind. Indeed, on p. 61
of the article just quoted, Brock warns that formal
agreement between a manuscript reading and Hebrew may
mislead, and gives six points which need consideration if
formal agreement is to be understood as fact rather than
fortuitous resemblance. The warnings are a valuable
reminder that a hasty use of the term "closeness to the
Hebrew" may owe much to unexamined presuppositions and
familiarity with Hebrew text criticism, statistical method and
taxonomy. This is hardly surprising, as much worthwhile
study has, quite appropriately, concentrated on the
transmission of the text, and has therefore debated the
reliability of individual manuscripts as witness to a text
tradition. This has been the first stage in assessing the
Peshiṭta as a derivative to be set against a presumed
Massoretic *Vorlage.* Albrektson's *Lamentations* is a model
of this approach.

Not surprisingly, attention in such discussions has been
focussed on those details of the text which Koster noted on
pp. 2, 3 of *Exodus* as being significant: the major differences
of transposition, omission, addition and alteration; and the
minor differences of preposition, particle or *waw*, endings of
verb or noun, final *waw* on verbs, pointing of nouns and
verbs or punctuation, *seyame* and orthography. The result
of these studies, for example Dirksen's *The Transmission of
the Text in the Peshiṭta Manuscripts of the Book of Judges,*
is of great value: it has indicated not only the relationships
between manuscripts and the establishment of stemmas, but
also the possibility of allowing for syntactic divergences to
be identified and editorial activity detected. Dirksen noted
on p. 69 that a study of 17a8 showed that Sergius Risius,
Maronite Archbishop of Damascus, had put a lot of editorial

work into his copying, adding an extensive record of variants. A development of this suggestion was made by Gelston on the basis of his work on the Twelve Prophets, where on pp. 37,38 he observed that in some cases the construction of manuscripts (e.g. 17a6-9) is the result of text critical work. All these manuscripts are the work of Sergius Risius, whose work as a text critic is thus given due recognition

With a view to demonstrating that in Leviticus the three groups of manuscripts may usefully be identified and their readings assessed, the Leiden edition's emended readings of 7a1 will be discussed in more detail than the Introduction to Leviticus permitted. The resemblances between 7a1 and its near-contemporaries, antecedents and successors can thus be set out the more clearly.

The first series of remarks touches on the 119 places where 7a1 has been emended in accordance with the rules of the edition given in the Preface to the Genesis and Exodus volume, p. viii: "The printed text . . . is chosen on the basis of a definite majority of the manuscripts dated to the tenth century or earlier". This has the advantage of presenting 7a1 as a representative text of those centuries, but, as the remarks which follow suggest, the emendations result in the manuscript being pulled in two different directions at the same time: towards the later, standard, text, and towards the older manuscripts. The printed text therefore is an artificial one, almost an average text inclining to where the majority readings indicate. It is the more important, therefore, to bear in mind the warning about any printed text which De Boer made in the Cambridge lecture previously quoted.

CHAPTER TWO

119 EMENDED READINGS

A re-appraisal of the edition's alterations to the text of 7a1
shows that apparently insignificant differences demonstrate
varieties of interpretation as well as errors in transcription.
What an underlying Hebrew text is thought to mean, rather
than merely what it was seen to say, may be at stake.

1. A re-appraisal

It is necessary to re-appraise the changes made to the text of
7a1 in order to establish the cumulative consequences as
well as the immediate significance of the alterations made.
This chapter on the Ambrosian manuscript considers some of
the reasons why its text gives the readings that it does, and
so prepares the way for Chapter 6 which discusses the
Peshiṭta of Leviticus as translation. The Leviticus edition
noted, p. xv, that of the 119 changes made to the text of 7a1,
only 25 were to be considered corrections of error. When
that number of errors is compared with those listed on pp.
xii-xxi it is easier to gauge the care and accuracy of 7a1 as a
manuscript. There are 21 in 6b1 (which lacks 1:1-3:6); 19
(other than concerning *seyame*) in 8b1 and 19 in 9a1 (which
begins only with 15:16). The comparison with 8a1 is more
difficult. There are (at least) 40 corrections made before the
work of the two or more pre-sixteenth-century correctors of
8a1; but the use of the term in 8a1 does not necessarily
signify that the original reading was an error, simply that
another reading was preferred.

Comparisons between 7a1 and printed editions, such as
that made by Cornill and quoted in Chapter 1, must be
treated with caution: the printed editions are based, as will
be shown in Chapters 7 and 8, on careful if unacknowledged
editing; there may also be a presupposition on the part of the
critic (as of Cornill) which leads to faulty judgment.
Howbeit, there is an exemplary level of care shown in the
copying of manuscripts of the standard or later text, many of
which come from the Mosul area and some of which are in
the Claude James Rich collection in the British Library. For
example, there are only two errors in 9b1, and eight
(including four concerning *seyame*) in 10b1. This accuracy
may be confirmatory evidence that the later text, closely
associated with the Mosul region, is comparatively lately
established but considered normative, and quite possibly
definitive.

The 25 readings considered errors and noted on p. xv of
the Leviticus edition are set out below. The note (a)
indicates that the reading appears in the list on p. xiv of
emendations of readings which possibly result from
assimilation. The lemma shows the Leiden text, and the
variant is the reading of 7a1.

2:1	ܐܚܣܡܘ.ܕ] ܐܚܣܡܘ
2:2$_{20}$	ܠܚܢܕ.ܪܚ.ܠ ܠܕ] ܠܚܢܕ.ܪܚ (a) 8b1+
5:22	ܠܕ] add ܠܒ (a)
8:8	ܘܗܡܣ - ܦܪܚܡ.] *om*
8:14	ܠܘܘܪ] add ܐܣܒܪ (a)
8:20	ܪܒܐ] *c. sey* (a)
10:4	ܠܡ] *om*
10:6	ܕ:ܐܘܩܪ.ܕ] ܐܘܩܪܐ.ܘ (a)
11:2	ܐܪܡܒܐ] ܘܐܪܡܒܐ (a)
11:42	ܠܚܕ] ܚܠܚ
13:56	ܐܘܩ.ܕ] ܐܘܩܦܒ

14:26	ܡܢܝܪܐ] ܡܢܝܪ
14:42	ܟܘܪܟ 2[0] s. sey
16:13	ܡܘܡܟܬܐ] ܡܘܡܟܬܗ
16:20	ܟܢܐܩ] c. sey
17:8[10]	ܬܟܒ] pr dalath
17:14	.ܐܡ 2[0]----------- ܐܬܟܐ] om homoe
20:26	ܒ] ܬܟܒ
21:22[20]	ܠܐܒܟ] pr ܐ (a)
23:15	ܒܠܬܠܐ] s. sey
24:14	ܐܡܢܬܟ] s. sey
25:31	ܟܐܩ - - ܟܠܐ] ܟܐܩ ܐܡܠ ܐܬܘܐ
26:46	ܡܩܝܒ] c. sey
27:3	ܠܐܬ ---------- ܐܐܡܠ] rep
27:9	ܬܝܒ]add ܟܒܐܩ

The re-appraisal of these altered readings of 7a1 is instructive, not least because it shows that it is important to make a distinction between the terms "emendation" and "alteration". One may indeed speak of emending the text, but to do so may mislead if it is taken that the text which is changed is always an error. In the first place it is the general principle of following the majority of the pre-tenth-century manuscripts which governs the alteration of 7a1. In the second place it is not always easy to distinguish an error from a variant which may be an admissible reading. Some readings are obviously erroneous: the major mechanical features of addition or omissions *per homoeoteleuton* or *homoeoarcton*, or by dittography or haplography are familiar. Yet in other instances there can be doubt. The rule of thumb method is to consider as error any reading that does not make sense, or to suspect as error a reading which does not have the support of a clear majority of pre-tenth-century manuscripts. But subjectivity comes in at this point.

There are readings which to a scribe and a reader do make sense: what appears to be an error, in that it is a minority (or even a unique) reading, may not be an error. Either the majority or the minority reading may be the result of unintentional or intentional clarification of sense, or be a simple matter of preference. Where the majority and minority reading are equally acceptable it may be impossible to establish the priority of reading. The cumulative effect of such changes is a development in the text. This was suggested in Chapter 1 and will be taken up in more detail in Chapters 4 and 5.

It is, therefore, a subjective judgment by an editor first as to whether a reading is an error, and secondly as to whether the reading comes from the scribe of the manuscript under review, or has its origin in a preceding manuscript or stage of the tradition. On p. 143 of his article "The Ancient Peshiṭta MSS of Judges and their Variant Readings" Dirksen reminds text critics that readings which are now peculiar to a manuscript may have been shared with other manuscripts, now lost. The present writer considers that another warning is necessary: Syriac is such that it is easy to miss the exact location of the error. What seems to be a minor error of one letter may be the more substantial one of a clause or phrase. The difference of a single *waw* or *dalath* may signify a different construction, and therefore be a difference of a whole clause. The editor of a text, who has access to a number of manuscripts, can have some check on assessing a reading, and may conclude how the reading came to be what it is. Yet considerations of what a reading should be are, inevitably, subjective. The hazards and complexities suggested in the preceding paragraphs are illustrated by the readings listed on pp. xiv, xv of the Leviticus Introduction and are discussed in the following paragraphs.

2. *Errors by assimilation*

The 36 readings mentioned on p. xiv as being possibly errors by assimilation have been re-appraised. Some of these 36 are included in the list of 25 errors listed on p. xv which was referred to above. Those which are listed there as being an *error* are marked (e) in the list below. Further comment than the length of the Introduction affords is needed, and therefore follows. It will be seen that some readings are now taken to be evidence of an interpretative choice, conscious or unconscious, rather than simple conformity to a nearby phrase.

1:2 ܡܢ] *pr waw*: the scribe had failed to note that ܒܥܝܪܐ was a generic term and that ܬܘܪܐ and ܥܢܐ were specific terms. So the writing of ܘܡܢ before ܬܘܪܐ made the list, wrongly, one of specific terms, "beasts and oxen and sheep".

1:9 ܢܩܪܒ] ܢܩܪܒܘܢ: the scribe wrote the plural ܢܩܪܒܘܢ instead of the singular, not noticing that the word was governed by the following noun ܟܗܢܐ rather than the preceding plural ܟܗ̈ܢܐ in vs. 8.

1:17 ܢܝܚܘܬܐ] ܢܝܚܐ : the emendation of 7a1's ܢܝܚܐ to the majority reading ܢܝܚܘܬܐ here and in 2:2$_3$o,9,12(+8b1); 3:5$_2$o,16(+6b1 8a1*(*vid*)); 23:13(+6b1),18$_2$o(+6b1) is evidence that the taking of a majority view may mislead (see below in the chapter on 6b1 and 9a1, pp. 73-5). The word ܢܝܚܘܬܐ also appears in 4:31; 6:14; 8:21,28; 17:6$_2$o and ܕܢܝܚܘܬܟܘܢ in 26:31. In these verses all the recorded manuscripts agree, except for 6b1 which reads ܒܣܡܐ (ܒܣܡܟܘܢ); some later manuscripts concur with 7a1's ܢܝܚܐ in 2:2. A text which illustrates the discussion is Gen 8:21, where the Peshiṭta manuscripts give a double translation: ܪܝܚܐ ܕܢܝܚܘܬܐ ܪܝܚܐ ܕܒܣܡܐ as the equivalent of MT ריח הניחח , except for 5b1 which gives only ܪܝܚܐ ܕܒܣܡܐ . In the previous verse 5b1 provides further evidence of its methodology, for it translates MT בהמה by Syriac ܒܥܝܪܐ rather than ܚܝܘܬܐ ,

keeping a generic term as equivalent for a generic term. All
recorded manuscripts give ܢܝܚܐ ܚܪܝܫ at Exod 29:18, 25, 41
as they do at Lev 6:8. At Lev 1:13 only 8b1 and some later
manuscripts give ܣܘܬܗܐ against the majority ܢܝܚܐ,
although all have ܣܘܬܗܐ ܚܪܝܫ at 1:9

Certainly the majority preference for an equivalent to the
Hebrew ניחח is Syriac ܣܘܬܗܐ, but the evidence of 5b1, 6b1,
and 7a1 suggests that ܢܝܚܐ was preferred, at least to start
with, as a formal equivalent, being cognate or indeed a
virtual transliteration. Then ܣܘܬܗܐ was accepted as a
doublet, a gloss, or a straight alternative. Rashi, at Exod
29:25 cites *Sifra* and comments ". . . as gratification of spirit
to Him who gave the command and found that his will was
carried out", in order to show that ניחח expresses divine
satisfaction, not at the sacrifice, but at the obedience shown
in thus responding to a command that had been given.
Perhaps ܣܘܬܗܐ as an alternative expressed that nuance, or
was preferred as a dynamic equivalent. LXX ὀσμὴ εὐωδίας
seems to have the same intention as the Syriac.
Interestingly, Payne Smith's *Thesaurus* cites, but rejects, the
suggestion that the root of the word ܣܘܬܗܐ is ܣܘܐ to
desire, rather than a root indicating something burning,
whether flesh or incense. 7a1, therefore, seems to stand at a
watershed where a dynamic rendering supersedes a formal
one.

2:2₂₀ (e) ܕܝܠ] *om dalath*: 7a1 is formally equivalent to MT
and also has the support of 8b1 and 10b2 for the reading ܝܠ
instead of ܕܝܠ . Rashi, citing *Sifra,* claims that the
frankincense is to the right hand side of the offering of fine
flour. ܝܠ here has the sense of "in addition to", and is the
correct reading. See also below, p. 25.

2:5 ܗܘܐ] ܘܬܬܐܦܐ: 8b1 reads ܬܬܐܦܐ against the majority
reading ܬܗܘܐ , which last agrees formally with the
imperfect found in MT. ܘܬܬܐܦܐ continues the sense begun

earlier in vs. 4, whereas 8b1 derives its verb from what is to follow, ܬܚܫܒ in vs. 7.

3:10 ܚܒܝܪܬܗ ,ܚܒܝܪܬܐ] : here 7a1, instead of relating the verb to the antecedent ܥܠܬܐ of vv. 6,9, has referred it, under the influence of the series of verbs in vv. 10 and 11 which have a similar ending, to ܩܘܪܒܢܐ . See 4:9 for a similar instance.

5:22(e) ܠܗ] *add* ܠܗ : this is a mistaken anticipation of the ܠܗ which comes three words later.

6:16 ܢܗܘܐ] ܬܬܘܩܕ : 7a1 may be mistakenly repeating the last word ܬܬܘܩܕ of vs. 15, or reproducing a correct understanding that every free-will offering of a priest is to be made entirely to God, and that nothing therefore can remain to be eaten. Rashi discusses the passage with reference to *Sifra*, ". . . every free-will meal offering of a priest . . . shall be wholly burnt".

8:14(e) and 20(e): see the preceding list.

9:20 ܠܡܕܒܚܐ] ܥܠ ܡܕܒܚܐ (+6k2): this is an interesting case of equivalents. The verse is to be taken with 1:15 (+8b1 12b1); 2:2 (+8b1 9l2),9 (+8b1); 6:8 (+6b1 8a1*); 16:25 (+8a1 9a1). The problem is that 1:15 makes it clear that ܠܡܕܒܚܐ usually translates the Hebrew אל המזבח , and that ܥܠ ܡܕܒܚܐ usually translates מזבחה . Hence the preposition ܥܠ usually indicates the presence of MT *he locale*. (MT 6:8 המזבח is an adverbial accusative, Samaritan Pentateuch giving there a locative). At 1:15 8b1 and 12b1 have repeated, wrongly, the ܠܡܕܒܚܐ of the first part of the verse, where *lamadh* = אל = to. The other manuscripts, rightly, anticipate the end of the action with the locative, "on the altar". At 2:2₀(e) 7a1 and 8b1 and 9l2 prefer *lamadh*, while the others, rightly, opt for the preposition ܥܠ ; at 6:8 6b1 and 8a1*, wrongly, prefer *lamadh* where there should be an equivalent for the locative (or adverbial accusative); at 9:20 *per contra* 6k2 and 7a1, rightly, go against the majority which prefer *lamadh*; at 16:25 8a1 and 9a1, rightly, go against the majority preference for the *lamadh*. In Syriac the *aph'el* of ܣܠܩ is the equivalent of MT הקטיר ; but the Syriac then has an ambiguity, since it can mean either "take up to" or "make an offering of". Hence the confusion.

10:6(e): see the preceding list.

10:15$_{10}$ ܘܕܬܝܪ] ܐܕܬܝܪ : this looks like a very common error, *waw pro dalath*. But there may be a matter of interpretation, namely reconciling 7:30 with this verse, to determine what it is that lies on top of what at different points of the handling of the wave offering. Rashi's comment on 10:15 reads: ". . . from this we learn that the fat portions were beneath the others at the time of the waving", and on 7:30 "the owner's hands are above . . . the priests' hands beneath".

10:15$_{20}$ ܒܗܪܝ] *add* ܕܐܡܗܪ ܘܒܢܘܗܝ, ܥܠܘܗܝ : in the MT this phrase occurs at the end of 8:31, but neither here nor at 10:18. 6k2[1] and 8a1* (*vid*) agree with 7a1 in putting the phrase here; 6b1 alone omits it from 8:31. Possibly these ancient texts sought consistency with the insertion, though a *verbatim* rendering would not insert it, and thus give the appearance of omitting it. See below, pp. 29, 31.

11:2   ܘܐܡܪܝ] ܘܐܡܪܝ (e) (+9b1 11b1): this is a singular/plural confusion. The subject is either "Moses and Aaron" together, or only the latter as spokesman. MT לאמר can signify either possibility.

11:26 ܠܟܘܢ] ܠܟܝܢ (+6b1): this is feminine, because of the antecedent. These two manuscripts are taking ܟܢܫܐ as feminine rather than masculine, see Nöldeke §87.

13:3 ܒܓܘܫܬܐ] ܒܓܘܫܬܐ (+6b1 11b1): later manuscripts read ܒܓܘܫܬܐ, whereas the majority reading omits *beth*. The text may be a misunderstanding, an assimilation to the fourth word following. 7a1 and its companions, with their relative particle and *beth,* better render MT בנגע .

14:6 ܘܡܢ ܒܗܝ] ܘܡܢ ܒܗܘܢ : this plural form comes from assimilation to the plural found in the following plural pronouns. This error should be added to the list on p. xv. It should be marked (a) in the preceding section and noted (e) here.

14:27 ܡܢ ܟܦܗ] ܒܐܝܕܗ (+6k2[1] 8b1): this is probably by assimilation to ܒܐܝܕܗ. in vs. 26. This too might be added to the list on p. xv and marked in the previous section (a) and here (e).

14:33 ܠܗܘܢ] *add* ܡܠܠܘ ܥܡ ܒܢ̈ܝ ܐܝܣܪܝܠ ܘܐܡܪܘ ܠܗܘܢ : this addition is an assimilation to the phrase in 15:1. MT does not have this addition.

14:36 ܘܢܦܢܘܢܗ] ܘܢܦܢܝܘܗܝ : this is by taking the subject as the singular ܟܗܢܐ rather than the indeterminate 3rd. plural.

17:8$_{2}$o ܒܝܢܬܟܘܢ] ܒܐܝܣܪܝܠ with some later manuscripts: MT has בתוכם , for which 7a1's reading would be an acceptable equivalent, though LXX ἐν ὑμῖν would seem to read, or at any rate to understand, בתוככם . The confusion is that MT is indirect speech, "among them". This can be turned into direct speech either as "among you", or with an interpretative element added, "among Israel". ܒܐܝܣܪܝܠ has been used earlier in vs. 6

21:2 ܒܐܒܘܗܝ] ܘܒܐܒܘܗܝ : this is by assimilation to the following nouns, which are preceded by a conjunction.

21:22$_{2}$o (e) is discussed below, 4 i, p. 26.

22:5 ܒܐܢܫܐ] ܕܐܢܫܐ : this is an erroneous anticipation of the initial *dalath* of the following ܕܛܡܐ. This should be added to the list of errors, p. xv of the edition, and noted (a).

24:2 ܫܪ̈ܓܐ] *s. sey*: this is as MT, which reads a singular. A plural is not required until vs. 5, of which the lemma reading may be an anticipation.

26:37 ܩܕܡ ܒܥܠܕܒܒ̈ܝܗܘܢ] ܩܕܡ ܒܥܠܕܒܒ̈ܝܟܘܢ (+some later manuscripts): here there are 2nd. masculine plural suffixes, against the majority reading of 3rd. masculine plural. See also vs. 39 where 7a1 reads ܕܐܒܗ̈ܝܟܘܢ against ܕܐܒܗܝܗܘܢ. Reference to the may explain what has happened. MT has 2nd. masculine plural, לכם and איביכם. The Syriac has gone astray earlier by adding a pleonastic ܠܗܘܢ. Whereas MT has simply ורדף אין the Syriac has ܟܕ ܠܝܬ ܕܪܕܦ ܠܗܘܢ. Next, the means of comparison have been confused with the object of the comparison, and so a repetition of ܠܗܘܢ has been supplied instead of an equivalent for לכם. 7a1 does not have ܠܟܘܢ as an equivalent of MT לכם and so must be presumed to have either created or inherited the confusion. 9b1 has grasped some of the point, namely that the suffixes are in disarray. It has supplied a 3rd. feminine suffix (appropriate for ܐܪܥܐ) instead of the correct 3rd. masculine plural suffix, thus reading ܕܬܚܬܝ̈ܬܗ for ܕܬܚܬܝ̈ܬܗܘܢ at vs. 38. The majority of manuscripts continue with incorrect suffixes. 7a1 again misjudges the situation by supplying 2nd. masculine plural suffixes, ܕܐܝܒ̈ܝܟܘܢ for ܕܐܝܒܝܗܘܢ in vs. 39. This, though mistaken, has the intention of being consistent.

3. *Omissions, additions, transpositions*

Consideration must now be given to the remainder of the readings which have been altered, beginning with 7a1's omissions, and further continuing the process of recognising the possible grounds for the readings. The readings included in the list of 25 errors on p. xv of the edition's Introduction will be left aside from discussion.

i. *Omissions*

$3:5_{10}$ ܘܠܘܝ̈ܐ] *om* (+8b1 and later manuscripts): MT provides only בני אהרון, as at vs. 8. It is therefore possible that the text's addition appears under the influence of its presence in the phrase at vs. 2. At vs. 8(e) only 8a1 and 8b1 add the word, rightly or not, for the sake of explanation.

4:13 ܠܗ] *om* (+10b2 and other manuscripts): the word's presence may be unnecessary, but formally it represents MT.

7:33 ܠܡܢܗ] *om*: the Syriac presents a different word order from the MT, which places למנה last. Vs. 32 begins ܩܪܒܐ ܕܢܚܒܪ which may have influenced the variant.

14:14 2⁰ܠܗܘܢ] *om* (+8a1): *BHS* records Samaritan Pentateuch, LXX miniscules and some Hebrew Mss as making the same omission. It seems that the other Peshiṭta manuscripts have added the word, rather than that 7a1 and 8a1 have omitted it, as also in 14:16 where neither 6b1 nor 7a1 supplies the second ܚܡܘܪ , nor does the equivalent appear in MT.

20:21/22 INSCR, and 23:4/5 INSCR: 7a1's omissions of these Inscriptions are better regarded as non-interpolations. Such headings are not found in all manuscripts.

23:8/9 INSCR ܪܫܗ ܕܚܒܠ ܕܚܦܘܟ ܕܗ 7a1 omits the word ܕܗ ܚܣܝ , which in fact is superfluous.

25:34 ܠܬܡܢ] *om*: the careless omission of a final adverb.

ii. *Additions*

There are now 7a1's additions to be considered.

16:3 ܠܚܛܗܝܐ] *add* ܬܪܝܢ , with other manuscripts. This is appropriate: there are two young goats for the sin offering of the people.

18:12 ܐܘܢܝܬܗ] ܘܡܢܕܗܘܢܝܬܗ ܡܛܠ : some Hebrew manuscripts present כי . *BHS* suggests that LXX and Vg indicate this reading. This expansion to a causal clause in 7a1 is comparable to a process observable in all the versions, and indeed sometimes in Hebrew manuscripts as well: it is a clarification of a meaning otherwise only implicit. More examples of this will be considered later, in Chapters 5 and 6. All the Peshiṭta manuscripts use the phrase at vs. 14, where MT gives ‎כִּי‎ .

23:3/4 INSCR, 7a1 has, with added *dalath,* (‎ܪܚܠ ܘܠܟܬܐ‎) the note that 9a1 has between vv. 4/5; 6b1^mg and 12b1 have a different inscription.

23:17 ‎ܠܣܬܐ ‎ܪܚܒܬܐ‎ ‎[ܚܒܬ‎ (+8a1* and later manuscripts): either in anticipation of the phrase in vs. 20, or to link with the beginning of the verse, as emphasis that this is the first of the meal offerings. A similar explanatory addition is made by Targums Onqelos, Pseudo-Jonathan, and Neofiti.

iii. *Transpositions*

There are seven instances of transposition, which, again, may indicate that factors other than textual derivation enter into matters.

7:23 ‎ܪܐܡܪ̈ܐ ‎ܪ̈ܬܘܪܐ‎ ‎[ܪ̈ܬܘܪ.ܐ ‎ܪܐܡܪ̈.ܐ‎ : 7a1 places the three groups, *viz* lambs, bulls and goats, in a different order: this is carelessness rather than assimilation.

$15:24_{10}$ ‎ܠܩܘܒܠ ‎ܠܥܡܐ‎[*tr* (+6k2 9a1^c): this word order, which corresponds to that of MT, may reflect literal, formal, equivalence. The remaining Mss place indirect object before the subject. The difference is one of syntax.

21:14 ‎ܣܡܟ ‎ܠܐ‎ / ‎ܗܘܐ‎ - ‎ܪܣܘ‎] *tr*: a transposition of object and verb/subject, the emended text printed being formally the same as MT, 7a1 here preferring verb/subject to stand first.

22:22 ‎ܠܟܬܘܢ‎/ .‎ܠܗ ‎ܡܢܚܣ̈ܝܗ‎] *tr*: this change of an adverb phrase and indirect object occurs in a phrase which is an expansion of MT for clarity, "not one of" for "them" or "from them".

23:11 ‎ܠܩܘܒܠܐ‎ / ‎ܠܒܬܪ ‎ܝܘܪܐ‎] *tr* (+ 9a1*): this might suggest a change of emphasis, the defining adverbial phrase standing first.

26:14 ‎ܠܐ ‎ܕܝܢ‎] *tr*: this is a change more apparent than real. ‎ܕܝܢ‎ does in fact stand second, but in other manuscripts it is a

matter of orthography whether the first word of the verse is
ܐܠܐ or ܐ ܆ .

27:23 ܠܚܡܐ ܕܢܒܫܗ] *tr*: the change of order leaves 7a1
formally closer to MT, and also gives a preferred Syriac
order of accusative before nominative.

In most of the examples given above the emended order
given in the lemma stands formally closer to MT. The
preceding paragraphs in this section suggest that scribal
preferences, conscious or unconscious, may have influenced
the readings of 7a1. The results may have been errors, in
that changes into the text have been introduced, but these
cannot be dismissed as being *mere* errors and were not
necessarily regarded as such in the edition.

4. *Single letters, pronouns, endings*

i. *Single letters*

The single letter emendations similarly raise questions
concerning the kind of equivalents which the Syriac displays,
and the possibilities reflected in different manuscript
traditions. It is easy to dismiss single letter or pronominal
differences as insignificant, and hence mere scribal slips.
However larger, syntactical matters may be at stake.

2:2$_{20}$ ܪܫܝ] *om dalath* (+8b1 10b2): this corresponds
formally to MT. The *dalath* wrongly tries to effect a
relative clause. The incense is on top of the oil, not *vice-
versa*. See above, p. 18.

11:15 ܒܠܝܫܬܗܘ] ܠܠܝܫܬܗܘ (+some later
manuscripts): the *lamadh* seems a Hebraism, see also vv.
16,19,22 and Gen 1:11. The majority of the manuscripts
might have been led astray by *beth* in ܘܒܝܬ immediately
beforehand. Both *lamadh* and *beth*, however, appear in
Syriac adverbial constructions. The difference is one of
syntax, see Nöldeke §§ 247, 248.

13:37 ܠܚܒܝܬ] *pr waw* (+6b1), as does MT: a matter of

syntax may underlie the difference. Without *waw* this is an inclusive comment on what has gone before, "the priest declares it clean"; with *waw* it is a consequential statement, "and so the priest declares it clean."

14:45₁₀ ,ܠܚܪ̈ܣܘܡ] *pr waw*: this is probably by assimilation to the form of the next word.

16:13 ,ܢܗܬܣܘܪܡ] *dalath pro waw* (e): this makes a final rather than a consecutive clause. It should not necessarily be considered an error.

19:34 ܠܚܩܘ _] ܣܠܝܬܚܘ _ (+later manuscripts): an expected phrase, as in 17:8,13, but here the word ܠܚܩܘ _ formally reflects MT אתכם .

20:12 ܗܢܣܡܘ _] *pr waw* : the printed text is formally that of the MT. In vs. 11 all manuscripts except 9a1 read ܗܣܡܝܘ _ , and there MT is without *waw*.

21:22₁₀ ܘܡ] *pr waw*: as MT. 7a1 has, however, confused matters, by mistakenly importing ܠܐ from the preceding phrase ܠܐ ܝܗܘܬܝܐ or by reproducing the ܠܐ from the phrase ܠܐ ܝܗܘܢ in vs. 23.

22:3 ܪܡܐܝ] *pr waw*: this is a mistaken addition, and should be listed among errors.

23:22/23 INSCR ܢܝܠ] *om dalath.* Manuscripts vary in the use of *dalath:* see above, under (ii) at 23:3/4 for the difference between 7a1 and 9a1.

25:9 ܘܝܩ] *pr waw*: there is no conjunction at this point in MT, which has a different word order, "on the day of Atonement you are to cause the trumpet . . . ". 7a1 repeats the word ܘܝܩ from the beginning of the verse. It is therefore an inner-Syriac matter.

27:21 ܢܗܣܡ] ܠܚܣܡ (+9b1): formally as the MT, and also dynamically. The majority of the manuscripts have misunderstood the sense. "The field is like a field under the ban - it belongs to the priests" is the intended sense. The misunderstanding is to take the field's yield as being under the priests' ban.

ii. *Pronouns*

The discussion now turns to the idiomatic use of pronouns.

2:3 ܗܘ] *om* (+8b1 and later manuscripts): these do not provide an enclitic, as 10b1 does at 2:10. The enclitic is the Syriac idiom found in verbless clauses, and so is not to be expected in the Hebrew, which may have an independent pronoun serving as predicate or complement without a verb. MT and Syriac have a 3rd. person pronoun in the same phrase as this at 6:10.

6:11 ܗܘ] *om* (+8a1 and later manuscripts): another example of the foregoing.

14:52 ܠܗܢܐ] *add* ܗܘ : the MT does however have an object particle את which might have suggested an appropriate use of the demonstrative pronoun.

iii. *Suffixes and other endings*

Suffixes and emphatic endings again show the need to consider Syriac idiom, although there is the added problem that some Syriac usage changes with time. For example, the emphatic form loses its particular significance over against the absolute state. The most notable usage where Syriac differs from the MT is that of anticipatory pronoun suffixes- either in a genitive relationship or in anticipation of an object.

6:10 ܣܢܝܐ] ܣܢܝܐ : *stat emph* for *absol* as predicate in a verbless clause. This became the later customary usage.

8:9 ܕܦܘܡܗ] ܕܦܘܡܗ : the text represents MT. The anticipatory pronoun object suffix is the expected Syriac idiom.

11:42 ܠܗ] ܠܗܬ : this shows an anticipatory possessive pronoun suffix, relating to ܐܪܥܐ , unless it is an error. See the list of errors given earlier, p. 14.

13:58 ܐܟܪܐ] ܟܘ ܠܘ (+8b1): this is the more idiomatic Syriac, *stat absol* with ܠܘ.

16:14 ܟܗܐ] ܗܘܐ: this is an example of a regressive suffix, going back to ܐܝܗܘ.

17:6 ܗܘܒܝܗܐ] ܟܘܒܝܗ : this omission of an anticipatory pronoun suffix seems an error.

17:10 ܗܝܒܒܐܟܐ] ܡܗܝܒܒܐܟܐ (+8b1): a different understanding of the antecedent, ܝܢܠ rather than ܟܗܘ. It is the emended, lemma, text that reflects the MT.

19:21 ܗܝܒܝܐܘ] ܟܘܒܝܐܘ : *stat emph*, rather than the expected 3rd. masculine singular suffix as MT.

25:28 ܟܚܘܒܝܠ] ܡܚܘܒܝ : this is as MT and the expected Syriac usage.

iv. *Conjunctions*

Concerning conjunctions, only two instances are worth comment.

19:6 ܟܗܘܠܐܘ] ܟܗܘܠ ܐܟܐ: MT has no conjunction. Stylistically, 7a1 is preferable, as being more emphatic: "furthermore", "and also".

25:11 ܟܠܐ] ܟܠ ܐܟ (+6b1): again MT has no conjunction. 7a1 is more emphatic than the lemma.

5.   *Syntactic preference and error*

i. *Syntactic preference*

Of more substance, however, the following changes indubitably indicate preferences in syntax, where MT may be understood and expressed in different ways. In each case the reading of the Hebrew is followed by that of the majority of Syriac manuscripts. 7a1's reading is placed after the lemma bracket.

Text	Hebrew	Leiden] 7a1
7:25	כל אכל	ܟܠ ܡܢ ܕܢܬܐܟܠ] ܟܠ ܕܐܬܐܟܠ 7a1
$8:35_{2o}$	ולא	ܘܠܐ] ܕܠܐ 7a1
13:16	ללבן	ܠܚܘܪ] ܕܢܚܘܪ 7a1 6b1
13:31	והנה אין	ܕܠܐ ܗܘܐ] ܘܠܐ ܗܘܐ 7a1
$15:24_{2o}$	ואם שכב ישכב	ܕܕܡܟ] ܕܬܕܡܟ 7a1
17:5	אשר הם זבחים	ܕܕܒܚܝܢ] ܕܕܒܚܝܢ 7a1

Here the reading of 7a1 may suggest a participle, a participial noun, or a mis-reading of the Hebrew based on dividing the text אשר המזבחים .

21:21 is a matter of punctuation, 7a1 placing the point before ܒܗܢܐ and the majority placing it after. The difference is explicable only in the Syriac: but it is not always certain which scribe was responsible for placing the points, whether in 7a1 or in other manuscripts.

25:48	אחרי נמכר	ܒܬܪ ܕܐܙܕܒܢ] ܒܬܪ ܕܡܙܕܒܢ 7a1
25: 51	ישיב	ܢܗܦܟ] ܢܗܦܘܟ 7a1

Formally, the lemma is nearer to the Hebrew; the majority reading of the Syriac manuscripts suggests "repay". 7a1 changes the subject to "the redemption".

Two further passages suggest differences of interpretation.

$10:15_{2o}$ ܡܪܝܐ 2°] *add* ܕܐܗܪܘܢ ܘܒܢܘܗܝ ܐܚܣܢܬܗ (+6k1 8a1*): this has already been mentioned in this section, and is linked with 7:29 and 21:22 as well as 10:18. The addition is made in the interests of consistency and emphasis.

$14:45_{2o}$ ܘܢܣܬܪܘܢܗ] ܘܢܣܬܪܝܗ̇ : this takes singular "the priest" as the subject, following MT; the remaining Syriac manuscripts take the subject as an indeterminate 3rd. masculine plural, "they".

ii. *Cognate*

There is only one example of a cognate, that is two words from the same Syriac root.

8:35 ܠܝܘܠܪܬܗ ܚܝܠܪܬܗ formally agreeing with MT word
משמרת . For the 7a1 reading, see Exod 14:24 (= MT אשמרת),
Jer 32:8 (= מטרה) .

iii. *Seyame*
The matter of *seyame* can be summarised briefly:

22:25 ܠܘܗܝܬ] *s.sey*: 7a1 may be right; the sense, as well as
the MT, suggest singular.

26:46 ܚܝܘܗܝ,] *c.sey*: 7a1 is in error. The word is a
preposition, not the plural noun.

For the remaining cases:

  8:20 ܪܝܫܐ] *c.sey*: error, there is one head only;

  11:4 ܘܗܝܬܘܗܝ] *c.sey*: error, a singular term is intended;

  14:42 ܟܐܦܐ 2°] *s.sey* (e): error, there are many stones;

  15:11 ܒܐܠܗܐ 1°] *s.sey* : error, the word requires *sey*;

  16:20 ܠܩܘܫܐ] *c.sey* (e): error, a singular is required;

  19:19 ܠܩܒܠܬܗ] *s.sey*: error, the verb requires plural;

  20:5 ܠܩܒܬܗܠ] *s.sey*: error, the sense requires plural;

  23:15 ܡܨܠܠܬ] *s.sey*: the sense and form require plural;

  23:18 ܘܗܕܐ ܫܠܡܐ] *c.sey*: error, there is one offering only.
Sey comes from assimilation to preceding plural;

  23:32 ܠܨܕ] *s.sey*: error, the idiom requires plural;

  24:14 ܟܐܢܘܗܝܡ] *s.sey*(e): error, the form requires plural.

6. *Conclusion*

This consideration of the places where 7a1 has been altered
confirms that 7a1 as a witness to the Peshiṭta tradition is a
median text, whether one's concern is with that manuscript's
additions, omissions and syntax (typology); or its position
between earlier and later manuscripts (chronology). It marks
a divide between its antecedents and its supplanters. It shows
some interpolations and expansions as the standard text does;
it is like the older manuscripts in that it is sparing of them;
but at the same time leaves out some that they already have

made. To use the vocabulary of Nida and Taber's *Theory and Practice of Translation,* pp. 202, 203, its character as an instance of translation stands between the formal and the dynamic. It lies between the mechanical on the one hand, and the linguistically and syntactically sensitive on the other.

That is not, however, to say that the mechanical approach to translating the Hebrew is always a mark of early attempts, and the linguistically sensitive always of later. In translation matters, as in early Israelite settlement patterns, there is dimorphism: that is to say, different patterns co-existing. Changes in the text tradition come as much, if not more, from a move towards further explication as from a "Syriacisation" of syntax and vocabulary: a point taken up in Chapter 6. But a warning must be given, that it is not easy to distinguish between readings which are result of deliberate attempts to explicate, and readings which are the result of an unconscious assimilation of words or phrases to such nearby words or phrases as are similar or even identical. Sufficient instances have been given above to demonstrate this difficulty with respect to 7a1, of which perhaps the most notable is at 10:15, see p. 20.

By way of conclusion to this chapter it may be useful to note some examples of emendations where the nature of the printed text and 7a1's text may be contrasted. It can be seen:

(a) that the following variants in 7a1 are examples of a tendency to be linguistically sensitive and show concern for the Syriac idiom: 6:16; 9:20; 13:37, 58; 16:3; 18:12; 21:14; 22:22; 23:17; (see pp. 19, 23, 24, 25, 28).

(b) that instances of the more idiomatic approach are to be found in the printed text at: 2:3; 6:10; 7:25; 13:31; 14:14; (see pp. 23, 27, 29).

(c) that readings formally closer to MT are found in 7a1 at:

11:15; 13:37; 15:24; 25:9, 28; 27:21, 23; (see pp. 24, 25, 26, 28, 29).

(d) that readings formally closer to MT are found in the printed text at 4:13; 17:10; 18:12; 19:34; 20:12; 21:14; (see pp. 23, 26, 24, 28).

But, as the writer warned in his article "'The best words in the best order'": closeness to, or distance from, MT is a subjective judgment: a warning to be heeded at such readings as those where MT is patent of more than one understanding. Instances are to be found in 7:25; $8:35_{20}$; $10:15_{10}$; 13:16, 31; 17:5; 19:6; 25:11, 48, 51; (see pp. 20, 28, 29). Further demonstration of this argument comes with an examination of the places where 7a1 is altered, despite clear support from manuscripts earlier than, and later than, the tenth century. It will be seen that these changes have made the Leiden text conform more closely to the standard text than its position as a median text might have suggested. But this was perhaps inevitable, given that so few of the ancient manuscripts survive.

It may be asked whether the original or the altered readings should be preferred. Obviously, where there is a clear error, the altered reading is preferable. But in other cases, no clear guidance can be given: the question of alternative possibilities must be allowed. As will be shown in the next chapter, there is a danger in permitting prejudices about resemblance to MT to influence thinking in this matter.

CHAPTER THREE

THE OLDER, THE NEWER, THE ORIGINAL

The comparison of 7a1 with manuscripts older and younger than itself bears out its designation as a median text. None of these three manuscript traditions has a monopoly of exact formal equivalence with MT: each has some evidence of the internal explanatory element already discernible in MT itself.

1. *7a1 and the older manuscripts*

More is needed than the statement that 7a1 is a median text, and the provision of merely quantitative support. It is important to show the kind of readings which are present in the older manuscripts, the later manuscripts, and in 7a1. As a result something may be said about the mechanical aspect of text transmission, the physical work of copyists. Something too may be said about the history of the text's transmission, and the kinds of text which were dominant in various places at various times. But, more important, something can be said about the process, indeed the organic nature, of text transmission and the consequences of that in the text that results. There is an inherent tendency for manuscripts to accumulate and to discard. M.H. Goshen-Gottstein noted this in "Prolegomena to a Critical Edition of the Peshiṭta", p. 38: ". . . the earliest manuscripts in existence generally show the same corruptions and exhibit on the whole the same text". "Corruptions" is a harsh word, the more so as MT itself bears witness to the same phenomenon, and this point will be touched upon later when principles of translation and text are under review. "Tendency to explication" might be a better phrase. This present chapter shows that the phenomenon of inner and cumulative interpretation is found in all three types of Leviticus text, pre-7a1; post-7a1, and 7a1 itself. So, to further the argument put forward in the last chapter, 27 instances of 7a1's being altered (despite the support of one or more older manuscripts) are set out in a different form. This is followed by a setting out of 77 instances where the generality of the later manuscripts (i.e. the standard text of Gelston or *Textus Receptus* of Koster) departs from the printed Leiden text.

The evidence of the manuscripts

There are 27 agreements between 7a1 and one or more of the manuscripts 6b1 6k2 8a1 and 8b1 which may be summarised as follows:

7a1 8b1	8	7a1 6b1	9
7a1 6b1 8a1	1	7a1 6b1 8a1 8b1	1
7a1 6k2	3	7a1 8a1	3
7a1 6k2^1 8a1	2		

The readings are given below. The lemma is the reading of the Leiden text, the variant is that of 7a1. The phrase "formally equivalent" has been discussed in Chapter 2, and is referred to later in this chapter, in section 3.

2:2$_1$0   ܠܚܡܐ] *om dalath* (+8b1 10b2): this is formally equivalent to MT; other manuscripts have interpreted, unless 7a1 *etc* have erred.

2:2$_2$0   ܠܗ ܡܢܗܕܡܐ] ܠܚܘܕܡܐ (+8b1): the text is the equivalent for locative in MT.

2:3   ܗܘ] *om* (+8b1): here the pronoun is a predicate in the Syriac idiom of a verbless clause; the phrase is not formally equivalent to MT.

3:5$_1$0   ܠܚܡܐ] *om* (+8b1): this is formally equivalent to MT, later manuscripts expand to give clarity.

3:5 2o ܢܝܚܘܬܐ] ܢܝܚܐ (+8a1*(*vid*)): this is formally equivalent to MT.

3:16 ܢܝܚܘܬܐ] ܢܝܚܐ (+6b1 8a1*(*vid*)) : this is the same as above.

6:11 2o ܗܘ] *om* (+8a1): *cf* 2:3.

8:14 ܘܩܪܒ] *add* ܡܘܫܐ (+6k2): this is an explanatory addition, with no equivalent in MT.

9:20 ܠܡܕܒܚܐ] ܥܠ ܡܕܒܚܐ (+6k2): this use of ܥܠ in an equivalent for locative in MT is the usual practice, *cf* 2:2 3o. The text then is an error.

10:15 ܡܪܝܐ 2o] *add* ܕܐܡܪܘ ܘܦܩܕܗ, ܠܐܠܗܘܢ (+6k2[1] 8a1*): this addition has a resemblance to the phrase in vs. 18, and makes for clarification. See Chapter 2 above, p. 20.

11:26 ܠܗܘܢ] ܠܗܝܢ (+6b1): here the antecedent ܒܥܝܪܐ is taken as feminine.

13:3 ܕܡܫܘܚܬܐ] ܕܒܡܫܘܚܬܐ (+6b1 11b1): here the phrase "which is in . . . " makes smoother sense within the passage. See p. 20, above.

13:16 ܠܚܘܪ] ܕܚܘܪ (+6b1), *cf* vs. 3: here ܠܚܘܪ is an assimilation to that word in the next verse, 17, unless it is an example of two ways of expressing the same MT phrase about turning white.

13:37 ܢܒܥܬ] ܘܢܒܥܬ (+6b1): this is formally equivalent to MT.

13:58 ܡܐܢܐ] ܡܐܢ (+8b1): here, idiomatically, the absolute state is used after ܟܠ.

14:14 ܟܗܢܐ 2o] *om* (+8a1): this is not a formal equivalence to MT. The Syriac of both the text and the variant expands for clarification.

14:16 ܟܗܢܐ 2o] *om* (+6b1): this is formally equivalent to MT.

14:27 ܟܦ ܝܕܗ] ܒܐܝܕܗ (+6k2[1] 8a1): the text is formally equivalent to MT.

15:24 ܠܘܬܗ ܓܒܪܐ] *tr* (+6k2 9a1c): this is a matter of Syriac idiom, a different ordering of subject and

	indirect object.
16:14	ܪܚܡܗ܄ 2⁰]ܪܚܡܗ܄ (+8b1): this is an assimilation (see next verse), or an explication.
17:10	ܐܦܩܪܒܘܢܗ܄] ܐܦܩܪܒܘܢ܄ (+8b1): the text is formally equivalent to MT, whereas the other manuscripts take the Hebrew איש or Syriac ܠܓܒܪ as the antecedent.
23:4/5	INSCR]*om* (+6b1): this has been added only to some manuscripts.
23:13	ܫܘܚܐ] ܣܘܚܐ (+6b1): *cf* 3:5.
23:18	ܫܘܚܐ] ܣܘܚܐ (+6b1): *cf* 3:5.
25:11	ܐܦ ܠܐ] ܠܐܘ (+6b1): this is more idiomatic Syriac, whereas the text is formally equivalent to MT.
27:23	ܕܗܒܬܟ ܠܘܐ] *tr* (+8b1): here there are different preferences for word order, but neither is formally equivalent to MT מסכת הערכך ; the variant places object first.
SUBSCR	(+ 6b1 8a1 8b1): the MT does not have this addition.

The relegation to the Apparatus of 7a1's readings in these cases indicates the assimilation of the printed text to the standard text. It will be seen that the divergences of reading are more by way of explanation than syntax. The figures in the previous table suggest that 8a1 is not entirely in accord with 7a1. It inclines to the pattern of later manuscripts, while 7a1 inclines more to that of the earlier. But nevertheless, 7a1 has shown a move towards that pattern which is seen most clearly in manuscripts of the ninth and tenth centuries. A check on the way in which 7a1 stands at the mid-point can be made by an examination of the readings where the later manuscripts deviate from the printed text of the Leiden edition, and by assessing the nature of the changes.

2. *7a1 and the later manuscripts*

The standard text, or *Textus Receptus*, is clearly seen when the revised 8a1 (8a1^c or, more rarely, 8a1^1) coincides with the series of manuscripts beginning with 10b1, although the series may begin, as in 10:6, with 9b1. Sometimes 8b1 accords with the later and sometimes with the earlier manuscripts; in Leviticus more often with the earlier. It seems that, in Leviticus, 10b1 marks the definitive start of the standard text. Manuscripts before that date may be said to have a tendency towards it; manuscripts after that date may be said to show resemblances if not similarities. There is, therefore, a common base which is the point of departure for the divergences in later text transmission. It is noteworthy that there are very few places where 8a1 has not been emended, either by addition or deletion, to concur with these later norms. It should be noted also that 9a1 sometimes joins the pattern of the later manuscripts, although it is more often to be found in the company of 6b1.

For the sake of simplicity material is set out in columns, with the manuscripts giving the earliest attestation of the standard text noted. The standard text is referred to by the indication "ff". This is used rather than *fam* or even *group* as those terms would demand a discussion of the history of the text beyond present purposes. This indication, "ff", suggests only that for the reading in question the range of manuscripts (9b1) 10b1.2 11b1 12b1.2 is present, beginning with the earliest manuscript in the series. As 8b1 does not fall sufficiently into the pattern of the standard text, it is excluded from the notation "ff". Full manuscript evidence must be sought in the Apparatus in the Leiden edition. In some instances it is suggested, by use of the sign = , that there is a formal equivalence between the Syriac and MT: the significance of this has been mentioned at the end of Chapter 2, p. 31, and is discussed in Chapter 6, pp. 99-101.

The 77 readings of the later manuscripts where they differ from the Leiden printed text, are as follows:

4:35 ܟܠ$_2$o] ܡܢ 8a1c (*ras*) 9b1ff: this is a partitive ܡܢ ("some, part of"), possibly through assimilation to the preceding phrase. The text = MT.

5:6 ܠܫܠܝܛܗܗ] ܠܫܠܝܛܗܐ 8a1c 9b1ff = MT: the text is probably by assimilation to the last word in the sentence.

5:16 ܘܢܬܠܝܘܗܝ] ܘܢܝܬܝܘܗܝ 8a1c 9b1ff: this is a change in the sense, in that what is given must first be brought. The text = MT.

7:16 ܐܦ] *pr waw* 6b1 9b1ff: the difference between the text and the variant is an inner Syriac syntactical difference. MT has only *waw*.

7:30 ܬܪܒܐ] *pr waw* 9b1ff: this use of the conjunction is to give a smoother reading; the text = MT.

8:19 ܡܢ] *om* 6b1 10b1ff = MT; the text adds partitive ܡܢ for clearer sense.

8:36 ܘܥܒܕ] ܘܥܒܕܘ 9b1ff: this takes the subject as plural, Aaron - and - his - sons; the text = MT.

10:6 ܒܢܘܗܝ] *add* ܕܐܗܪܘܢ 9b1ff: this is added for explication; MT lacks the equivalent of ܕܐܫܬܪܘ ܠܗ, *cf* vs. 12.

10:8 ܘܐܡܪ - ܠܐܗܪܘܢ] ܘܡܠܠ ܡܪܝܐ ܥܡ ܐܗܪܘܢ ܘܐܡܪ ܠܗ 6b1 9b1ff = MT; the text omits these words *per homoe.*

10:12 ܒܢܘܗܝ] ܒܢ̈ܝ ܕܐܗܪܘܢ 6b1, *add* ܕܐܗܪܘܢ 9b1ff: both these variants are explanatory; MT has בניו הנותרים.

11:10 ܒܟܠܗ] *pr waw* 8a1c 9b1ff: this is an assimilation to the beginning of the following phrase. MT has a partitive מכל.

11:20$_{10}$ ܕܡܗܠܟܐ] ܕܡܗܠܟܢ 8a1c 9b1ff: this takes ܠܝܕܐ as the subject.

11:20$_2$0   ܡ ܐܪ̈ܠܝ] ܐܡ ܟܠܝ 9b1ff: this is a consequence of the choice of subject as above.

13:4$_1$0   ܟܘܝܣܐ] add ܡ, 8a1^C 9b1ff: this adds a pronoun to a Syriac verbless clause; the text = MT.

13:4$_2$0   ܝܘܣܝܗ̣ܪ] ܝܘܣܠܝ 8a1 9b1ff: a difference of syntax; the Syriac provides alternative ways of rendering the Hebrew as either a consecutive clause (variant) or a final clause (text). MT לבן.

13:13   ܚܘܕܗ̣ܪ] add ܚܣܡ 8a1^C 9b1ff: this is an explanatory addition. Text = MT, though the Syriac has made of it a succession of clauses.

13:15   ܟܣܝܐ] pr lamadh 8a1 9b1ff = MT את direct object marker.

13:20   ܟܘܣܐ] ܚܘܣܝܚ 8a1^C 9b1ff: this is a Syriac idiom, a pronoun suffix added. The text = MT, which has וראה.

13:25   ܟܣܚܒ] pr waw 9b1ff: this provides a smoother reading, where two phrases are linked. The text = MT.

13:43   ܡ̈ܝܘܣܗ̣ܪ] ܟܣܝܘܣܗ̣ 6b1 6k2 8a1 10b1ff = MT: the text gives a suffix, an inner Syriac change for clarity.

13:44   ܡܘܟܣܠܝ̣ܪ]·ܚܘܟܠܝ̣ܒ 8a1^C 10b1: there are two interpretations of MT. The text indicates that the individual is declared unclean, the variant that the spot is declared unclean.

13:52   ܡܘܣܣܘܢ 1^0] add ܟܣܡ 8a1^C 10b1ff: this is an addition which makes for clarification.

13:55$_1$0   ܟܣܘܣܠ 2^0] om 8a1(ras) 10b1ff: MT does not have the equivalent of ܟܣܘܣܠ 1^0. It is the text which makes the addition.

13:55$_2$0   ܣܠܡ ܟܠܐ] om 8a1(ras) 10b1ff: the text = MT.

13:57   ܡܣܘܣܐܢ] ܡܘܣܣܘܢ, 8a1^C 10b1ff: this is a difference of singular or plural subject, "the priest" or "they"; it is a matter of interpretation. MT has תשרפנו.

14:32   ܟܠܐ] ܟܠܗ 6b1 9b1ff: the text and the variant

provide two ways of rendering אשר, as a consecutive or a final clause respectively.

14:36 ܢܣܝܬܗ ܒܗܢܐ] *tr* 8a1c 9b1ff = MT: the text is a Syriac preference of word order, the object/verb being placed first.

14:38 ܡܢ] *pr* ܠܒܪ 8a1c 9b1ff: the added word is Syriac idiom; the text = MT.

14:48 ܡܚܘܬܐ 2°] ܡܚܘܬܗ 9b1ff: a suffix is added for clarification; text = MT.

14:51₁o ܨܦܪܐ] ܠܨܦܪܐ 9b1ff: Syriac usage can omit direct object marker, although usually *lamadh* represents את.

14:51₂o ܘܠܙܘܦܐ] ܘܙܘܦܐ 6b1 9b1ff: both the text and the variant give a different order of words from MT; the text presents object marker.

14:57/15:1 Syriac interpolation: a heading.

15:12 ܕܢܩܪܘܒ] ܕܩܪܒ 8a1c 9b1ff: the text and the version give different equivalents (*pt* and *impf* respectively) of MT אשר יגע which is understood as a concessive clause.

15:19 ܡܢ] *om* 6b1 8a1c 9b1ff = MT: the text adds ܡܢ to represent accusative of manner, taking דם with זבה.

15:26 ܠܛܡܐܘܬܐ] ܒܣܘܬܐ 8a1c 9a1 9b1ff: the text and the variant give different interpretations of MT כטמאת נדתה, the text as a similarity of kind, the variant as one of time.

16:27 ܡܫܟܝܗܘܢ] ܡܫܟܗܘܢ 8a1c 8b1ff: the text = MT, plural ערתם; the variant prefers a singular noun "skin" as each of them has but one, rather than "skins".

17:7 ܠܥܠܡ - ܢܗܘܐ] ܠܗܘܢ ܢܗܘܐ ܠܥܠܡ 8a1c 9a1 9b1ff: the text prefers to place an adverbial phrase last; the variant, first. Both readings differ from MT תהיה זאת להם לדרתם.

17:10₁o ܐܢܫ] *pr* ܒܪ 9a1 9b1ff: this is an addition for explication, MT has בית.

17:10 2° ܒܐܝܣܪܐܝܠ] ܒܝܢܬܟܘܢ 6b1(*vid*) 6k2 8a1^c 9a1 9b1ff: the verse is a paraphrase in Syriac. MT has בתוכם as in vs. 8, where some manuscripts read בתוככם as MT does in vs. 12.

17:11 ܕܒܣܪܐ] ܕܟܠ ܒܣܪ 8a1^c 9b1ff: this is an assimilation to the phrase in vs. 14, where MT has נפש כל בשׂר דמו (*bis*). *Cf* Gen 9:4.

17:12 ܟܠ] *pr dalath* 8a1^c 9a1 9b1ff: this is Syriac idiom, to introduce speech. The text = MT.

18:10ff ܦܘܪܫܝܗ̇] ܦܘܪܫܝܐ 6b1 9a1 9b1ff: the text is Syriac idiom, a suffixed form. MT has a construct phrase ערות.

18:11 ܐܒܘܟ 2°] *add* ܠܐ ܬܓܠܐ 8a1^c 9b1: this is an expansion for clarification. MT has these words only at the end.

18:28 ܠܥܡܐ] ܠܥܡ̈ܡܐ 8a1^c 9b1: the variant is a plural for a singular, *cf* vs. 24. MT has a singular.

18:30 ܬܥܒܕܘܢ] *add* ܐܦܢ ܚܕ 8a1^c 10b1: this adds a Syriac idiom for emphasis ("even a single one"), a dynamic equivalent of MT infinitive construct לבלתי עשׂות מחקות.

20:8 ܐܢܐ 3°] *om* 6b1 8b1ff: both the text and the variant give idiomatic equivalents, in which two kinds of verbless noun clause are found. The pronoun is repeated for the divine name: MT אני יהוה מקדשכם.

20:26 ܘܬܗܘܘܢ] *add* ܠܝ 6k2 8a1^c 9a1 9b1ff = MT. The text is an omission.

21:10 ܐܝܕܗ] ܐܝ̈ܕܘܗܝ 8a1^c 8b1ff: the variant prefers the plural noun "his hands" instead of the singular, which would be the formal equivalent of the Hebrew idiom, "fill the hand", "consecrate". The text = MT.

21:20 ܫܘܪܘܪܐ] *c.sey* 8a1 8b1 9a1 9b1ff: The text = MT.

22:6 ܢܦܫܐ] *pr* ܟܠ 8a1^c 9b1ff: the addition is for the sake of idiom.

22:22 ܘܓܘܪܒܐ] *c.sey* 8a1^c 9b1ff. The text = MT.

23:15 ܢܗ̈ܘܘܢ] *add* ܠܟܘܢ 8a1^c 9b1ff: this is an assimilation to the phrase at the beginning of the verse. The text = MT.

23:30   ܐܘܒܕܘܢܝ ܠܒܢܝ] ܠܟܗܢܐ ܘܒ̈ܢܝ 8a1ᶜ 9b1ff: this is an assimilation to the phrase in the previous verse; unless it is an explanation by the variant on the lines found in later times, a "death at the hands of heaven" signified by a premature and childless death. See Rashi on this verse. The text = MT

23:37   ܩܘܡܬ] c.sey 8b1ff: the text = MT.

23:39   ܥܠܠܬܐ] ܥܠܠܬܗ 9b1ff: this is a preference for the suffixed form of the plural ("its products") rather than for the emphatic state of the singular ("the produce").

24:2   ܕܟܝܐ ܙܝܬܐ] tr 9a1 8b1ff = MT: this is an idiomatic difference; the change in word order shows two ways of rendering MT construct, noun, and adjective. MT שמן) זית זך(.

25:7   ܗܘܐ] pr waw 8a1 9a1 9b1*ff: this is a smoother linking of words; the text = MT.

25:16   ܕܥܠܠܬܐ ܕܙܒܝܢ] tr 8a1ᶜ 9b1ff: both the text and the variant are an explication of the earlier part of the verse. MT has no equivalentfor ܕܙܒܝܢ 3°. The problem is the rendering of a Hebrew which contains an adjective, an absolute noun and a construct: there can be ambiguity as to which noun the adjective modifies. In this verse the modification of the price does not depend on the size of the produce in one year, but on the size of the crop taken over a number of years yet to elapse: the Syriac attempts to make this clear.

25:25   ܘܦܢܩ] pr waw 8a1 9b1ff = MT.

25:30   ܕܒܩܪܝܬܐ] ܕܩܪܝܬܐ 8a1ᶜ 9a1 9b1ff: this is a difference of syntax, where the variant omits the preposition beth which gives a relative clause. The text = MT.

25:33   ܕܩܪܝܬܐ] ܕܒܩܪܝܬܐ 8a1ᶜ 9b1ff: the text and the variant both interpret the Hebrew; MT has ועיר.

25:41 ܕܐܒܘܗܝ] ܕܐ̈ܒܗܘܗܝ 8a1c 9a1 9b1ff: = MT. The text may simply be an assimilation to the end of ܒܢ̈ܘܗܝ earlier in the verse; or (rather, see the next entry,) a deliberate change on grounds of sense, that the return is to the territory of his father (specific), rather than his ancestors (general).

25:45 ܫܪ̈ܒܬܗܘܢ] *s.sey* 8a1c 8b1 9a1 9b1*ff: possibly this is a change to give better sense; "their family" rather than "their families". The variant = MT.

26:5 ܠܣܒܥܟܘܢ] ܠܣܒܥܐ 8a1c 9b1ff: the text = MT.

26:6 ܕܡܙܝܥ] *pr* ܡܢ 8a1c 9b1ff: this addition is Syriac idiom to form an equivalent to the Hebrew participle, indicating an indefinite clause.

26:18 ܬܘܒ ܒܗܠܝܢ] *tr* 8a1c 9b1ff: this is Syriac idiom as an equivalent for Hebrew עד אלה.

26:22 ܘܬܒܨܪܟܘܢ] ܘܬܒܨܝܟܘܢ 6b1 8a1c 8b1ff: these are forms from the roots ܒܨܐ and ܒܨܪ respectively, which are each weak in one letter, but have no difference of meaning.

26:25 ܕܩ̈ܛܝܠܝ ܚܪܒܐ] ܕܩ̈ܛܝܠܝ ܚܪܒܟܘܢ 8a1 9a1 9b1ff: these are different equivalents, both plural, but the variant has suffix. MT has simply איב.

26:27 ܒܗܠܝܢ ܬܘܒ] *tr* 8a1c 9b1ff: this is a Syriac idiom preference in word order. (*cf* vs. 18). MT בזאת.

26:40 ܒܥܘܠܐ] ܒܥܘܠܗܘܢ 8a1c 9b1ff: = MT: the text is assimilation to ܘܥܘܠܐ earlier in the verse; or the variant is an assimilation (or explicatory addition) because of ܥܘܠܗܘܢ earlier.

27:3 ܘܠܟܠ] *om* 8a1 8b1 9b1ff = MT: the text is an explanatory addition.

27:6 ܕܟܣܦܐ 2°] *om* 6b1 8a1 8b1 9b1ff: the word "silver" is redundant here, although the text = MT.

27:8₁ ܟܗܢܐ ܕܢ̈ܦܫܗ] *tr* 6b1 8b1 9a1 9b1ff: = MT. There is a difference of syntax, in that the variant places the object before the subject of the verb.

27:8₂ ܐܝܟ] *pr waw* 9b1ff: this is an assimilation to

ܟܐ preceding.

27:9   ܚܝܐ ܗܘܐ ܬܪܝܢ .ܬܪܝܢܐ] ܬܪܝܢܐ ܗܘܐ ܚܝܐ   8a1
            9b1ff: these are different equivalents of the Hebrew,
            reflecting different division of the text. The text =
            MT.

27:10   ܬܪܝܢܐ] om 6b1 8a1 9a1 8b1ff = MT: the text is an
            interpretative expansion.

27:32   ܟܘܣܬܐ] s. sey 8a1(vid) 9a1(vid) 9b1 (vid), and
            other manuscripts: probably in error; the text = MT.

The material set out above suggests that the printed text
inclines to formal equivalents to MT in 27 instances, and the
standard text does so in 20. Both together deviate from
formal equivalents in 30 instances. Of particular interest are

(a) the 10 instances where 6b1 concurs with the formal
agreement of the standard text with MT: 7:16; 8:19; 10:8;
13:43; 14:32; 15:19; 17:10$_{20}$; 26:22; 27:8$_{10}$, 10 ;

(b) the 6 instances where 6b1 concurs with the standard
text against MT: 10:12; 14:32; 14:51$_{20}$; 18:10; 20:8; 27:6;

(c) the 9 instances where 9a1 agrees with the standard text
against MT: 15:26; 17:7, 10$_{10}$,12; 18:10; 21:20; 25:7, 30;
26:25.

There is no monopoly of formal resemblance to MT on the
part of either the older or younger manuscripts, or indeed of
7a1.

3. Non-correlation with formal rendering of MT

It is disappointing that there is no conclusive demonstration
that the incidence of dynamic rather than formal equivalents
increases with the lateness (or priority) of the manuscripts.
It must be admitted that, as so often in Peshiṭta material, the
evidence runs in contrary directions: to the evidence of the
previous paragraph there can be set the following instances.

(a) Evidence of assimilation of an inner Syriac kind can be seen in the standard text in such readings as 11:10; 17:11; 23:15, 30.

(b) The Leiden text shows formal equivalents to MT in such passages as 5:16; 8:36; $13:55_{20}$; 26:5.

(c) The standard text shows formal equivalents to MT in e.g. 5:6; 8:19; 10:8; 13:15, 43.

(d) Divergent understandings by the Leiden text and the standard text of the same Hebrew are to be observed in such passages as 10:12; $13:4_{20}$, 44; 14:32, 51_{20}; 15:12, 26; 20:8; 25:16; 27:9. Both understandings are explicatory; it does not seem possible to assign priority to either.

(e) Explanatory additions are to be found in the standard text at, e.g. 10:6; 13:13, 52; 18:11, 30.

(f) Explanatory additions are to be found in the Leiden text at, e.g. 8:19; 13:43; 15:19; 27:3.

Maori's comment, on p. iii of the English summary of his unpublished doctoral dissertation, *The Peshitta Version of the Pentateuch,* is pertinent here: "Despite the obvious attempt at painstakingly literal translation, proper Syriac usage is not sacrificed to that end".

There must now be an examination of the oldest text available for Leviticus in order to see whether this does in fact, with some degree of consistency, reflect an unadventurous rendering of the Hebrew known in MT. It is regrettable that so little is known of pre-MT texts; for the present purpose there can only satisfactorily be a comparison of the known with the known. The present writer has considered the material from Qumran Caves 4 and 11, but is of the mind that no firm conclusions can yet be drawn. While, too, there is value in consulting the Temple Scroll, matters of distinction between Leviticus quotation and Leviticus hermeneutic need to be clarified before a comparative study can be part of such a discussion as this present one. The next chapter will, therefore, compare 6b1 and 9a1 with MT.

CHAPTER FOUR

EARLY STAGES: EARLY TEXT

A survey of the available manuscripts which might give evidence of an earlier form of the Peshiṭta than 7a1 does not suggest that there was an "original" Peshiṭta in some way more identifiable with MT than later forms of the version. The interpretative element is present at all stages of the Peshiṭta's life.

1. *Expectation for an "original" Peshiṭta*

It might be hoped that the consideration of earlier manuscripts would lead to the discovery of the "original" Peshiṭta. It is to be regretted that Leviticus does not have the witness of manuscripts earlier than the sixth century. If manuscripts older than 7a1 are required, only the manuscripts 6b1 6k2 and the *ci-devant* 9a1 are available, even if some resemblances with the manuscripts 7a1 8a1 and 8b1 merit note. 9a1 is termed *ci-devant,* because reference must be made to Weitzman's work on 9a1, "The Originality of Unique Readings in Peshiṭta MS 9a1", where he indicated that 9a1 might be classed as a witness to an "early" text form, and concluded that the manuscript does reflect an early text with a close relation to MT. He observed, p. 227, ". . . a MS can preserve the original text uniquely if fed by a source not available to the rest". Perhaps the siglum 9<?a1 would suggest the true state of affairs, that it is a ninth-century copy of a much older text. The present study shows that while the judgment on the "early" nature of 9a1 is admissible, the comment on "close relation to MT" requires

modification. What follows therefore is a list of places where one or more "early" manuscripts give readings which are different from those of the Leiden printed text, and which may be presumed to give an earlier form of the Peshiṭta than that of 7a1 upon which that edition is based. There can be no question of an "original" text or text family, and certainly none of an identifiable ancient and distinct recension. It is merely that where the manuscripts which suggest a text earlier than 7a1 concur there is a broad family likeness: consanguinity in general terms rather than proved direct descent. Yet, nevertheless, it is useful to have set out in accessible form material which suggests an early Leviticus and which otherwise must be looked for in the Apparatus to the Leiden edition.

The conclusions of this survey are that the "early" manuscripts or text do show a relation to MT which deserves comment. But it is the kind rather than the number of the resemblances which merits discussion. This discussion follows in Chapters 5 and 6. A warning is needed again at this juncture, that such a phrase as "identity with MT" requires caution. The evidence of Leviticus shows that a reminder such as Gelston uses on p. 156 of *Twelve Prophets* is timely:

> Considerable liberties were taken by the translators in respect to the syntax and vocabulary . . . They were not afraid to make minor additions or adjustments either in order to explicate the meaning of the text as they understood it or occasionally for theological reasons . . .

More than one possibility for translation may therefore be suggested by the same Hebrew phrase; the consequent hazards for retro-translation are discussed in Chapter 5.

2. *The divergences of early manuscripts*

The following list of variants cannot be a complete record: the older manuscripts are defective. 6b1 lacks 1:1-3:6; 9a1 lacks 1:1-15:13; 6k2 attests only the fragments 6:21-7:24; 8:14-10:18; 13:42-14:47; 15:15-16:2; 17:7-19:9; 20:18-21:14; 23:3-24; 26:41-27:14.

The sign = signifies that there is *formal* agreement with the MT; * indicates a lemma to be found in the discussion of the relevant manuscript in the Introduction, not the Apparatus, in the Leviticus volume. The phrase "majority of manuscripts" indicates that the standard text is joined by 12a1 *fam,* so that it is the majority of *all* manuscripts which supports the reading.

3:7	‏ܐܘ‎] *om waw* 6b1 8b1 = MT; but the text and the variant both paraphrase.
3:9	‏ܗܪܝܢ‎] *c.sey* 6b1: the text = MT.
3:12*	‏ܠܚܬܐ‎] *om* 6b1 = MT. The text systematises the passage, with the use of this extra word.
3:16	‏ܣܘܬܐ‎] ‏ܘܚܡ‎ 6b1 7a1 8a1*(*vid*) = MT, see p. 17.
4:7	‏ܗܪܒܣܬܐ‎] *s.sey* 6b1 8a1*(*vid*): *?err*; a plural is expected, as in the text and MT.
4:8	‏ܘܣܠܐ‎] ‏ܗܪܒܐ‎ 6b1: = MT. The text uses ‏ܗܪܒܐ‎ twice, and ‏ܘܣܠܐ‎ once, to distinguish two kinds of fat. The variant uses ‏ܗܪܒܐ‎ three times, MT חלב three times. *cf* 6k2 at 7:3.
4:11	‏ܥܠ ܡܢ‎] ‏ܡܢ ܥܠ‎ 6b1 8a1* = MT: the difference is irrelevant as Syriac has confused the matter, using ‏ܡܢ‎ for על.
4:15*	‏ܘܣܘܡܟܘܗܝ,‎] ‏ܘܣܘܡܟܘܗ,‎ 6b1 = MT: the text, as LXX, has been assimilated to plural ‏ܘܣܘܡܟܘ‎ at the beginning of the verse.
4:20$_1$0	‏ܐܝܟ‎] ‏ܐܟܙܢܐ‎ 6b1: this shows a preference in style for the longer form, *cf* vv. 31, 35.
4:20$_2$0	‏ܠܟܗܢܐ ܥܠܘܗܝ‎] *tr* 6b1 8b1: there is a syntactic

difference in placing the subject first. The text = MT.

4:31₁o ܒܣܡܘܬܐ] ܢܝܚܐ 6b1 = MT. *cf* 3:16.

4:31₂o ܩܘܪܒܢܐ] *om* 6b1 8a1* 8b1 = MT: the text expands to emphasise the role of the offering.

4:34 ܩܪ̈ܢܬܗ ܕܡܕܒܚܐ] ܩܪ̈ܢܬ ܡܕܒܚܐ 6b1 = MT: this is a construct noun followed by an emphatic, rather than an anticipatory pronoun suffixed one followed by *dalath* and emphatic. These are two ways of rendering a Hebrew construct phrase.

4:35 ܐܝܟ] ܐܝܟܢܐ 6b1: this is another example of a preference, *cf* vs. 20.

5:3 ܢܛܘܪܒ] ܢܛܪܒ 6b1: *pa'el* for *pe'al*. The use of *beth* as governing preposition suggests there is no difference in meaning.

6:2 ܠܨܦܪܐ] ܠܝ ܦܪܐ 6b1: this is a difference of nuance; the text suggests "to moment of daybreak"; the variant: "moment before daybreak".

6:4 ܘܢܥܠܘܢ / ܘܢܥܠܢ 6b1: the difference is orthographic.

6:8 ܠܡܕܒܚܐ] ܥܠ ܡܕܒܚܐ 6b1 8a1*: the text is correct in representing MT adverbial accusative.

6:14 ܒܣܡܘܬܐ] ܢܝܚܐ 6b1 *cf* 4:31₁o.

6:15 ܒܬܪܗ] *pr* ܡܢ 6b1: this is an idiomatic preference for the longer phrase.

7:3 ܘܚܠܒܐ] ܘܬܪܒܐ 6k2: text has ܚܠܒܐ and ܬܪܒܐ to indicate different kinds of fat; MT has חלב twice. *cf* 4:8.

7:6₁o ܕܟܪ̈ܐ] *s.sey* 6b1: with ܟܠ these are different ways of rendering the MT כל זכר .

7:6₂o ܕܟܗܢܐ] ܕܒܢ̈ܝ ܐܗܪܘܢ 6b1 6k2(*c.sey*): these are two ways of completing the preceding phrase. MT reads בכהנים . The text is an expansion.

7:7 ܕܡܚܣܐ] ܕܢܚܣܐ 6b1 9b1*(*vid*): *impf* for *pt*; MT has אשר יכפר . The text and the variant provide different equivalents, participle and finite tense respectively.

7:14$_1$o ܘܢܩܪܒ] ܘܢܩܪܘܒ 6b1: this is another instance of syntactic difference, *cf* 5:3.

7:14$_2$o ܦܘܪ̈ܫܢܐ] *s.sey* 6b1 6k2 and other manuscripts = MT.

7:15 ܠܠܝ ܦܪܐ] ܠܨܦܪܐ : *cf* 6:2.

7:16$_1$o ܗܘ] *om* 6b1 6k2 = MT: this is a syntactic difference, the text using a pronoun in a Syriac verbless clause.

7:16$_2$o ܐܦ] *pr waw* 6b1 9b1 and majority of manuscripts: this is a preference of conjunction. MT provides a simple *waw*.

7:16$_3$o ܬܘܒ ܢܬܐܟܠ] *tr* 6b1: this is a difference in idiom, with respect to word order.

7:20 ܕܡܪܝܐ] *om* 6b1: the text = MT אשר ליהוה.

7:24 ܕܦܓܪܐ] *c.sey* 6b1: the variant takes this as a plural rather than as a generic singular.

7:25 ܕܢܐܟܘܠ] ܕܐܟܠ 6b1: the variant prefers a participle for customary action, rather than an imperfect for possible action. These are two ways of rendering MT participle אכל.

7:32 ܫܠ̈ܡܐ] ܕܫܠܬܐ 6b1: this is an error, *cf* vs 33, showing confusion over respective meanings of ܫܠ̈ܡܐ / שלמים.

7:38 ܕܦܩܕܗ] *add* ܡܪܝܐ 6b1: this is an expansion to clarify the meaning. The text = MT צותו.

8:2 ܠܡܫܘ̈ܚܐ] *s.sey* 6b1: this is an error.

8:5 ܠܟܠܗ̇ ܟܢܘܫܬܐ] ܠܟܢܘܫܬܐ 6b1 = MT: the text is explicative.

8:11 ܘܠܟܠܗܘܢ] ܘܠܟܠ 6b1 = MT: the text is idiomatic, adding a pronoun suffix.

8:14 ܘܩܪܒ] *add* ܡܘܫܐ 6k2 7a1: this is an expansion to clarify the meaning. The text = MT.

8:15 ܩܪ̈ܢܬܗ]ܩܪ̈ܢܬܐ 6b1 = MT: the text is idiomatic, adding a pronoun suffix.

8:19 ܡܢ] *om* 6b1 and majority of manuscripts = MT: the text is idiomatic, adding partitive ܡܢ "some of", for clarification.

8:21 ܣܘܬܐ] ܢܝܚܐ 6b1 *cf* above, 3:16.

8:24 ܡܕܒܚܐ] *pr* ܟܠܗ 6b1: the variant is an addition, referring to "the whole altar", for greater clarity.

8:28 ܣܘܬܐ] ܢܝܚܐ : 6b1 *cf* above, 3:16.

9:2$_1$o ܚܕ] *om* 6b1 = MT: the text adds the word to indicate an indefinite article.

9:2$_2$o ܥܓܠܐ] ܕܥܓܠܬܐ 6b1 6k2 = MT, *cf* 7:32.

9:3 ܘܐܡܪܐ] *s.sey* 6k2 8b1: this may be an assimilation to the preceding singular.

9:7$_1$o ܩܕܡ] ܠܘܬ 6b1: the text and variant show two ways of representing MT אל, "towards" or "before".

9:7$_2$o ܥܡܐ] ܥܡܟ 6b1: the text = MT; the variant makes a closer identification, "your people".

9:11 ܘܡܫܟܐ / ܘܒܣܪܐ] *tr* 6b1: the text = MT; the variant prefers a different order of words.

9:20 ܠܡܕܒܚܐ] ܥܠ ܡܕܒܚܐ 6k2 7a1: the variant is to be preferred for MT *he locale.*

9:23 ܩܕܡ] ܥܠ 6b1: *cf* vs. 7, the text and the variant provide two ways of rendering MT אל , here with reference to the appearance of the glory of the Lord "in front of" or "over" all the people.

10:8 ܘܐܡܪ - ܠܐܗܪܘܢ] ܘܡܠܠ ܡܪܝܐ ܥܡ ܐܗܪܘܢ ܘܐܡܪ ܠܗ 6b1 and majority of manuscripts = MT. The text has assimilated the phrase to the opening words of vs. 6, but kept ܡܪܝܐ as the subject.

10:12 ܒܢܘܗܝ] ܒܢܝ ܐܗܪܘܢ 6b1: this is an expanded phrase. All manuscripts expand here, in order to clarify the meaning that the sons of Aaron are intended.

10:13 ܘܐܘܒܠܘܗܝ] ܐܘܒܠܘܗܝ 6k2: the variant omits the *waw init* because it is considered either unnecessary or an error.

10:15$_1$o ܘܫܘܩܐ] *om waw* 6b1 = MT; here the text adds *waw*, although it is not necessary.

10:15$_2$o ܡܪܝܐ 2°] *add ex* vs. 18, or 8:31,6k2[1] 7a1 8a1*

10:18 ܕܐܗܪܘܢ - ܠܒܢܘܗܝ] *om* 6b1 = MT; this phrase is added by the text, *cf* vs. 15, 8:31.

10:19 ܘܩܘܪ̈ܒܢܝܗܘܢ] ܘܩܘܪ̈ܒܢܐ 6b1: the text = MT. The variant avoids the repetition of the suffix on two consecutive words.

11:19 ܘܛܘܣܐ] ܘܦܪܚܕܘܕܐ 6b1: the variant provides "bat", rather than "peacock," which accords with MT עטלף ; but Rashi takes vs. 18 תנשמת as "bat". *cf* Deut 14:16. For further discussion, see Chapter 6, p. 118.

11:21 ܕܢܕܪ] ܕܢܥܒܪ 6b1: "pass over", rather than "scratch". This seems to be an inner Syriac error; MT לנתר.

11:26 ܠܗܘܢ] ܠܗܝܢ 6b1 7a1; the antecedent ܒܥܝܪܐ is taken as fem, *cf* Nöldeke §87.

11:32 ܡܐܢܐ] *c.sey* 6b1: the sense might require the plural "items", "utensils", if it is to include the specific items which follow rather than be one among them.

11:35 ܬ̈ܦܝܐ] *s.sey* 6b1 8b1 and majority: better sense is given by the singular "stove"; MT is dual, considering it to have two parts.

11:38 ܘܢܦܠܘ] ܘܢܦܠ 6b1 8a1 8b1: the variant takes ܙܪ̈ܥܐ as sg., *cf* Nöldeke §146, or perhaps it is the simplest form of verb as it stands first.

11:43 ܢܬܛ̈ܢܦܘܢ] *pr* ܒܗܘܢ 6b1: if this is not an error, then it is a resumptive rather than anticipatory word.

11:45 ܐܠܗܟܘܢ] *om* 6b1 = MT: the text is an explanatory addition.

11:46 ܗܘܝ] ܗܢܐ 6b1 9b1 and majority: the text is an idiomatic addition of an enclitic pronoun.

11:47/12:1] INSCR *om* 6b1.

12:8 ܥܠܬܐ ---ܚܕ] ܚܕ ܠܥܠܬܐ ܘܚܕ ܠܚܛܗܬܐ 6b1 = MT; the text follows a logical order.

13:2 ܟܗ̈ܢܐ] *s.sey* 6b1: the text = MT.

13:3$_1$o* ܕܒܣܪܗ 2° --- ܐܢ] *om* 6b1 = MT: the text has added an explanatory phrase. Yet all manuscripts share error of ܡܫܘܬܢܗ for ܡܫܢܗ, dittograph, *cf* vs. 2.

13:3$_2$o ܕܡܟܘܫܬܐ] ܕܒܡܟܘܫܬܐ 6b1 7a1 11b1 = MT, though MT is complex and the Syriac confused. The problem lies in the elements of the blemish. The Syriac, both text and variant, consider the blemish to be superficial, and so to be examined for the bleaching of the hair and possible penetration of the blemish: its increase in size draws attention to its potential danger. The Hebrew does not mention this increase in size.

13:3$_{30}$ ܢܣܚܠܘܐ] ܗܣܚܠ 6b1: text and variant provide alternative equivalents, with infinitive and imperfect for MT לבן [הפך], cf 13:16,20.

13:5 ܘܣܚܝܚܬ] ܣܚܝܚܐ 6b1: the text = MT, and retains suffix.

13:8 ܣܚܝܚܐ] ܘܣܚܝܚܬ 6b1: the text = MT; here the variant introduces the suffix, for clarity.

13:12$_{10}$ ܒܣܥܪܗ] ܒܣܥܪܐ 6b1 = MT: here the text introduces the suffix, for clarity.

13:12$_{20}$ ܘܣܥܪܗ] ܣܥܪܐ 6b1 = MT: the text here also introduces a suffix for clarity.

13:16 ܢܣܚܠܘܐ] ܗܣܚܠ 6b1: the text = MT; the variant is an alternative rendering of ללבן.

13:17* ܘܢܚܙܝܗ] pr waw 6b1 = MT; the text is an example of asyndeton.

13:20$_{10}$ ܘܡܥܡܩܐ] ܡܥܡܩܐ 6b1: the text = MT, but the variant drops the suffix, perhaps by sound.

13:20$_{20}$ ܢܣܚܠܘܐ] ܗܣܚܠ 6b1: cf above, 13:3$_{30}$.

13:20$_{30}$* ܘܠܒܝܟܬܐ] pr waw 6b1 = MT: cf vs. 17, but here it is the variant that retains, and the text which omits, the conjunction.

13:22 ܒܓܠܕܐ] om 6b1 8a1 = MT: the text adds a word, and so clarifies the sense.

13:25 ܘܣܚܝܚܬ] ܣܚܝܚܐ 6b1 = MT ושער אחד.

13:27 ܒܡܫܟܐ] om 6b1 = MT: the text adds a word, and so makes the phrase explicit.

13:30 ܣܚܝܚ] ܘܣܚܝܚܬ 6b1 = MT, cf vv. 32, 34, 43.

13:37 ܘܢܚܙܝܗ] pr waw 6b1 7a1 = MT; the text omits the conjunction, whereas the variant gives a sense of consecutive action.

13:43 ‏ܕܟܼܡܪܗ] ‏ܕܟܼܡܪܗ 6b1 6k2 8a1 8b1 and majority of manuscripts: the text makes explicit by the use of the suffix.

13:50 ‏ܟܡܐ 2°] *om* 6b1 = MT: the text makes explicit with the addition, *cf* vs. 51.

13:51 ‏ܐܘ ‏ܟܒܠ] ‏ܘܟܒܠ 6b1 = MT: there are two interpretations here. The text continues the list of elements into which the disease has spread; the variant has the sense of whatever use the skin may have been put to.

13:52₁0 ‏ܕܠܬܠ] ‏ܠܬܠ 6b1: there is a syntactic difference between text and variant; the former has an indirect object the other has a genitive.

13:52₂0 ‏ܒܩܢܝܐ ‏ܘܣܕܩܢܘܗܝ, / ‏ܒܚܠܠ -- ‏ܒܒܝܬܐ] *tr* 6b1 = MT: *cf* vs. 57. The choice here is of word order, whether the explanatory clause comes first or second.

13:52₃0 ‏ܘܣܩܕܘܗ 2°] ‏ܘܣܩܕܘܗܝ, 6b1 6k2 8a1 and majority of manuscripts: the difference is that of antecedent and object, whether the priest or unspecified persons do the burning, and whether it is the whole item or the blemish alone. The variant seems closer to the MT, though this may be a case of the part for the whole.

13:54₁0 ‏ܘܐܫܠܠܐ ـ] ‏ܐܫܠܠܐ ـ 6b1: the text = MT.

13:54₂0 ‏ܟܡܐ 2°] *om* 6b1 = MT: the text makes explicit with the addition.

13:55* ‏ܐܟܠ] ‏ܕܐ ـ ܟܠ 6b1: the variant uses *dalath* after verb of seeing, and so gives a syntactic difference.

13:57 ‏ܟܠܣܐ ‏ܐܩܕܘܗܡ, [ܘܣܩܕܘܗ ‏ܟܠܣܐ 6b1 6k2 8b1. MT ‏באש תשרפנו , Syriac text and variant give different subjects, 3rd. person indefinite plural and 3rd. person singular, and a different order of words. *Cf* vs. 45.

14:16₁0 ‏ܟܡ 1°] *add* ‏ܗܘ 6b1: the addition of a demonstrative pronoun is by way of explication. The text = MT.

14:16₂0 ‏ܟܡܐ 2°] *om* 6b1 7a1 = MT: the addition by the text makes explicit, *cf* vs. 17.

14:21 ܚܕܐ] *om* 6b1 6k2 8a1 = MT: the text adds, and so makes explicit.

14:26 ܕܣܡܠܐ] ܕܣܡܠܗ 6b1: the text = MT, the variant uses an anticipatory suffix.

14:32 ܘܠܐ] ܕܠܐ 6b1 9b1 and majority of manuscripts = MT: the text signifies a consecutive clause, variant a final one.

14:34 ܐܪܥ ܝܪܬܘܬܟܘܢ] ܐܪܥܐ ܕܝܪܬܘܬܟܘܢ 6b1: difference of syntax; the text = MT. Here there are two ways of rendering a Hebrew construct and absolute noun. But all render ארץ כנען by ܐܪܥܐ ܕܟܢܥܢ.

14:40 ܠܟܐ̈ܦܐ] ܟܐ̈ܦܐ 6b1: text = MT: the variant does not give a direct object marker.

14:41 ܩܪܝܬܐ] ܡܥܡܪܬܐ 6b1: two different equivalents, or interpretations, "village" and "habitation" for the MT עיר.

14:42 ܘܢܚܠܘܢ] ܢܚܠܘܢ 6b1: the text = MT.

$14{:}43_1$o ܗܘܝ] *om* 6b1: this is an idiomatic difference, the variant using ܒܬܪ to govern its verb in the first instance.

$14{:}43_2$o ܘܗܘܝ ܒܬܪ] ܘܒܬܪ 6b1: again the variant prefers the single word to govern its verb.

14:45 ܘܢܦܩܘܢܗ] ܘܢܦܩܝܘܗܝ 6b1: the variant has the subject singular, "priest", as does MT; the text gives the impersonal 3rd. plural as subject.

14:45* ܠܛܡܐܐ] ܕܛܡܐ 6b1: there is a difference of syntax between the text (adjective) and the variant (relative clause).

$14{:}48_1$o ܗܘܝ] *om* 6b1: *cf* $14{:}43_1$o.

$14{:}48_2$o ܗܘ̇] *om* 6b1 = MT: the text uses demonstrative, for clarity.

$14{:}51_1$o ܘܠܙܘܦܐ] ܘܙܘܦܐ 6b1 9b1 and majority of manuscripts: the text = MT and keeps object marker.

$14{:}51_2$o ܠܗܠܝܢ] ܗܠܝܢ 6b1: *cf* vs. 53.

14:53 ܠܨܦܪܐ] ܨܦܪܐ 6b1: the text = MT, as above, with object marker.

14:57 ܗܢܐ] *add* ܗܘ 6b1 8a1* 8b1: this is Syriac idiom, an enclitic pronoun in a verbless clause.

15:10 ܕܢܩܪܘܒ] ܕܩܪܒ 6b1 = MT participle: there are two different equivalents here; *pt* in the variant and *impf* in the text.

15:12 ܐܘ ܕܢܚܫܐ] ܘܕܢܚܫܐ 6b1: the difference is one of syntax, "and" against "or". MT has simply "wood", both the text and the variant add "brass".

15:14 ܘܢܝܬܐ ܐܢܘܢ] ܘܬܐܬܐ 6b1; ܘܢܥܘܠ 9a1: the text explicates, "and brings them," *cf* vs 29. LXX οἴσει. The variants are different equivalents, "and comes" or "and enters" for MT ובא.

15:15 ܠܕܒܚܐ] ܠܝܩܕܐ 6b1 9a1: MT עלה ; the standard equivalent is ܝܩܕܐ, hence the text is in error.

15:17 ܐܘ ܡܫܟܒܐ] ܕܡܫܟܒܐ 6b1 8b1; ܘܡܫܟܒܐ 9a1* = MT: different interpretations according to context, *cf* vs. 4. The first variant and the text are explicatory, unless they are an inner Syriac error.

15:19 ܡܢ] *om* 6b1 8b1 9a1 and majority of manuscripts = MT: the text takes ܐܢܬܬܐ as subject, adding a causal or partitive ܡܢ, and the variant takes ܕܡܗ̇ as subject.

15:24 ܠܘܬܗ̇ ܓܒܪܐ] *tr* 6k2 7a1 9a1[c]: here there are two preferences for word order.

15:26 ܠܛܡܐܘܬܐ] ܢܕܬܐ 8a1[c] 9a1 and majority: the text = MT, whereas the variant provides a different interpretation. The comparison is not of uncleanness, but of the time of exclusion.

15:28 ܬܬܕܟܐ] ܬܕܟܐ 9a1 = MT; the text has an interpretative element, "is made clean" rather than "is clean".

15:30 ܐܢܘܢ] *om* 6b1 = MT: the text puts a pronoun as object for the sake of clarity or emphasis.

15:32 ܕܢܦܘܩ] ܕܢܦܩ 6b1 6k2 8a1 9a1 and majority of manuscripts: here there are different equivalents for MT imperfect; the text has *impf*, and the variant has *pt*.

16:1* ܩܕܡ ܡܪܝܐ / ܚܕܐ ܒܫܢܬܐ] *tr* 9a1: the text = MT, the difference is in preference of word order for emphasis, depending on the adverb phrase coming first or second.

16:4$_1$o ܕܩܘܕܫܐ] ܠܩܘܕܫܐ 9a1: the text = MT; the variant offers different interpretation, "for holiness" rather than "holy".

16:4$_2$o ܒܡ̈ܝܐ ܒܣܪܗ] *tr* 6b1: the text = MT; the variant is a different preference for the placing of an adverbial phrase.

16:5 ܨܦܝܪ̈ܝܢ] ܨܦܝܪ̈ܐ 6b1 9a1: the text prefers the absolute state with numbers, *cf* vv. 7,8.

16:7 ܟܕ ܚܝܝܢ] *om* 6b1 9a1* = MT: the text is an addition for interpretation, "while alive".

16:13 ܘܠܐ] ܕܠܐ 9a1: the text = MT; the variant is a final clause, rather than a consecutive one.

16:14$_1$o ܒܨܒܥܗ] ܒܨܒܥܗ 9a1: the text and the variant provide two related forms, with no difference in meaning.

16:14$_2$o ܘܩܕܡ] ܘܥܠ 9a1: the text = MT ולפני ; the variant may wish to distinguish this from the preceding ܐܦ̈ܝ.

16:16$_1$o ܠܡܥܘܠܬܗܘܢ] ܠܡܥܘܠܬܐ 6b1: the text = MT; the variant is idiomatic, providing an anticipatory suffix which also gives precision.

16:16$_2$o ܘܡܢ 1°] *om waw* 6b1: the text = MT; the variant is an error, by assimilation to the preceding ܡܢ.

16:17 ܚܘܣܝܐ] *om* 6b1 9a1 = MT: the text's addition makes explicit the purpose - "to make atonement".

16:18$_1$o ܠܩܕܡ] ܡܢ ܩܕܡ 6b1: these are different syntactic preferences, the variant's being more idiomatic.

16:18$_2$o ܩܪ̈ܢܬܗ] ܩܪ̈ܢܬܐ 6b1: this is syntactic preference; the text is more idiomatic in supplying an anticipatory suffix in a genitive construction.

16:21 ܬܪ̈ܬܝܗܘܢ] ܬܪ̈ܬܝܢ 9a1: here the text is again more idiomatic in providing an anticipatory suffix, which also emphasises "both".

16:25   ܠܟܕܗܕܒܪܐ [ܠܟܕܒܗܪܐ 8a1 9a1: MT *he locale.* The
variant is to be preferred, *cf* 9:20.

16:29   ܠܟܣܐ] ܠܚܣܐ 9a1: the difference is in syntax, the
text being preferable in that it uses the absolute state
after ܠܟ .

16:32$_1$0   ܠܩܘܬܐ] *s.sey* 9a1: the text = MT, and this is
correct.

16:32$_2$0   ܠܩܘܬܠܐ] ܠܪܐܝܪܐ 6b1 9a1(*s.sey*): these are
different equivalents for MT בגדי , indicating a
difference of understanding; the use by both of the
conjunction is an error. The text has understood two
types of clothing, the variant one type with two
characteristics - "linen" and "holiness".

16:34   ܐܝܟ] ܐܝܟܢܐ 9a1: here the variant prefers the
shorter form.

17:2   ܠܟܠܗܘܢ] *om* 6b1: the text = MT; the variant is an
error, by assimilation to the previous phrase.

17:6   ܠܚܘܐܗ] ܠܚܘܣ 6b1: the same difference as has
occurred earlier, *cf* 3:16.

17:7   ܠܬܠܬ ܠܚܘܡ ܠܗܘܢ ܨ [ܠܚܘܡ ܐ - ܠܬܠܟ 8a1^c 9a1 9b1
and majority of manuscripts = MT: the difference is
one of preference for the placing of an adverb.

17:9$_1$0   ܠܗܠܐ] ܠܩܕܡ ܠܗܠܐ 9a1 = MT: here there are two
equivalents; the variant uses *lamadh* for dative; the
text ܩܕܡ for actions done in the presence of God.

17: 9$_2$0   ܠܓܘ] *om* 6b1 9a1 = MT: the text is idiomatic in the
use of this element; the variant loses the sense of
"inside", "among", through its omission.

17:10$_1$0   ܠܐܝܣܪܝܠ] *pr* ܒܝܬ 9a1 9b1 10b1 and majority of
manuscripts: here there are two equivalents forבית
ישראל .

17:10$_2$0   ܠܐܝܣܪܝܠܐ] ܒܘܬܟܘܢ 6k2(*vid*) 6b1 8a1^c 9a1 9b1
and majority of manuscripts: here there are different
equivalents for MT בתוכם , 2Mss בתוככם , *cf vs.* 8.

17:10$_3$0   ܠܗܢ 1^0] *pr* ܡܢ 6b1: the variant uses a partitive
"some of", MT כל דם .

17:11₁o ܕܢܦܫܐ] ܕܢܦܫܗ 6b1: the variant is probably an error, by assimilation to the customary use of an anticipatory suffix.

17:11₂o ܘܐܢܐ ܝܗܒܬܗ] ܘܝܗܒܬܗ 6b1: here there are two preferences in word order, the variant placing ܐܢܐ after ܠܟܘܢ; text = MT.

17:12₁o ܟܠ] *pr dalath* 8a1ᶜ 8b1 9a1 and majority of manuscripts: the variant is more idiomatic in its use of the particle to introduce speech.

17:12₂o ܥܡܟܘܢ] ܒܝܢܬܟܘܢ 6b1 9a1: the different prepositions give different equivalents to MT בתוככם; the variant is formally closer to MT.

17:12₃o* ܢܐܟܠܘܢ] ܢܐܟܘܠ 9a1 = MT: the Hebrew has a singular subject הגר, and the Syriac a plural subject, ܐܝܠܝܢ ܕܡܬܬܘܬܒܝܢ. This passage might suggest a correction towards the MT by 9a1, but only if there were sufficient other similar instances to corroborate. As it is, it is an inner Syriac error. The sentence is punctuated with a break after ܥܡܟܘܢ and the verb has reverted to a singular, albeit masculine, subject from the beginning of the verse. The feminine would be expected, in agreement with ܟܠ ܢܦܫܐ.

17:13₁o ܒܢܝ̈] *om* 9a1: the text = MT.

17:13₂o ܕܦܪܚܬܐ] *om dalath* 6b1: the difference is a choice of syntax; the text repeats *dalath* after ܐܘ.

17:13₃o ܘܢܟܣܝܘܗܝ] ܘܢܟܣܝܗ̇ 9a1: the variant is in error having taken the wrong antecedent ("animal" or "bird") rather than "blood".

17:15 ܕܥܡܪܝܢ ܒܝܢܬܟܘܢ] *om* 6b1 9a1*; but *cf* vs. 10 above: the text has an addition which is an assimilation to the earlier verse, or provides a double translation of גר as a noun and as a participle by way of explication.

17:16₁o ܢܣܒܠ] ܡܣܒܠ 6b1: these are two equivalents for MT *impf*, the text giving the sense of indefinite time, and the variant the sense of habitual action.

17:16₂0   ܡܘܠܗܝ] ܠܘܡܚ 6b1: here the text = MT, and the variant loses definition by omitting the suffix in error.

18:6   ܠܩܘܪܒܬܗ] ܩܘܪܒ 6b1 = MT: in the context the text (*ethpa'al*) has an interpretative element, as against the variant (*pe'al*); the former suggests "touching" as well as "approaching".

18:8   ܩܘܪܒܗ]ܩܪܘܒ 6b1 9a1: this is an error, by similarity of sound, and the text is more idiomatic. The text and the variant alter the syntax in this passage; they place the predicate after "nakedness", not, as MT, after the personal noun at the end; *cf* also vv. 9, 10, 11, 14, 16.

18:12   ܓܝܪ] *om* 9a1: the text is idiomatic; the variant omits the particle.

18:13   ܩܪܘܒ] ܩܘܪܒܗ 6k2 *etc*: here there is the reverse of the example in vs. 8.

18:21   ܘܠܐ] *om waw* 6b1: the text = MT; the variant loses the force of the connection between the clauses.

18:24   ܒܟܠܗܘܢ ܗܠܝܢ] ܗܠܝܢ ܟܠܗܘܢ 6b1 9a1 = MT: this is a preference in word order.

18:26   ܟܠܗܘܢ] *om* 9a1: MT כל, *cf* vs. 29. The text has an explicitness that MT and the variant do not show.

18:28   ܐܝܟ] ܐܝܟܢܐ 6b1: this manuscript's preference for the longer form has been seen earlier, e.g. 4:20.

18:29   ܟܠܗܘܢ] *om* 9a1: *cf* vs. 26.

18.30   ܘܬܝ] *pr waw* 9a1 = MT: the text does not link this verse with the preceding one, but makes a new start.

19:6₁0   ܬܐܟܠܘܢ 2⁰] *om* 6b1 8b1: here the text is expanded to clarify the sense that it is eaten on each day.

19:6₂0   ܘܠܐ] *om waw* 6b1: here the variant makes a break between the clauses. The phrase "and it is not eaten" is not in MT, but is an interpretive addition in the text and the variant.

19:9₁0   ܘܡܐ] *s. sey* 6b1 8b1 9a1(*vid*) = MT: the difference between text and variant is that the latter uses the singular for that of which each has one; the former uses plural as there are many who have one.

19:9₂0   ܐܘܠܬܐ] *c. sey* 6b1: the text = MT; the variant considers that more than one occasion is involved.

19:10   ܐܘܢ] *om* 6b1: the text = MT, the variant an error, omitting the object.

19:12   ܠܐ] *pr waw* 6b1 8a1(*vid*) = MT: the text prefers brevity in giving instructions.

19:13₁0   ܠܐ 2⁰] *pr waw* 6b1 8a1: this is a further example of the foregoing. The text = MT.

19:13₂0   ܠܥܒܕܟ] ܠܦܝܗ 6b1: the difference is in choice of word, *cf* 6:2.

19:16   ܐܘܡܝ ܟ] *s. sey* 9a1: the variant is probably an error. Both text and variant are an exposition of MT, which has "do not go around as a tale-bearer among your people"; the Syriac has "do not slander your people".

19:17   ܬܠܝܬ ܡܗ ܢܗܘ] *tr* 6b1 = MT: the difference is choice of word order. The text places verb second for emphasis.

19:20₁0   ܢܒܝܕ] *pr dalath* 9a1: the variant makes a syntactical change, to make a relative clause, unless there is an error by assimilation to ܢܒܝ earlier in the verse.

19:20₂0   ܘܠܐ] *om waw* 6b1 = MT: the text here prefers a conjunction.

19:27   ܢܘܣܪܝܗܕ] ܢܘܣܪܝ 9a1 = MT: this is preferable as idiom, and is another example of a choice between singular and plural where each person has only one.

19:28   ܢܘܡܬܗܕ] ܢܘ ܡܘ 9a1: the text = MT and is an explanatory expansion.

19:30*   ܥܬ ܗܘܩܕܝܢ] 9a1* = MT: a change has been made to 9a1 by the original or a later scribe. All other manuscripts read as the text does, showing that the reference is to commands in general rather than to a single specific one, *cf* 26:2. See also, below, pp. 70, 84, 96.

20:2   ܠܒܝܐ ܗܘ] *om* 6b1 9a1 = MT: the text adds the words and clarifies.

20:8 ܐܢܐ 3°] *om* 6b1 8b1 9b1 and majority of manuscripts: the difference is in the addition of pronouns in a Syriac verbless clause; the verse is a paraphrase of MT, *cf* 19:30.

20:9 ܘܠܐܡܗ 1°] ܐܘ ܠܐܡܗ 6b1: syntactic difference, in the preference for "or" rather than "and".

20:11 ܘܕܡܗܘܢ] ܕܡܗܘܢ 6b1: the text prefers a conjunction.

20:12 ܫܘܚܠܦܬܐ] ܡܛܠ ܕܫܘܚܠܦܬܐ 9a1: there is a syntactic difference, the text preferring a causal clause.

20:13 ܘܕܡܗܘܢ] ܕܡܗܘܢ 6b1 *cf* above, vs. 11.

20:15 ܬܬܪܓܡ] ܬܬܩܛܠ 6b1 8b1 9a1 = MT: the text explicates, giving "stoned" rather than "killed".

20:17$_1$o ܥܘܠܗܘܢ] ܚܛܗܘܢ 9a1*: here there are two different equivalents for עונו , "knavery" and "wickedness".

20:17$_2$o* ܚܛܗ] *add* ܐܘ 9a1: this is explication, unless it is an error.

20:19 ܕܚܬܗ ܕܐܡܟ ܘܕܚܬܗ] ܕܚܬܗ -- ܕܐܡܟ ܕܐܒܘܟ 9a1: the difference is of word order; the text = MT.

20:20 ܕܕܕܗ] ܕܕܗ 8b1 9a1 9b1*: the variant is an error by assimilation to the word in the preceding phrase.

20:25$_1$o ܬܛܡܐܘܢ] ܬܬܛܡܐܘܢ 6b1: the difference is between "make defiled" and "be defiled"; the text = MT.

20:25$_2$o ܢܦܫܬ̈ܟܘܢ] ܢܦܫܟܘܢ 6b1: the difference here is idiomatic, as before, between singular and plural where each of many has only one; the text = MT.

20:25$_3$o ܘܒܟܠܗ] ܘܒܟܠ 6b1: the text is more idiomatic, adding a suffix.

20:26$_1$o ܘܬܗܘܘܢ] *add* ܠܝ 6k2 8a1^c 9a1 9b1 and majority of manuscripts = MT: the difference is of word order, when compared with the following lemma.

20:26$_2$o ܩܕ̈ܝܫܝܢ] *add* ܠܝ 6b1 and other manuscripts: this variant relates the adjective rather than the verb to the pronoun ܠܝ.

20:26₃o   ܐܪܟ ܡܪܟ] *om* 9a1: the text adds the words to MT for emphasis.

21:10   ܩܡ‌ܣܪܝܐ‌ܐ] ܩܡܣܝܐ 6b1 = MT: the text is consistent in using a passive participle in this and the preceding phrase. MT has a finite tense (ומלא) in this phrase.

21:12   ܢ‌ܠܝ‌ܢܐ] ܒ‌ܠܝ‌ܫ 6b1 9a1: the text and the variant give different equivalents, with no difference in meaning, for MT יחלל.

21:14   ܩ‌ܣ‌ܝܒ‌ܠ‌ܣܐ‌ܟ] *om waw* 8a1 9a1 9b1 and majority: the difference between the text and the variant is that the text prefers a conjunction to link the clauses.

21:20₁o   ܩ‌ܣ‌ܝ‌ܐ‌ܝ‌ܩ] *c. sey*   8a1(*ras*) 8b1 9a1 9b1 and majority of manuscripts: the text is correct.

21:20₂o   ܩܡ‌ܪܝ‌ܐ‌ܝ‌ܣ] ܐ‌ܝ‌ܪ‌ܟ   9a1. Neither the text nor the variant ("mono-testicular"/ "blear-eyed") is the correct equivalent for MT מרוח אשך , signifying "enlarged/crushed testicle". This is a difference of interpretation of a difficult Hebrew.

21:21   ܩ‌ܣ‌ܝ‌ܒ‌ܝ‌ܐ‌ܩ] ܠ‌ܣ‌ܣ‌ܐ 9a1: these are two different equivalents for אשי, "offerings . . .".

21:22₁o   ܚ‌ܣ‌ܝ‌ܟ‌ܐ‌ܣ‌ܩ] ܟ‌ܣ‌ܝ‌ܟ‌ܣ 6b1: text and variant give different interpretations of MT מקדשי.

21:22₂o   ܩ‌ܝ‌ܟ] ܣ‌ܝ 9a1* = MT: the text interprets the Hebrew prefix *mem* as an indication of a noun, the variant understands it as a preposition "from".

21:23₁o   ܩ‌ܝ‌ܪ] *om* 6b1 = MT: the text adds this to smooth the reading.

21:23₂o   ܩ‌ܠ‌ܐ] *om waw* 6b1: the text = MT.

21:23₃o   ܩܝܪ 2°] *om* 9a1*: the variant is probably an omission; the text provides two pronouns in a Syriac verbless clause.

22:3₁o   ܩ‌ܝ‌ܣ‌ܠ‌ܐ] ܝ‌ܣ‌ܠ‌ܐ 9a1: the difference between the text and the variant is syntactic. The variant uses *st absol* after ܠ‌ܣ.

22:3 2o ܟܕ ܛܘܡܐܬܗ] ܘܛܘܡܐܬܗ 6b1 9a1 = MT: the text clarifies the meaning of the Hebrew with a temporal clause.

22:3 3o ܡܩܕܡ ܐܦ̈ܝ] ܡܩܕܡܝ 6b1 9a1: the text and the variant provide different equivalents; MT מלפני .

22:4 1o ܙܪܥܗ] ܙܪܥܐ 6b1: the text provides a Syriac idiom, an anticipatory suffix for MT construct, seed - of - Aaron.

22:4 2o ܢܬܕܟܐ] ܕܕܟܐ 6b1: the text and the variant provide a difference of syntax, *impf* and *pt* respectively, for MT *impf*

22:7 ܘܒܡܥܪ̈ܒ] ܘܡܥܪ̈ܒ 6b1: the text and the variant provide slightly different idiom as equivalents for MT(השמש) ובא .

22:9 ܐܢܐ 3o] *om* 6b1 9a1: the text provides a further pronoun with the participle, to render an infinitive construct with suffix, as well as providing two pronouns in the verbless clause. The syntax is different from the Hebrew which has only one אני .

22:10 ܕܟܗܢܐ] *c. sey* 9a1: the text = MT.

22:11 ܟܣܦܗ] ܟܣܦܐ 6b1: the text = MT.

22:15 ܩܘܕ̈ܫܐ] *s.sey* 6b1: the text = MT, the variant is an error.

22:16 ܘܚܛ̈ܗܐ] *s.sey* 6b1: the text and the variant provide an interpretation of MT עון אשמה in ܚܘܒܐ ܘܚܛ̈ܗܐ ; the variant is an error.

22:18 ܒܝܬ] *pr dalath* 6b1: the preceding ܡܢ was taken for ܡ̇ܢ , or the addition is an independent error.

22:30 1o ܘܒܗ] *om waw* 6b1 = MT.

22:30 2o ܠܡ ܨܦܪܐ] ܠܨܦܪܐ 6b1: the text and the variant make different choices of equivalents, *cf* 6:2 *etc.*

22:32 ܬܛܢܦܘܢ] ܬܛܡܐܘܢ 9a1: the text and the variant make different choices of equivalent, without difference of meaning, *cf* 21:12. MT has תחללו .

23:2 ܕܬܩܪܘܢ] *om dalath* 6b1: the difference is syntactic; the text (=MT) prefers a *dalath* to introduce speech.

ܕܬܛܪܘܢ 9a1: the variant here provides a different equivalent, "observe" rather than "proclaim".

23:4 ܬܩܪܘܢ] ܬܛܪܘܢ 9a1: as in the previous lemma.

23:7 ܝܘܡܐ] *pr waw* 6b1: the text and the variant provide a difference of idiom to represent the temporal adverb MT ביום.

23:11 ܡܢ ܡܕܒܪܐ / ܠܡܘܒܠܐ] *tr* 7a1 9a1*: the text = MT; the difference is one of preference in word order.

23:12 ܒܝܘܡܐ] ܒܗ ܒܝܘܡܐ 6b1: idiom, the text = MT.

23:13 ܣܘܬܐ] ܢܝܚܐ 6b1 7a1: *cf* 3:16.

23:18 ܣܘܬܐ] ܢܝܚܐ 6b1 7a1: *cf* above.

23:21 ܒܟܠܗ ܒܝܬ ܠܕܪ̈ܝܟܘܢ] ܒܟܠܗ ܒܝܬ ܡܥܡܪܟܘܢ. ܡܥܡܪܟܘܢ. ܠܕܪ̈ܝܟܘܢ 6b1 9a1* = MT: the difference between the text and the variant is one of syntax, viz. the placing of an adverb phrase.

23:22$_1$o ܣܦܪ̈ܐ] *s.sey* 6b1 8a1(*vid*): the text = MT; the difference is the text's preference for a plural where there are many items, and the variant's for a singular where each has only one.

23:22$_2$o ܐܠܗܟܘܢ] ܐܠܗܐ 6b1: the text = MT.

23:25 ܥܒܕ̇] ܥܒܕܐ 6b1 9a1: the text = MT, "work-of", (construct state).

23:27 ܩܘܪܒܢܐ] *c.sey* 6b1: the text = MT; the variant uses plural as it understands there is a frequency of offerings.

23:30 ܠܢܦܫܐ] *om lamadh* 6b1: the text = MT; it has an object marker.

23:31 ܘܟܠ] *om waw* 9a1: the text = MT.

23:32 ܒܝܬ ܪ̈ܡܫܐ] *om* 9a1 = MT: the text is an expication.

23:35$_1$o ܦܪܝܐ] ܦܪܐ 9a1: the text prefers the emphatic, and the variant the absolute state.

23:35$_2$o ܦܘܪܝܫܐ] ܦܘܪܝܫ 8a1 9a1: the same preference as above.

23:35$_3$o ܥܒܕ̇] ܥܒܕܐ 6b1: see vs. 25.

23:36$_1$o ܘܩܪܒܘ 1°] ܩܪܒܘ 6b1 = MT.

23:36$_2$o ܟܢܫܝܢ] ܟܢܘܫܝܢ 6b1 9a1: both the text and the variant have ܗܘܝܬܘܢ immediately before, and so provide different equivalents of MT עצרת הוא , "day of assembling", an active (text) or a passive (variant) *pt* meaning "assembling" or "assembled".

23:37₁₀ ܒܗܘܢ] *om* 6b1 = MT: an addition for clarification by the text.

23:37₂₀ ܘܢܘ̈ܣܟܐ ܘܕܒ̈ܚܐ] *tr* 9a1: MT זבח ונסכים .

23:38 ܘܡܘܗܒܬܟ - ܘܡܘ̈ܗܒܬܟܘܢ 1°] *om* 6b1 9a1 = MT: the text provides a double translation of מתנותיכם .

23:39 ܡܛܠܠܬܐ] *c.sey* 8a1 9a1 9b1: the text = MT.

23:40 ܣܒܘ] *pr waw* 6b1 = MT.

24:2 ܕܒܣܡܐ ܕܙܝܬܐ] *tr* 8b1 9a1 9b1 and majority of manuscripts: the text and the variant provide different equivalents of the Hebrew construct, adjective, and noun. MT has זית זך (שמן).

24:8 ܐܝܟܢܐܝܬ] *om* 9a1. The text = MT.

24:9* ܘܢܐܟܠܘܢܗ] ܕܢܐܟܠܘܢܗ 9a1: the variant provides a final clause, and the text a consecutive clause; MT has *waw* and a finite verb.

24:11 ܘܓܕܦܐ] ܘܓܕܦܗ̇ 6b1: the variant provides an idiomatic anticipatory suffix.

25:2 ܪܘܚܬܐ] *om* 6b1 9a1* = MT: the text adds the word for explication.

25:5* ܕܫܒܬܐ] ܕܫܒܐ 9a1: the variant is an error, or a different equivalent with no difference in meaning, for MT שבתון .

25:7 ܬܗܘܐ] *pr waw* 8a1 9a1 9b1* and majority. The text = MT.

25:8 ܕܫܢ̈ܝܐ] *c.sey* 6b1 8b1 9a1: the text = MT.

25:11₁₀ ܐܪ̈ܥܟܘܢ] ܐܪ̈ܥܬܟܘܢ 6b1: neither the text nor the variant is in MT; both expand in order to clarify the meaning.

25:11₂₀ ܘܠܐ] ܐܦ ܠܐ 6b1 7a1: the difference is of idiom for emphasis.

25:12₁₀ ܘܡܢ] *om waw* 9a1 = MT.

25:12₂₀ ܥܠܠܬܐ] ܥܠܠܬܗ̇ 9a1 = MT, suffixed, but singular.

25:14   ܐ] *om* 9a1. The text = MT.

25:15[1]0   ܩܢܘܒܣ̈ܐ]ܩ ܣܒܘܢ̈ܣܘ 6b1: the difference is of syntax, the variant prefers a construct, and the text an absolute with *dalath,* for the construct in MT here.

25:15[2]0   ܢ.ܐܘܒܕ 2[0]] *om dalath* 6b1: *cf* construction above.

25:15[3]0   ܢ.ܐܠܠܬܐ] *c. sey* 6b1: the variant thinks that there is a multitude of harvests, the text that there is one each year.

25:16[1]0   ܢ.ܐܠܠܬܐ] *c. sey* 9a1: *cf* above.

25:16[2]0   ܢ.ܐܒܘܒܣ 3[0]] *om* 6b1 8b1 9a1* = MT. The text adds to clarify the meaning.

25:20   ܐܣܢܘܣ]ܐ ܣܢܘܣܐ 6b1: the variant prefers the longer form.

25:21   ܐܠܠܬܐ] *c. sey* 9a1, *cf* vs. 16.

25:23[1]0   ܐܗ]ܗ.ܒܘ.ܐ 6b1: this may reflect unpointed Hebrew חמכר instead of MT's pointing, which is *ni ph'al.*

25:23[2]0   ܐ.ܒ̈ܣܩ̈ܐܪ]ܐ ܝܒܣܩ̈ܐܪ 9a1: the addition of a suffix clarifies the meaning.

25:24   ܢ.ܒ̈ܗܐܗܐܩܗ] ܩ.ܐ̈ܗܐܒܣܩ 9a1: the text and the variant present different equivalents, "inheritance" or "heritage". The text is consistent with vv. 27, 28, 33. But the word ܩܒܐܗ̈ܪ is found in vv. 45, 46. MT has אחזה in all these places.

25:27[1]0   ܒܣܩܣܒ] *pr waw* 9a1 = MT.

25:27[2]0   ܢ.ܒܘܒܣܗܩ]ܢ ܐܗܒܣܣܗܘܗ 9a1: the difference is one of form, though the variant is not listed in Payne Smith. It may therefore be an error, *cf* vs. 29.

25:28   ܩܕ̈ܒܐ]ܩ ܒܣܕ̈ܐ 6b1 9a1: the text and the variant give different equivalents here, *pt* and *impf*, where the former stresses continuous action, and the latter indefinite future action. MT has מצאה , with יד as subject.

25:29   ܢ.ܒܘܒܣܗܩ]ܢ ܐܗܒܣܣܗܗ 9a1: the text = MT, the variant without suffix loses definition.

25:30[1]0   ܢ.ܒܣܠܐܪ]ܢ ܐܒܣܠܪ 9a1 = MT: the text has assimilated ܢ.ܐܒܣܠܪ to ܢ.ܒܣܠܐܪ in vs. 29, and is consistent with

ܫܠܡܬܐ 3 words later.

25:30₂° ܕܒܩܪܝܬܐ] ܕܩܪܝܬܐ 8a1^c 9a1 9b1 and majority of manuscripts: the text = MT, with its sense of a relative clause.

25:31₁° ܒ̈ܬܐ] *pr waw* 9a1 = MT.

25:31₂° ܕܠܡ] *om* 9a1*: the text's use of the particle is idiomatic.

25:31₃° ܕܚܩ̈ܠܐ] *s. sey* 6b1: the text = MT, the variant considers the singular "open space" to be more suitable.

25:33₁° ܢܦܘܩ ܡܢ] *om* 9a1*: the text = MT.

25:33₂° ܘܩܪܝܬܐ] *c. sey* 6b1: MT is confused, בית ועיר . Perhaps this was originally בתי ערי . Probably the variant is right in its interpretation, "cities (of the Levites)".

25:38 ܕܐܬܠ] ܘܐܬܠ 6b1 9a1: the text and the variant are different equivalents for MT infinitive, לתת ; the text is preferable.

25:40 ܢܗܘܐ 2°] ܢܦܠܘܚ 9a1: the text and the variant are different equivalents for יעבד , "be" and "serve", unless the text erroneously repeats ܢܗܘܐ 1°.

25:41₁°* ܠܝܪܬܘܬܗ] ܠܝܪܬܘܬܐ 6b1: the variant's ending is an error by assimilation to that of the next word. The text = MT.

25:41₂° ܕܐܒܘܗܝ] ܕܐ̈ܒܗܘܗܝ 8a1^c 9a1 9b1* and majority of manuscripts = MT: the text distinguishes "father's" from "fathers'" inheritance.

25:45 ܝ̈ܪܬܘܬܗܘܢ] *s. sey* 8a1^c 8b1 9a1 9b1* and majority of manuscripts = MT: the difference between the text and the variant reflects the previous lemma.

25:46 ܦܘܪܩܢܐ] ܦܘܩܪܢܐ 6b1: the difference is a preference for one form rather than another, *cf* vs. 24.

25:47₁° ܘܕܬܘܬܒܐ] ܘܬܘܬܒܐ 9a1 = MT: the text makes a syntactic change, adding a *dalath* as in the previous word of the pair.

25:47$_2$o ܥܡܗ] *pr dalath* 6b1: the text = MT suggests "with him", not "who is with him".

25:52$_1$o ܢܚܫܘܒ] *pr waw* 6b1 9a1*: the text = MT, the variant prefers a conjunction.

25:52$_2$o ܘܐܝܟ] *om waw* 9a1 = MT: the reverse of the previous lemma.

25:55 ܐܢܘܢ 3°] *om* 6b1: the text = MT, and the difference from the variant is that of the number of pronouns used in a verbless clause.

26:2 ܠܡܩܕ̈ܫܝ] ܥܡ̈ܝ 6b1 = MT: a difference of interpretation, *cf* 19:30 above.

26:4 ܘܐܪܥܐ ܬܬܠ] ܘܬܬܠ ܐܪܥܐ 6b1 = MT: the text balances the two parts of sentence, showing a preference in word order and rhythm.

26:5 ܒܐܪܥܟܘܢ ܒܬܘܟܠܐ] *tr* 9a1 = MT: the text places the adverb second.

26:6 ܐܪܥܐ] ܐܪܥܟܘܢ 6b1; the text = MT, the variant's suffix emphasises it as the possession of the Israelites.

26:8 ܒܥܠܕܒ̈ܒܝܟܘܢ ܩܕܡܝܟܘܢ] *tr* 9a1: the variant places the adverbial element first; the text = MT.

26:10 ܕܥܬܝܩܐ] ܕܥܬܝܩ 6b1: the text and the variant are different equivalents for a Hebrew participle.

26:13 ܘܗܠܟܬܟܘܢ] ܘܗܠܟܬܘܢ 6b1 8b1: the text = MT. There are different equivalents, the text is "I made you walk"; the variant "you walked".

26:14 ܗܠܝܢ ܟܠܗܘܢ] *tr* 6b1: there is a difference in word order. Neither that of the text nor thevariant conforms to MT.

26:15 ܘܦܘܩܕ̈ܢܝ ܬܒܛܠܘܢ] ܘܬܒܛܠܘܢ ܦܘܩܕ̈ܢܝ 9a1 = MT: the text gives difference of emphasis through a difference in word order.

26:18 ܬܘܒ] *om* 9a1: the particle was interpolated in the text for the sake of idiom.

26:20$_1$o ܘܐܪܥܟܘܢ ܠܐ ܬܬܠ] ܘܠܐ ܬܬܠ ܐܪܥܟܘܢ 9a1*: the variant places the verb first, for emphasis, the variant = MT.

26:20$_2$o ܥܠܠܬܗ̇] ܥܠܠܬܐ 9a1: the text = MT, the variant loses effect with loss of suffix, which may result from assimilation to the end of the following word.

26:22$_1$o ܕܚܩܠܐ] ܕܕܒܪܐ 9a1 (ܕܐܪܥܐ 10b2): here there are two equivalents, with no difference in meaning, for MT שׂדה.

26:22$_2$o ܘܬܒܙܝܟܘܢ] ܘܬܒܘܙܟܘܢ 6b1 and majority: the difference is one of the roots ܒܘܙ and ܒܙܐ, each weak in one letter, but with no difference in meaning. MT has ושכלה אתכם.

26:23$_1$o ܬܘܒ ܒܗܠܝܢ] *tr* 6b1: the difference in word order is a matter of idiom.

26:23$_2$o ܬܘܒ] *om* 9a1*: *cf* vs. 18.

26:25$_1$o ܘܐܝܬܐ] ܘܐܬܠ 9a1: the text and the variant provide different equivalents. MT has והבאתי.

26:25$_2$o ܕܒܥܠܕܒܒܐ] ܕܒܥܠܕܒܒܝܗܘܢ 8a1 9a1 9b1 and majority: here there are two different interpretations of ביד אויב.

26:27$_1$o ܒܗܠܝܢ] ܒܗܕܐ 6b1 = MT בזאת: the text and the variant provide different idiom.

26:27$_2$o ܬܘܒ] *om* 9a1*: *cf* vs 23.

26:28$_1$o ܘܐܦ] *om waw* 8a1 9a1: the text is more idiomatic; MT has *waw* only.

26:28$_2$o ܘܒܚܪܝܢܘܬܐ] ܕܚܪܝܢܘܬܐ 6b1 9a1 = MT: the text is idiomatic. There are different equivalents, the text giving the force of a separate element: "in anger and in contrariety", instead of "in the anger of contrariety".

26:31 ܕܒܣܡܘܬܟܘܢ] ܕܒܣܡܝܟܘܢ 6b1: *cf* 3:16.

26:34 ܬܬܪܥܐ] ܬܪܥܐ 9a1: different equivalents are provided by the text (*ethpe'el*) and the variant (*pe'al*), with no difference in meaning. MT has תרצה.

26:35 ܕܚܕܘܬܗ̇] ܕܚܪܒܘܬܗ̇ 6b1: the text and the variant provide different words, "lying waste" and "poverty", unless there is an inner Syriac error. MT has השמה.

26:37 ܐܝܟ ܕܡܢ] ܡܢ 6b1: the text = MT.

26:39 ܘܐܦ] *om waw* 9a1 10b2 and majority of manuscripts: the text = MT.

26:40 ܒܡܪܚܘܬܐ] ܒܡܚܪܘܬܐ 9a1^{txt}: here there is a difference of interpretation, "contrariety" against "laying waste". MT is בקרי; probably the variant is an error.

26:45$_{1^o}$ ܐܠܐ --- ܕܡܕܒܪܢܐ / ܡܛܠ --- ܐܠܗܗܘܢ] *tr* 6b1 9a1: the variant places cause before consequence.

26:45$_{2^o}$ ܐܠܗܗܘܢ] ܐܠܗܟܘܢ 6b1 8a1*: the text and the variant show a difference of interpretation, the text = MT, and variant making the references to the current generation by using the suffix "your" rather than "their".

26:46$_{1^o}$ ܘܢܡܘ̈ܣܐ ܘܕܝ̈ܢܐ] *tr* 6b1 8a1* 9a1* = MT: the variant has ܕܝ̈ܢܐ first, as in vs. 43.

26:46$_{2^o}$ ܒܐܝܕܐ] ܒܐܝܕܗ 6b1 9a1: the variant is more idiomatic in that it adds a suffix.

27:6 ܕܟܣܦܐ 2°] *om* 6b1 8a1 9b1 and majority of manuscripts. The text = MT; the variant lets the sense of the first use of the word carry over.

27:8$_{1^o}$ ܢܩܝܡܘܢܗ] ܢܩܝܡܘܗܝ 9a1 = MT. The text takes an indefinite 3rd. person plural subject.

27:8$_{2^o}$ ܟܗܢܐ ܕܢ̈ܘܗܝ] *tr* 6b1 8b1 9a1 9b1 and majority of manuscripts: the difference is the relative position of subject and object.

27:10 ܠܡܒܪܐ] *om* 6b1 8a1(*ras*) 8b1 9a1 and majority 0f manuscripts = MT: the text has added the word for clarity.

27:15 ܕܕܢ̈ܘܗܝ] ܕܢ̈ܘܗܝ 6b1 10b2: the variant considers this word to be in apposition to the previous word.

27:17 ܕܦܘܢܝܐ] ܕܡܬܦܢܝܐ 6b1 9a1: there are two different equivalents, a participle and a noun. The text = MT, *cf* vs. 18.

27:20 ܠܚܒܪܐ] *pr* ܢܦܠܐ 6b1: the variant repeats the word found two words earlier, for the sake of clarity. The text = MT.

27:22	ܗܘܐ] ܗܘܬ 6b1 9a1: the variant uses a feminine, to agree with ܐܠܘ.
27:25₁0	ܠܟܝܡ] pr waw 6b1 8b1 9a1: the text = MT.
27:25₂0	ܡܢܬܚ]ܡܕܬ 6b1: the text and the variant have two different equivalents: "modius" against "farthings". MT has גרה.
27:25₃0	ܗܘܐ] ܢܗܘܐ 9a1: there is a syntactic difference, the text preferring *pt* and the variant *impf*, both indicating continuing custom. MT has *impf*.
27:30	ܠܡܥܣܪ] c. *sey* 6b1 8a1 9b1*(*vid*) 9a1: in this lemma and the next, the difference between text and variant is orthographic, the presence or absence of *seyame* on a numeral.
27:32	ܠܡܥܣܪ] s.*sey* 8a1ᶜ(*vid*) 8b1 9a1(*vid*).
27:34	ܦܘܩܕܢܐ] *om* 9a1: the text = MT. The variant concentrates on the giver of the commands.

3. *Assessment of the divergences*

There are, then, some 350 variants. Some 75 show the Leiden printed text to be formally equivalent to MT, and some 125 show 6b1 and/or 9a1 to be formally equivalent to MT. Some 12 instances show that both the text and the variants of 6b1/9a1 differ from MT. The remaining (138) places do not suggest any significant conclusions. It might seem, therefore, that 6b1/9a1 are examples of a preference for formal equivalents, word for word renderings, identity of syntax, matching order of words, and even cognates. Yet the number of approximations to MT on the part of 7a1 (as emended and printed) shows that the matter is not so clear-cut. This is confirmed when it is seen that a number of the unclassified differences are of Syriac idiom: small matters of particles and enclitics. The figures by themselves conceal as much as they reveal, and some account must be given of the kind of divergences which appear.

(a) 16 readings are worth noting, as suggesting lexical

differences, and each is noted above: 3:16; 4:8; 6:2; 11:19; 16:32$_2$o; 17:15; 19:30/26:2; 20:17$_1$o; 21:12, 20$_2$o; 23:38; 25:24; 26:13, 35, 40; 27:25$_2$o. The question is one of interpretation, in that the Hebrew is not understood, or is capable of being understood in more than one way: hence translation demands exegesis. The divergences in 17:15 and 23:38 suggest that the text has a double rendering of a single Hebrew phrase. Such differences indicate equally valid methods of giving equivalents to the same Hebrew original, rather than a revision of the text to conform to MT or to depart from it.

(b) The most typical of the changes fall into two groups. The first group contains variants which indicate that an addition has been made in order to explicate. Most commonly 6b1/9a1 provide the shorter text. When this is compared with the longer text, 7a1 or 7a1 (as emended and printed), the shorter text appears to demonstrate (and indeed in the Apparatus is recorded as being) *omission*. On the contrary, it is the longer text which is *addition*. When the evidence can be set out in a different way, as above, the additional matter can be noted differently and the matter made plain. Hence the use of the term "non-interpolation" might be an appropriate way to signify matter which, although added to later manuscripts, is not added to earlier ones. The confusion caused by noting down what has not been added as an omission is an interesting consequence of having to collate different kinds of text against one base. Less extreme examples of explanatory changes, which do not add to the substance of the text, merely to an understanding of it, are: 4:31$_2$o; 7:6$_2$o; 9:2$_1$o; 10:12, 18; 13:3$_1$o, 27, 54$_2$o; 16:7, 17; 19:6$_1$o and 25:11$_1$o. 10:12 and 19:6$_2$o show an expansion by the earlier text, 6b1, although all texts clarify the Hebrew in these two places. But for the rest of these examples it is 7a1 and later manuscripts which provide the expansions and additions.

(c) The second of the most typical changes is that of syntax, and particularly the change of word order. Examples of places where a change of order has been made for such purposes as placing subject of clause first, placing adverbs and adverbial phrases later, keeping to an ordering of pairs, or selecting order for emphasis or for perceived logic are: $4:20_{2}$o; 9:11; 12:8; $13:52_{2}$o, 57; 16:1; 17:7, 11_{2}o; 18:24; 26:4, 45_{1}o. The later text, 7a1 and later manuscripts, prefers the adverb to follow the verb, and causal clauses to follow the main clause.

(d) Examples of readings which are syntactic differences other than word order may be found at: 7:7; $9:7_{1}$o; 13:16, 57; 15:10, 12, 32; 16:5,13; $17:13_{2}$o; 20:9; $22:4_{2}$o; $25:11_{2}$o; and 27:17. There is no clear-cut distinction to be made, such as that the earlier, 6b1 text, prefers imperfects, whereas the 7a1 and later text prefer participles and infinitives in indefinite clauses. The evidence runs in both directions.

4. *The development of a tendency*

From the evidence set out and discussed above it can be seen that the relation between the Syriac and MT is not as straightforward as it might appear at first sight. Certainly there is a link between 6b1 and 9a1, but it is not one which might demonstrate dependence. Nor yet is it the case that 6b1 and 9a1 are consistent in presenting a text which is demonstrably closer in the matter of formal equivalents to MT. Many of the differences between 6b1+9a1 and the printed Leiden text are in the realm of syntax, particularly word order, rather than major interpretative difference of vocabulary. They speak of different ways of representing an identical Hebrew *Vorlage*, but in style rather than substance. Yet despite that, it is hard to avoid the conclusion that in the kind of text they represent, anterior to the kind of text represented by 7a1, there was a tendency to cling to the shape of the Hebrew text, or the ordering of its words. The change, however, was one of degree and not of kind: an inherent process had an added impetus. Whether there was at that period, in the seventh century, a desire for greater flexibility or merely a tolerance of a more idiomatic approach cannot be finally demonstrated. Certainly there was a concern for a greater clarity: but while biblical transmission might reflect current cultural trends, the nature of the material exercises a restraint on scribal activity. Furthermore, as the previous chapter suggested, after the ninth and tenth centuries the influence of a common base for a text confirmed whatever interpretative consolidation had been reached by that time. Both exegesis and syntax had reached a stability, leaving later deviations to be matter of ignorance and error rather than of acceptable alternatives.

Hence the interpretative element necessary in changing a Hebrew text into a Syriac one should be understood as a process, evidence of which can be found in the later stages of the text transmission as well as at the presumed beginning. 7a1 represents something of a watershed, as the difference in character between the standard text and the earlier (6b1/antecedent of 9a1) text indicates. Again it can be said that the absence from Leviticus of 5b1 is regrettable. Its lack prevents an assessment of 6b1/9a1 against that kind of text. Confirmatory evidence of the findings of this paper comes from the comments of three writers who allude to the question of an "original" Peshiṭta. De Boer warned on p. 355 of his Cambridge lecture "Towards an Edition", previously referred to, that the search for an "original" Peshiṭta could be unrealistic:

An attempt to reconstruct "the" Peshiṭta version enters the danger zone in which easy wishful thinking, or unrealistic ideas about the purity and perfection of the first, original copy call the tune.

Gwilliam pointed out on p. 66 of "The Materials for the criticism of the Peshitto New Testament",

It ought to be unnecessary to repeat that exemplars are witnesses to texts which are older than the leaves of the exemplars.

This might suggest that a process of infinite regression from extant manuscripts might lead to the "original" after all; but this notion is countered by a comment of Dirksen on p. 146 of "The Ancient Peshiṭta MSS of Judges and their Variant Readings":

No text edition can establish a text which is (much) older than the text of the MSS which have been used for it.

What must remain in doubt is the appropriateness of the term "closeness to MT". Closeness is a subjective judgment, and can be expressed in different ways: most typically in the difference between closeness to what MT says, and closeness to what MT may mean. Hence the use of the term suggests that there should be further examination of what the translators intended, and the influences which were brought to bear on the text in the process of its transmission through the years.

CHAPTER FIVE

TEXT AND INTERPRETATION

Attempts to use the Peshiṭṭa as a mechanical aid in text
criticism of MT fail because of the interpretative element in
the version. The interpretative element is inherent from the
outset, not secondary and found only in the transmission of the
text. The aims and methods of the translators must be
identified.

1. *Three related problems*

There are three related problems which become recognisable
when the Peshiṭṭa is identified as a translation; none of the
three can readily be addressed in isolation, but it is now
necessary to disentangle and identify them. They are the
problems of the text itself and criticism of it; the
transmission of the text and its history; and the methods of
translation which result in the text. The purpose of this
chapter is to set out the terms of the discussion, so that the
chapter which follows can give detailed evidence. For the
sake of clarity the conclusions can be anticipated. First, that
attempts to use the Peshiṭṭa as a tool for textual criticism of
MT will fail, if it is forgotten that the Peshiṭṭa is a version
which has interpretation inherent in its making: it is not a
mechanical replication. Secondly, the Peshiṭṭa, in common
with other versions and indeed the Massoretic Text itself, has
a history of transmission. In the course of this, the inner
dynamic of the text influences the conscious or unconscious
unacknowledged changes which scribes may introduce.
Thirdly, the recognition of the method and scope of the

translation is fundamental to an understanding of the nature of the Peshiṭta: this basic character influences the process of transmission.

Three separate issues can therefore be identified as problematic. The first has to do with *Vorlage*: it looms large in the discussions on the Peshiṭta such as Dirksen summarised in his contribution to *Mikra* referred to earlier; basically they regard the Peshiṭta as representation. That is to say, the version is regarded as an attempt to make a Hebrew text comprehensible to those who required a Syriac basis for an understanding of it in exegesis and homily. This view sites the interpretative element in a text other than the translation itself. One possibility is to site it in an identifiable Hebrew text, distinct from MT, which is already charged with the interpretative element which could be the basis of the version. Alternatively, the interpretative element might be sited in a middle term between the Hebrew and the translation; hence the search for an identifiable Targum which might be this medium of exchange.

The second issue to be identified is that of the nature of the Peshiṭta as a version; it has to do with kind rather than content, with the literary quality and adequacy of the version. It concerns the accommodation of the translation to those who needed a Syriac rendering; those who, moreover, required one which was familiarly comprehensible. The ease with which the Syriac could be understood was of more immediate necessity than the explication of the Hebrew: that, after all, could be taken for granted once the Syriac version had come to birth. If the translators were more familiar with the Hebrew, the transcribers and users were more (if not only) familiar with the Syriac language. This has led to the view that the transmission rather than the origin of the text determines its interpretative character. This character could derive from the cumulative effect of small but significant changes, conscious or otherwise; or it could come from deliberate re-shaping along the lines of discoverable principles.

The third issue is that of definition of terms. The terms Targum and Peshiṭta are commonly used in discussions, but imprecisely or ambiguously. They may be used descriptively, that is "Targum" refers to known and identifiable material, such as Onqelos, Ps Jonathan or Neofiti; and "Peshiṭta" refers to the Syriac text of the Old Testament which is to be distinguished from the Syro-Hexaplar and from Jacob of Edessa's revision. Alternatively, the terms may be used expressively, to indicate a type of approach: an oral tradition of interpretation which sticks closely to the Hebrew, provides enough explication for comprehension, but leaves homiletic to a further stage of text handling.

Quite clearly, text criticism, text history and translation criticism can indeed be separated: yet all three interact. Their interaction is seen where, in the present study and in the Introduction to the Leviticus edition, certain passages have been considered under each of these three heads. Text history is summarised in the Introduction to the edition, and in the present study text criticism is addressed primarily in Chapter 2 and translation criticism in Chapter 6. This latter chapter shows that their interaction is seen even more clearly when it is recognised that the term "Peshiṭta" indicates both hermeneutic method and a version which ante-dates the present forms of recognised Targum. Hence the present chapter starts with a salutary warning to those who would use the Peshiṭta to reconstruct a Hebrew *Vorlage*, goes on to discuss the term Targum as applicable to Peshiṭta studies, and concludes with general remarks on problems and opportunities facing a translator from Hebrew into Syriac.

2. *The hazards of retro-translation*

The traditional concern with the Peshiṭta version has been to assess its contribution to text criticism of the Hebrew bible. *Biblia Hebraica Stuttgartensia,* in De Boer's editing of Samuel at any rate, has recognised the problem that neither "the Hebrew text" nor "the text of the Peshiṭta" is a fixed term, and thereby suggests the axiom that text criticism is a study of variables by means of variables. Hence its apparatus cites different editions of the Peshiṭta: Lee, Walton, Urmia and Mosul, together with four specified and several unspecified codices. But not even this care in identifying different kinds of Peshiṭta text leads to satisfactory conclusions.

The problem is, simply, that to construct a putative Hebrew which the Peshiṭta is supposed to reflect is a hopelessly subjective enterprise. Even if the purpose of *BHS* was only to offer a number of readings different from MT, leaving it to the user to decide whether the version was an interpretation of MT or a translation of a different *Vorlage,* the implication was that a retro-translation was possible. The subjectivity of such an enterprise is shown by a sampling of the evidence. In the following selection the evidence from *BHS* is set out after the MT lemma: the listing of the witnesses corresponds with that of *BHS.* Comment is also provided, by which it is shown that the Syriac text does not provide evidence of a different *Vorlage,* but does give evidence of interpretation or explication. The word "but" makes the point clear that the comment refers to the Peshiṭta rendering. It will be seen that while the evidence of the apparatus is set out below, the present discussion is concerned only with the Peshiṭta, and no conclusions can be drawn about the methodology of the other versions or their relationship with the Peshiṭta.

1:1   יהוה] Pesh *tr post* ויקרא : but this is a necessary change to show that יהוה is the subject for the first as well as the second verb of the verse.

1:2   קרבניכם [קרבנכם Sam LXX Pesh: but this is a difference of idiom (attaching the suffix to a plural rather than a singular), suggesting that more than one offering comes from each person, or that individual offerings are taken together. The conjunction of Sam and LXX with Pesh suggests a different *Vorlage*. It is, however, an example of shared method.

1:4   העלה[קרבנו Pesh: but Pesh in Leviticus is systematic in its rendering, and in this passage uses the general term ܩܘܪܒܢܐ until definitions later in the text make it possible to use a specific one. In 1:14 it is not yet clear which of the terms ܩܘܪܒ, ܥܠܬܐ, or ܥܠܬܐ is appropriate.

1:7   הכהנים בני אהרן [בני אהרן הכהן Pesh: but this is an order of words to make clear that the subject of the sentence is explicitly "the priests".

1:8   ואת הראש [את הראש Mss Sam LXX Pesh TgMss: this conjunction of witnesses again suggests a different *Vorlage*, but a shared use of the conjunction for making an express link is as likely. The Syriac has ܪܝܫܐ, without object marker.

1:14   מן התרים] *add* ליהוה Pesh: but the Syriac has added this indirect object for clarification, following the pattern of the previous part of the verse where there is the same indirect object.

1:16   בנצתו [בנצתה Sam Pesh Tg Tg^J , prp *pr* ואת : but the Syriac takes a different meaning from that of MT, "the crop and *its content*" rather than "the crop and *its feathers*". The Syriac second noun's suffix requires a masculine antecedent, which is "crop" and not "bird".

4:14   פר] *add* אחד Pesh: but this is the Syriac indefinite article, provided as the equivalent of a Hebrew anarthrous noun.

5:11   וישים [יצק Sam LXX Pesh: but the Syriac uses ܪܡܐ to render נתן in the next phrase; in this phrase ܢܣܝܡ is an obvious root to use where oil is concerned.

5:24   מכל] add דבר Sam LXX Pesh Tg^J: Pesh has ܟܠܡܕܡ which is the appropriate term to render MT, unless כל is understood as a plural "everything" rather than "anything".

6:14   חפתנה [תפיני sec Pesh: but the Syriac is an attempt at explication. The Hebrew is not straightforward and an interpretation has been offered, mentioned in the discussion in Chapter 6.

6:20   תכבס [יכבס Sam LXX Pesh Tg^J Vg: but in Pesh the verbs are passive verbs (ܢܬܚܘܪ and ܢܬܬܫܝܓ). The whole syntax of the translation "shall be washed" is different from the Hebrew "You shall wash".

7:21   שרץ [שקץ pc Ms (sic) Sam Pesh TgMs: but Pesh aims at consistency, cf 5:2, and prefers a general term at this stage in the text because definitions have not yet been established.

7:32   ליהוה [לכהן Pesh: but this is to avoid anticipation of the next phrase. It is only by virtue of its being an offering to the Lord that there is a participation by the priest.

8:8   על [אל Sam LXX Pesh: but Pesh has a completely different understanding of what is described: it understands words rather than objects. ܠܝ is the appropriate term when the items are understood as an *inscription* upon the breastplate. This is mentioned in the discussion in Chapter 6, p. 124.

8:19   וישחטהו משה [וישחט Pesh, cf vs. 14: but there is an error in the Syriac, partly a conflation of phrases in the passage, and partly a misunderstanding as to who slays the ram.

9:4   נראה [נראָה LXX (Pesh Tg Tg^J Vg): but here there is a difference between possible renderings of an unpointed text, cf vv. 6,23; 16:2. In vs. 21 there is a similar instance: צוה is taken by Pesh as passive צֻוָּה .

13:42 בגבחת, בקרחת [בגבחתו, בקרחתו Sam LXX Pesh TgMs: but the suffix is added for precision, see p. 122.

13:50,54 [והסגירו add הכהן Ms LXX Pesh (Tg): but the addition has been made for explication.

15:31 [והזרתם והזהרתם Sam Pesh: but the MT word has been understood as "to warn" rather than as "to separate"; *cf* the use of the word at Ezek 3:18, 33:7,8,9.

19:18 [לא תקם *om* Pesh: but the lemma is in fact represented in the Pesh, which renders these words and ולא תטר together in the phrase ܠܐ ܬܛܪ ܒܣܢܐܬܐ, see p. 111.

23:21 [יהיה לכם *om* Pesh: but Pesh casts the verse in a different way, mainly in order to render a Hebrew construct phrase מקרא קדש by a Syriac participle and adjective ܝܘܡܐ ܡܩܕܫܐ so as to denote the character of the day in itself, rather than what it was to be for Israel. The two Hebrew words of the lemma are then not necessary.

23:26 [לאמר add דבר לבני ישראל לאמר Pesh: but this is an expansion so that this verse corresponds with vs. 2.

24:23 [אבן add וימת Pesh: but this is an addition for explication.

26:2 [שבתתי מצותי Pesh: but this is interpretation. See the comments in Chapters 3 and 4 on this verse and on 19:3, 30. See pp. 62, 70, 96.

27:22 [יקדיש add איש Ms Pesh: but in fact all manuscripts have ܢܩܕܫ . איש is not in fact necessary, though Pesh does add this word for explication. Further, to an English ear at least, a Hebrew יקדיש איש קדיש is hardly euphonious.

Two comments are appropriate at this point. First, that there is a clustering of witnesses, Sam LXX and Pesh, at 1:2, 8; 5:11, 24; 6:20; 8:8. This suggests that where these three

witnesses concur a *Vorlage* other than the MT is to be
assumed. The *BHS* apparatus for Leviticus suggests 50
places where Sam and LXX readings agree against the MT.
By far the greatest number of these indicate additions and
omissions which suggest explication rather than evidence of
a Hebrew text to rival the Massoretic. The evidence shows
that the expansion and contraction is in the translation
process rather than the basic text. Were it in the basic text
greater variations would be present.

Some examples of the 50 may be given, using the
reconstructed Hebrew suggested by *BHS*:

1:10	ליהוה *add* [קרבנו ;
4:5	אשר מלא את ידו *add* [המשיח ;
5:6	על חטאתו אשר חטא ונסלח לו [מחטאתו , *cf* 4:35;
9:3	זקני [בני ;
9:21	יהוה את *add* [צוה ;
13:3,5,17,	
27,36	וראה [וראהו ;
17:4	לעשת אתו עלה או שלמים ליהוה לרצונכם*add* [הביאו
	לריח ניחח וישחטהו בחוץ ואל פתח אהל מועד לא הביאו.

The second comment is that at such places as 1:16; 6:14;
15:31; 19:18; 26:2 MT presents texts which are difficult and
problematic. It is it least as likely that the Peshiṭta
translator(s) resolved the problem independently of other
versions as that the *Vorlage* differed from MT. The
evidence above shows that there can be no simple
assumption that the Peshiṭta is a mechanical reproduction of
MT. What once seemed to be evidence of another Hebrew
text proves to be evidence of the familiar one with some
minimal explication. Nor yet is there need to postulate a
middle term between Peshiṭta and MT in which the
interpretative element might lodge. A comment made by

Gwilliam in "Materials for the criticism of the Peshitto", p.
48, touches on this theory of the relation between the
Peshiṭta and the MT:

> . . . it is not so obvious that the Peshitto Old Testament was
> derived immediately from the Hebrew, without the intervention
> of a Targum or some ancient version . . ..

This section therefore concludes that the interpretative
element in the Peshiṭta is in the translation of MT and not
in an intermediary between MT and Peshiṭta: this
interpretative element is evidence of the freedom and the
constraint of a particular approach to MT.

3. *The Targum character of the Peshiṭta*

These questions of the origins and nature of the Peshiṭta
were raised by Hayman in his review of Koster's *Exodus*, p.
270:

> It remains to be seen whether Koster's statement that "the origins
> of P (at least as far as the Pentateuch is concerned) are to be
> looked for in an authentic translation of the Hebrew basic text
> and not in a number of erratic targums (p. 536)" will be
> confirmed by the collations of Leviticus and Deuteronomy.

Chronologically and typologically (that is, in its date and in
its character) the Peshiṭta has a setting resembling those of
such different kinds of contemporary (or at least near-
contemporary) versions Targums Onqelos and Ps Jonathan,
the Qumran material from Caves 4 and 11, and possibly the
Temple Scroll. It is unrealistic to expect that the origins of
the Peshiṭta will ever be other than shrouded in mystery, but
it is in this area of origin that reference is most frequently
made to the word "Targum", even if there is uncertainty as

to whether its appropriateness relates to dependence upon
Targum or to similarity of method.

The fixed points of the discussion are the instructions
about Targum set out in *mMeg* 4:4, 9 and consideration of
the major relevant Targums: Onqelos, Ps Jonathan, and
Neofiti. From the first reference it is clear that Targum is an
oral presentation, and is intended to supplement rather than
displace the Biblical Hebrew: it is an exegetical aid rather
than a source of exegesis. *mMeg* 4:4 instructs the reader of
Torah to read one verse at a time to the translator, and the
reader of prophetic books to read no more than three verses
at a time. 4:9 prohibits the use of euphemism in the reading
of such scripture as Leviticus 18:6-18 or 18:21, on which last
verse see below in Chapter 6, p. 115. *bSabb* 63a can be
quoted in support of this approach, that authority resides in
scripture, not the exegesis of scripture: אין מקרא יוצא מידי
פשוטו . As against this, Aejmelaeus in "Translation
Technique and the Intention of the Translator", p. 30, notes:
"Once the translation had been completed it was used on its
own. It was read and understood without reference to the
original". That writer had already pointed out, p. 25, that the
work of a translator is to realise an understanding: but that
leaves aside an important issue. This issue is that if the
Targum was in origin an oral Torah, by what stages and at
what time did the written Targums have their present form:
with the consequence that what should not be written came
to have been written. (York, "The Targum in the Synagogue
and the School", pp. 74-79, discusses this point). This kind of
discussion, of oral tradition in the period of the Second
Temple, led Heinemann in "Early Halakah in the Palestinian
Targumim", p. 115, to speak of "The New Targum Studies".

But "Targum" as a descriptive term carries a wide range
of meanings. Targum, as Aramaic version corresponding to
the Hebrew, must clearly have had its origin in discussion of

the Hebrew text and such meanings of that text as might be incorporated into a rendering. York refers with approval in his article "The Dating of the Targumic Literature", p. 62, to Geiger's comment over a century ago, in *Urschrift und Uebersetzungen der Bibel,* ". . . the Targumim are the remains of a lively dynamic activity that was centered on the biblical text"; but it is, of course, to be noted that discussion may have varied purposes and a variety of methods.

Alexander, in "The Targumim and the rabbinic rules", p. 17, marks out two kinds of Targum. The first, Type A, is like Ps Jonathan, in which it is possible to bracket out the interpretative elements. The second, Type B, is like *Tg Lam,* or *Tg Sheni* to Esther, virtually a "re-written bible". Other relevant comments made by Alexander in that article are that while Targum may be pre-determined it is not pre-written, albeit copies came to exist. (We might understand, therefore, that Targum is like another liturgical act, the sermon: the outcome of a prepared mind, not a prepared document). It is also to be noted that the mark of Targum, as against Midrash, is that the interpretative element is not supported by argument or reference to authorities, even scriptural authority. It is hardly surprising, therefore, that Targum has an element of the unofficial about it: it is of a different order from Mishnah and its successors. Diez Macho comments, appropriately, in "The recently discovered Palestinian targum: its antiquity and relationship with the other targums":

> . . . already in the days of the Tannaim, the M[e]targ[e]mim had to be directed not to change the explanation of the Biblical Text according to their private ideas; R. Yehuda said "Whoever translates a verse . . . and makes additions to it is a liar".

This conclusion, that Targum is private rather than public

opinion, matches Alexander's judgment that its setting is in liturgy and popular discussion, and will be taken up in the next chapter. Here, however, it can be noted that a consideration of its purpose and audience is an important element in understanding the targumic nature of the Peshiṭta. The terms "Targum" and "Peshiṭta" are concepts rather than descriptive terms. What they have in common is a shared search for meaning, rather than direct textual dependence. The background for that shared search is the need for a running translation rather than a commentary, whether verse-by-verse or topically arranged. In each case the translator's task was to provide an equivalent which did justice to the writing in the base language, Hebrew, but which was both comprehensible and significant in the target language, Aramaic or Syriac. There must be, therefore, an intention which is directed towards the basic text, in that an understanding of that basic text is to be realised in another language.

The study of the Peshiṭta as translation is, therefore, an attempt to enter the mind of the translator and identify the influences which informed it; to determine whether the translator was attempting to penetrate the text in order to discover its meaning, or to impose upon the text an understanding which reflected a communal agreement. The next chapter will give evidence that Targum and Peshiṭta work against the same background, with the same expectations and understanding of what renderings are legitimate or illegitimate.

4. *The work of a translator*

To speak of the work of a translator invites reference to the work of translators in the ancient and contemporary world of rhetoric and literature. The present writer has discussed translation at some length in "'The best words in the best

order"'. The main point of the discussion in that article was
that the translator had to come to terms with what the text
was understood to mean, as well as with the constraints and
possibilities of the target language. It is important to have
some knowledge of this, as the inherent nature of the
translation determines the shape of the changes that take
place in the course of the transmission of the text. This
concurs with the comment made by Barnes in his article "A
New Edition of the Pentateuch in Syriac", to the effect that
7a1 is suggestive of the tone for subsequent patterns of the
text. However he is leaving open the question as to why
changes were contained within certain limits which were not
exceeded. The changes within the tradition of the Peshiṭta
text are of the same kind as those between the Hebrew and
the Syriac. They include vocabulary, syntax, and style: the
presence of which suggests that there are resemblances
between translation and transmission.

Translation, it must however be noted, is not of exactly
the same order as transmission. Verbal inerrancy is a
requisite for the transmission of the text. But a theory of
exact mechanical equivalence enters the world of translation
only where legal necessity or certain theories of inspiration
hold the attention, in order to demonstrate that the authority
of the version is of the same order as that of its base. In
such circumstances it is not so much translation as
transliteration, or *verbatim* trans-authentication, that is
sought. Generally speaking, translation is a matter of finding
equivalents in the target language which correspond to terms
in the basic language and which are suited to the presumed
requirements of those who use the version. Rightly, then,
oratory or rhetoric is the genre into which translation is to
be placed. Quintilian's definition of rhetoric *Scientia bene
dicendi* may be too gnomic, but Grierson provided a
suitable definition in the Preface to *Rhetoric and English*

Composition, p. v,

> ... the study of how to express oneself most correctly and
> effectively, bearing in mind the nature of the language we use,
> the subject we are speaking or writing about, the kind of
> audience (often only vaguely definable) we have in view, and
> the purpose, which last is the main determinant.

This approach is similar to that of Knox, summarised in
the present writer's article on the 'Syriacing' of Leviticus,
mentioned earlier. Translation may fall into one of two
classes: the first of these is where the equivalents are formal
or mechanical. The base text is taken to be the "real" text,
and the translator's chief purpose is to signify that such is the
case, so that the hermeneutic and exegesis is based upon the
"original" which carries the whole freight of authority and
inspiration. The second class is where the translator's
purpose is to establish the version as the "real" text, so that
this in turn may carry the freight of authority and
inspiration. The version therefore must use the resonances
of the translation language, and choose carefully among
possible words, phrases and syntax: "the best words in the
best order".

Similar ground was covered by Brock and Alexander, who
referred to classical models in their discussions of Syriac and
Aramaic translations. The former, in "Aspects of Translation
Technique in Antiquity", p. 69, cites Cicero's definition of a
translator as ... *nec ut interpres, sed ut orator.* Brock goes
on to say that the kind of interpretation given will depend
on a number of factors, among which are the nature of the
text (legal or literary); the relative status of the languages
involved; whether or not the culture is bi-lingual; whether
the translation is oral or written; and whether the text or the
user of the text is considered to have priority. Alexander,
"The Targumim and the rabbinic rules for the delivery of the

Targum", p. 15, uses other classical terms, *fida interpretatio* and *expositio* in discussing the alternatives of *uerbum de uerbo* or *sensus de sensu,* and puts the discussion, as has been shown above, into the different kinds of targumic rendering.

5. *The philologist and the linguist*

But an approach which touches upon text and meaning brings the discussion into the realm of linguistics as well as that of philology. Miles touches upon this in *Retroversion and Text Criticism*, stating that Biblical versions are made for content, not art: there must be a range of fidelity to the meaning of the text. This would include the recognition that a rendering which is formally close can be changed if to maintain it would render the translation false. His contrast between the mechanical translation and that which is gratuitous or playful does not immediately strike a chord in Peshiṭta studies, but his warning that a translation may have more nuance than the original is most pertinent, as the next chapter will show.

A significant summary of linguistic and syntactic studies is to be found in Hospers, "Some Remarks with Regard to Text and Language of the Old Testament Peshiṭta". This study suggests that, in comparison with lexical studies, syntactic and linguistic ones have been neglected. Avinery noted in his unpublished doctoral dissertation *Taḥbir ha-lašôn ha-sûrît* that there had not been any kind of detailed grammar since Nöldeke (English version based on 2nd German edition, 1904), and that not even that pretended to be more than a compact work, drawing few examples from the Peshiṭta. Articles by Avinery and Muraoka have brought syntax and grammar to the fore, and have confirmed that it is in the whole area of language rather than the narrow one of lexicography or philology that the translator's art is to be found. Examples of this follow in the next chapter.

Reference has been made above to the purpose of translation as part of that art of oratory which Grierson describes. Translation, after all, demands that the original be comprehended before it can be rendered into another medium. It is necessary to come to terms with any ambiguities and opacities beforehand in order to present a version that is acceptably comprehensible, even if it may in some instances depart from what the constructor of the original may have intended.

This chapter presents the view that the Peshiṭta translator (though to speak of such an individual is a *façon de parler* rather than an established fact) made an accepted and acceptable rendering, which made use of understandings of a Hebrew text at the time of the translation. This, as the next chapter will show, is to understand that the Peshiṭta is not related to a specific Targum, but to the pre-history of Targums in general. It is not possible to say how much of a conscious exercise the making of the Peshiṭta might have been, with the consultation of possibly available written record, whether LXX or a Targum. Much of the construction of the material may not have been critical and analytic, but unconscious and imaginative. LXX and Targums alike contain traditions of interpretation: but while LXX texts had perhaps stabilised by the time the Peshiṭta was made, the Targum texts had not.

Translation is in part mechanical, an attempt to represent what is under the eyes, and in part it is imaginative, indeed intuitive. This is a point well made and developed by Aejmelaeus in the paper already noted, "Translation Technique and the Intention of the Translator". Brock's contribution to *III Symposium Syriacum*, "Towards a history of Syriac translation technique", goes further in that he discusses, pp. 4-7, the aims and intentions of users as well as translators of the text. His fastening on the social nature of translation, its societal aspect, is relevant for the next two chapters as well as for the present one. For if it is the intention of the translator to bring the basic text to those who know only their own, that is the target language, then the constraints and possibilities of that language are determinative. Lexical possibilities and constraints will shape what can be done in the same way as understanding of the meaning creates the material to be shaped. Translation and rhetoric are, like politics, the art of the possible. Hence Mulder commented in his contribution to the Leiden Symposium, 1988, p. 174:

> . . . the P translator was continually also alive to the syntactic and idiomatic differences by which the two languages can be told apart.

Later, p. 177, he speaks of "a rather literal translation smoothly fitting itself into the syntactic and idiomatic peculiarities of the Syriac language". Hence this chapter concludes with an approach to the constraints which faced the translator of Leviticus: those of the text to be rendered, and of the language into which it was to be rendered.

6. *Leviticus as Targum*

Hebrew Leviticus is a text which is of a piece. With the exception of chapter 10 there is no narrative; hence there are few proper names and no topography. Consequently there is no necessity for the typical Targum additions: no expansions of narrative to explain place, to suggest motive, or even to bridge a cultural gap. There is nothing of Ps Jonathan's addition of "I should not enter . . ." at Lev 9:1, or Neofiti's explanation that the prohibition of eating camel was

a warning against Gentile relationships, because גמל in
Chapter 11 suggests the homonym in Ps 137: את גמולך שגמלת
לנו. Departures from the mechanical equivalents to the
Hebrew text are penetrations of meaning or a response to a
stylistic imperative, yet are more modest than the passages
found, for example, in a variant in the left margin of Neofiti
at 18:29 ". . . who do such things against the Law [shall be
destroyed] from the life of the world to come and there will
be no portion for them in the midst of their people". Or
again a variant in the right margin at 20:6 "[and I will
destroy] him from the life of the world to come and there
will be no portion for him among his people". (See Lund and
Foster, *Variant Versions within Codex Neofiti I*). Further,
the Peshiṭta is more modest by far than some of the
enlarged text in Neofiti, which expands the basic Hebrew.
For example, the passage in 22:26 about the three typical
sacrifices of calf, lamb, or kid is developed so as to
correspond with the three sacrifices of the three fathers of
the world, Abraham (the calf), Isaac (the lamb), and Jacob,
(the kid).

The nature of the book translated also provides constraint
for the translator. Leviticus is a repository of prescriptions
and definitions: the definition of terms and the prescription
of actions whose significance is determined by conformity to
the definitions. There is therefore a considerable amount of
repetition, with the use of stock phrases. These repetitions
are not merely repetitions of phrases but of passages. Hence
there is that "block" presentation by topic: sacrifice, impurity,
festival, which is typical of the Priestly writer's work. Hence
there are problems, in that the book makes use of technical
terms whose presence is important. These may define
categories of person, action, creature, or physical
characteristic, each one of which needs to be given an
equivalent.

In the nature of things, provision of equivalent presents difficulties. There may be lack of knowledge concerning the term, or a simple disinterest in the significance of the term as originally conceived: it has become a matter of antiquarian interest. Yet an equivalent must be found if justice is to be done to the text, even if the text does not suggest immediate practical relevance, or has become a vehicle for other concerns. For example, in 19:3, 30; 26:2 ܗܟܘܬܝ is substituted for ܥܬ : general obedience rather than obedience in one instance only seems to be at stake. For the Jewish congregation Sabbath observance was mandatory; for Christian congregations the issue was different. But Rashi's comment that the passage was a summary of all the ten commandments has already been mentioned: the re-ordering of the text could represent Jewish, not Christian, understanding. It is at this point that the difficulty of discerning the kind of community for which the Peshitta was prepared makes itself felt. Christianity and Judaism both have a concern with the meaning of Torah; both therefore are concerned with exegesis, but differ concerning the point of reference which controls the exegesis.

These terms, Judaism and Christianity, are blanket confessional terms which refer to communities of faith whose conviction is that a proper human existence finds its definition and prescriptions in biblical terms. The relationship between Syriac Christianity and Judaism is simpler to describe in outline than to document in detail, but it is clear enough that the early period suggests that early Christianity and a Judaism which sat (or had to sit) loosely towards the Temple had much in common. In later times there were periods and occasions of hostility, of mutual tolerance, or of a combination for defence or survival. It is not possible to come to a final conclusion concerning the precise relationship between the Syriac Christians who used

and preserved the Peshiṭta, and the Jews through whom the
version came, whether this was by derivation or through
influence.   Fiey, *Jalons pour une Histoire de l'Eglise en
Iraq* comments on the difficulties of drawing conclusions,
saying that the evidence is negative rather than positive, pp.
46,7.   While there may be evidence of the proximity of
Jewish and Christian communities (as at Sos, to be
mentioned in the last chapter), Neusner's *The History of the
Jews in Babylon* suggests that some Jewish communities
were permeable by Christians or followers of Islam, and
others were not.   Communities which were influenced by
Tannaitic - Amoraic circles, for example Babylon
(Nehardea), would be more resistant.

But granted that there were communities where there was
association, it is hardly surprising that the Peshiṭta shows
elements of Jewish exegesis which did not come to have
formal approval in official or rabbinic circles; hardly
surprising that, while it is easy to see Jewish influence in the
Peshiṭta, it is less easy to find evidence of Jewish authority.
The Peshiṭta must be seen to have a value within the history
of Jewish exegesis as well as Christian church history.   That
is to say, it is more profitable to study the Peshiṭta in order
to understand the history of Jewish exegesis than it is to
study the history of Jewish exegesis in order to understand
the Peshiṭta.   Understandings of a text are various: an
understanding that starts as a possibility may become a
probability, and could end as being authoritative.   Or, *per
contra*, an understanding might start as being a possibility to
be retained, go on to be an opinion to be considered, a
meaning to be tolerated, or an interpretation to be rejected.
Hence the next chapter contains a selection of readings
where Peshiṭta and Hebrew seem to separate, yet one of
them may have LXX or a Targum as a companion.   The
ground common to Peshiṭta, Targum and LXX can be

shown, while the selection demonstrates the purpose and method of the translator.   In this way there is a demonstration of the range of problems that had to be faced, of the Peshiṭta's belonging to the literary *genre* of rhetoric, and its home in the traditions of making accessible to others the Hebrew scripture.

CHAPTER SIX

THE TRANSLATOR

A study of selected readings in Leviticus shows that the
Peshiṭta is of a piece with other versions, in particular LXX and
Targums Onqelos and Ps Jonathan. All approach the Hebrew to
display the meaning of the text. But they have their
convergences and divergences, by which it may be understood
that the Peshiṭta ante-dates the Targums as they are known.

1. *The translator's task*

The role of the translator is to find equivalents for the
meaning of the text to be translated. These equivalents may
be formal, in which case cognates, transliterations, and
homophones are used: the emphasis is on the external
resemblance between text and version. Alternatively, the
equivalents may be dynamic, in which case more than the
single word is taken into account: the emphasis is on the
inner meaning of the text, so that its sense may be conveyed
in the version. The Peshiṭta inclines to the second kind of
rendering, though both kinds are found, without there
necessarily being a clear-cut move from the one to the other.
In the light of this the material is grouped into four
categories: syntax, idiom, equivalent, and interpretation. Yet
it must be admitted that the boundaries between the
categories are not always clearly definable. The reason for
this lies as much in the difference between the languages of
Syriac and Hebrew as in the method of the translator. The
sense unit of the translation is not the word, nor yet the
phrase; it is more than the single verse, for there is a

tendency to make wording and logic consistent within paragraphs. Hence the unsatisfactory nature of a unitary statistical approach to the Peshiṭta, an approach which leaves out more than it includes: the version is a series of sense unit by sense unit equivalents. Further, it is to be remembered that Hebrew and Syriac differ in their range of words and syntax: a point that holds good even when it is a contrast of syntax and vocabulary between biblical Hebrew and biblical Syriac.

The lexical difference is less important than the syntactic. To give a few examples, biblical Hebrew links by *waw*, leaving context to determine the kind of clause: temporal, final, or consecutive. It also uses infinitive construct, with or without suffix, so leaving indeterminate the time and type of action suggested. The construct expression of genitive relation makes the nature of that relation elusive; there is difficulty in establishing the determinate or indeterminate nature of nouns; the paucity of adverbs and adjectives makes the qualification of noun and verb opaque. All these are characteristics of the Hebrew: Syriac is both more flexible and more capable of giving precision. For all that the nature of the text determines the Syriac as biblical, indeed Levitical, Syriac, there is a flexibility and an ability to give nuance which gives a non-Hebraic character to the version. Hence the phrase "faithful to the Hebrew" is Janus-like. The version looks backwards towards a Hebrew text; forwards to the Syriac language and understanding.

The Peshiṭta comes from the same world as the Targums and LXX, which versions faced the same kind of difficulties and opportunities: some examples from the Targums and LXX illustrate the shared difficulties and approach. In the case of the Targums they have been taken for the most part from Onqelos and Ps Jonathan; only occasionally, when some particular interest may be found, has reference been

made to Neofiti. Similarly, comparatively few instances
have been drawn from the LXX. The purpose is to show
that all these versions were coming to terms with an original
text which was not free of problems, and which was in a
language different in character from that into which the
versions were to be made. This was in despite of the fact
that the Targums were in a cognate language Onqelos and
Ps Jonathan are close in style to the Peshiṭta; Neofiti is more
expansive. The LXX differs, inevitably, in syntax. Its
propinquity to the Peshiṭta is more in the lexical range:
either these two versions have in this respect some
background in common, or (more likely) both faced the
same problems in a similar way.

2. Problems and method

The first range of problems is comparatively
straightforward, and may be broadly classified as idiom and
syntax. MT has a way of presenting material which requires
adaptation rather than mechanical reproduction.

  (1) Hebrew idiom.

  (a) There is the indeterminate noun, for example אדם at
1:2. This is rendered אנׁ אנׁ . Onq and (PsJ) use the single
word אנש , (אינש) just as LXX uses the single word
ἄνθρωπος in this verse, though repeating the word in 10:10
and using ἀνδρὶ twice, where MT repeats איש , in 15:2.

  (b) There is the distributive numeral, for example שש at
24:6. Here the Syriac repeats the word ܫܬ , contrary to the
usage in Onq. PsJ repeats the whole phrase.

  (c) Difference of idiom underlies the rendering of
Hebrew at 25:8: שבע שבחת שנים שבע שנים שבע פעמים . Syriac
ܥܒܕ ܥܢܘ ܕܝܢ.ܟܐܒ ܥܒܕ ܥܢܘ ܥܒܕ ܝܢ ܟܠ ܥܒܕ ܟܠ ܥܢܘܗܝ adds ܟܠ to the
construction, which then indicates that seven is multiplied by
seven. Onq and PsJ closely follow MT.

  (d) The Hebrew positive word תמים (1:3) is rendered by

a negative term דלא מהם in Syriac, LXX has the negative noun ἄμωμος. Both Onq and PsJ render MT by שלים . Similarly עירים (20:20) is translated by the Syriac with the negative particle in the expression דלהא כלמ . Onq ולד דלא and PsJ דלא וולד also use a negative term.

(e) Hebrew can express a command in narrative prose with a perfect tense prefixed by *waw,* as at 1:2 ואמרת . The Syriac uses an imperative, ואמרי , whereas Onq and PsJ follow the pattern of MT and have ותימר . A similar idiomatic change appears later, at 10:13, where MT has ואכלתם אתה which the Syriac renders ואכולתהון , as does LXX which has φάγεσθε. Onq and PsJ follow the pattern of MT and have ותיכלון יתה .

(f) MT infinitive construct can also suggest an imperative, and is understood as such by the Syriac at 11:2, where Hebrew לאמר is rendered ואמרתי להון . Onq and PsJ provide a formal equivalent to MT and have למימר .

(g) In fact the reluctance of the Syriac to have an exact, formal, equivalence for the infinitive construct is most noticeable.

(i) At 8:11 two verbs are used to avoid this construction. MT וימשח --------- לקדשם is rendered ומשח מזגא אנון , and LXX has ἔχρισεν and ἡγίασεν. Onq and PsJ again have a formal equivalent to MT, that is לקדשותהון for the infinitive construct and suffix.

(ii) Two finite verbs are used as equivalents for a finite verb and an infinitive construct at 8:15: for MT ויקדשהו לכפר עליו Syriac has ומשחה . וקדשה , whereas Onq and (PsJ) have the formal equivalents וקדשיה לכפרא עלו(ה)י .

(iii) At 16:17 the two Hebrew infinitives בבאו -- עד צאתו are rendered by the two Syriac participles כד עאל -- ועדמא דנפק ; Onq has the formal equivalent עד -- במיעליה מיפקיה

(h) The Syriac frequently uses participles to represent

either MT imperative or imperfect where continuity is understood, or where it is a matter of indicating customary action.

(i) At 19:32, where MT has תקום , Syriac gives ܗܘܐ ܩܐܡ, whereas Onq has תקום, Ps J has תקומון , and LXX ἐξαναστήσῃ .

(ii) In the same verse MT has והדרת , rendered as Syriac ܘܗܡܐ ܠܘܡ, and by Onq והדר, and PsJ ותיקר .

(iii) At 4:22, MT אשר לא תעשינה is rendered ܕܠܐ ܠܡܠ ܡܠܠܘܕܒܘ by the Syriac, and by Onq and PsJ as דלא כשרין לאתעבדא .

(iv) At 7:2, MT אשר ישחטו is rendered as Syriac ܘܠܚܡܠ, and by Onq and PsJ as דיכסון .

(v) At 11:2, MT החיה אשר תאכלו is rendered by Syriac as ܠܚܠ ܗܡܘܡܐ ܚܘܠܐܐ, by Onq as חיתא דתיכלון, and by PsJ as חייתא דמיכשרא למיכלכון .

(vi) Even a passive verb can be taken as inceptive, as at 6:5, where MT והאש על המזבח תוקד בו is rendered as Syriac ܘܢܘܪܐ ܕܥܠ ܡܕܒܚܐ ܠ ܡܘܩܕܐ, and by Onq and (PsJ) as ואישתא על מדבחא תהי י(ו)קדא ביה .

(vii) The Syriac use of an adverb provides another way of indicating continuity in place of MT adjective. At 6:6 MT has אש תמיד תוקד , which Syriac renders as ܘܢܘܪܐ ܐܡܝܢܐܝܬ ܬܗܘܐ ܡܘܩܕܐ, and Onq and (PsJ) as אישתא תדירא תהי י(ו)קדא.

2. It is, however, in the matter of clauses that the difference between the two languages is made plain.

(a) Here the Syriac is more concerned with preciseness in meaning, even if, as a result, the clause or phrase is made longer. This is especially the case when Hebrew can use one single word.

(i) At 1:3, MT לרצנו is rendered by Syriac as ܠܨܒܝܢܗ ܠܗ, by Onq as לרעוא ליה, by PsJ as לרעוא עלוהי, and by LXX as δεκτὸν ἐναντίον κυρίου.

(ii) At 14:19, MT על המטהר is rendered by Syriac as ܟܠܡܐ, ܗܘܐ ܗܘܗ܂ܕ܂ܟܢܗܐܕ by Onq and (PsJ) as דכי(י)דם , and by LXX τοῦ καθαριζομένου.

(iii) At 20:26, MT להיות לי is rendered by the Syriac as ܗܐܗܘܡ ܂ܠ, and Onq and (PsJ) as (פלחין) קדמי למהוי פלחון .

(b) A particular difficulty is that the Hebrew ways of expressing time, purpose, or consequence (temporal, final, consecutive clauses) are distinguishable largely by context; the form alone is not sufficient guide to determine difference. Syriac has to come to a conclusion on the nature of the clause before offering an equivalent, and this fact is reflected in the syntax.

(i) At 20:4 an imperfect with *dalath* and negative particle is equivalent to Hebrew לבלתי and infinitive construct to express "lest". MT לבלתי המית אתו is rendered by the Syriac as ܗ܂ܠܟ ܢܡܠܠܬܘܗܝ , whereas Onq renders the words as בדיל דלא למקטל יתיה and PsJ as מטול דלא למיקטול יתיה , but LXX as μὴ ἀποκτεῖναι αὐτόν.

(ii) At 26:13, where MT uses מן and an infinitive construct מהית להם עבדים , the Syriac ܗ܂ܠܟ ܐܗܘܘ ܠܒܗܘ ܂ ܠܬܒ.ܕܟ is used to express "so you will cease being". Onq and (PsJ) have מלמהוי עבדין (משעבדין) להון , and LXX has a genitive absolute ὄντων ὑμῶν δούλων as verbal element.

(iii) At 7:18, where MT uses a participle והנפש האכלת , the Syriac *dalath* and imperfect render the indefinite relative clause by ܘܢܦܫܐ ܕܗܐܟܠܐܘ , Onq by ואנש דייכול , PsJ by ואינש די יכול , and LXX by ἐὰν δὲ φαγὼν φάγῃ.

(iv) At 25:20, where MT introduces an open conditional clause with כי and an imperfect, the Syriac uses ܐ ܢ and a participle: MT has וכי תאמרו , which the Syriac renders by ܘܐ ܟܝ ܐܡܬ܂ܝܢ ܐܟܗ ܢ , Onq by וארי תימרון , PsJ by וארום אין תימרון , and LXX by ἐὰν δε λέγητε.

(v) In the same verse there is an example of a negative form of a similar construction, this time introduced by הן in

MT: it has הן לא נזרע , which the Syriac represents by ܠܐܕ
ܘܠܚܡ ܣܠܝ , and Onq and PsJ render as הא לא נזרע .

(vi) At 19:23 there is an indefinite temporal clause, introduced by כי in MT: it has וכי תבאו , which the Syriac renders as ܘܡܐ ܕܬܥܠܘܢ , using ܡܐ with an imperfect. Onq and (PsJ) have וארי תיעלון (וארום).

(vii) At 15:2 the same MT particle needs to be translated differently where a different indication of time is required, "while" rather than "when". כי יהיה זב is translated by ܟܕ ܢܗܘܐ ܕܐܒ , and by Onq and (PsJ) ארי (ארום) יהי דאיב . This pattern is found earlier, at 1:2, where MT has כי יקריב . The Syriac renders this as ܟܕ ܢܩܪܒ , Onq as ארי יקריב , and PsJ as די יקרב .

(viii) At 5:3 the matter is one of substance as well as syntax. MT והוא ידע ואשם "he has knowledge and is guilty" leaves unclear whether the knowledge accompanies the act or is given later. The Syriac interpretation uses a *dalath* for a Hebrew *waw* and gives definition ܘܡܐ ܕܝܕܥ ܕܚܛܐ , "he knew that he sinned". PsJ expands considerably, specifies the occasion, and the action, and relates that information was given to the individual, but Onq stays close to MT, והוא ידע וחב , and LXX gives further definition: μετὰ τοῦτο δὲ γνῷ καὶ πλημμελήσῃ, "and afterwards he knew, and had offended."
But it is not easy to draw a firm line between Syriac syntax and Syriac idiom, with which the next paragraph is concerned.

(3) Although Syriac and Hebrew are cognate languages, their idiom can differ in ways that make the finding of equivalents difficult.

(a) A further hazard is that similar roots may have different significance.

(i) At 20:17 MT uses the word חסד , usually translated

"loving-kindness". That equivalent will not serve here, and a term such as "shame" is more appropriate. The Syriac has ܚܣܕܐ , which has just that meaning; Onq has קלנא , which has that sense also. PsJ and Neofiti both expand, but are in the same tradition of interpretation. Either there is another Hebrew root חסד, or a sense of "shame", as well as "loving-kindness", comes from such a basic meaning as "liability". LXX has ὄνειδός ἐστιν.

(ii) At 13:51 Hebrew ממארת is, incorrectly, given the Syriac ܡܪܝܪܐ as its equivalent, by near-transliteration. Perhaps the translation has associated the word with the root מרר "to be bitter" instead of with the root מאר "to break open", or מרה "to be obstinate". MT is not clear, but the context suggest that "persistent" or "running" would suit best. Onq has מחסרא , possibly suggesting "diminish by consuming".

(b) A need for equivalence of idiom underlies some renderings.

(i) At 19:18 MT כמוך has as the Syriac equivalent ܐܝܟ ܢܦܫܟ , which is capable of expressing "as you yourself do" or "as you do yourself". Onq renders כותך , and PsJ paraphrases: דמן אנת סני לך לא תעביד ליה . LXX ὡς σεαυτόν resembles the Syriac.

(ii) At, e. g. 1:15, the locative ending on המזבחה is represented in Syriac by ܠܗ , in Onq and PsJ by על כתול , and in LXX by ἐπί. Where interpretation plays a small part the matter of idiom is straighforward.

(iii) At 22:7, idiom rather than a need for interpretation explains the rendering of Hebrew ובא השמש by the adverbial phrase ܒܡܥܪ̈ܒܝ ܫܡܫܐ . Onq has וכמיעל שמשא , PsJ has ויטמוע שימשא , and LXX has καὶ δύῃ ὁ ἥλιος.

(c) The greater clarity that Syriac commands underlies a number of instances where a Hebrew phrase which includes a construct state is ambiguous. There are many ways in which Syriac can express a relation between noun and adjective. There may be an anticipatory pronoun suffix on the first noun, the second noun being prefixed with *dalath*; two nouns may be linked simply with *dalath*; the first of two nouns may be in the construct or bound state; two nouns may be joined by *waw*; or recourse may be had to finite tense and pronoun (enclitic or object).

(i) At 23:35 the Hebrew phrase מקרא קדש is rendered by a Syriac participle and an adjective joined by *waw* ܩܪܝܐ ܘܡܩܕܫܐ ܗܘܐ. Onq has מערע קדיש, PsJ has מארע קדיש (דחגא) and LXX has κλητὴ ἁγία.

(ii) At 26:36 MT phrase מנסת חרב, "as the sword puts to flight", is rendered more lengthily (and to the writer's mind less attractively) as ܥܡܩܒܐ, ܕܥܪܩܝܢ ܡܢ ܩܕܡ ܐܝܠܝܢ, "as men flee before the sword", Onq ויערקון מעריק כיד מן קדם דקטלין, PsJ ויערקון הי כמערוקי חרבא בחרבא; and (to the present writer least attractively of all), by LXX ὡς φεύγοντες ἀπὸ πολέμου, "like those who flee from battle".

(d) The use of the word אין by MT also occasions the use of longer phrases in the Syriac.

(i) At 14:21 the Hebrew ואין ידו משׂגת, "does not have the means", is rendered in Syriac ܘܠܐ ܡܛܝܐ ܐܝܕܗ, ܘܡܘܬ. Here there is an instance of a Syriac participle and preposition; Onq has ולית ידיה מדבקא, PsJ has ולית ידיה מספקא, and LXX has καὶ ἡ χεὶρ αὐτοῦ μὴ εὑρίσκῃ.

(ii) At 26:6 the similar MT construction with אין is translated by a verb: ואין מחריד becomes ܘܠܐ ܢܗܘܐ ܡܢ ܕܡܕܚܠ ܠܟܘܢ. Onq has ולית דמניד, PsJ has ולית דמניט; LXX is nearer to the Syriac and has καὶ οὐκ ἔσται ὑμᾶς ὁ ἐκφοβῶν. To the writer this is a further example of a forceful expression being regrettably toned down in translation.

(e) A characteristic Syriac usage is that of the anticipatory pronoun suffix.

(i) At 4:12 MT והוציא את כל הפר is translated ܘܢܦܩܘܗܝ, ܠܟܠܗ ܬܘܪܐ: there is also an element of precision in that the suffix is placed on the verb and on the adjectival element.

(ii) At 8:19 Syriac provides another instance of the anticipatory suffix, here involving a change of word order to effect it: MT וישחט ויזרק משה becomes ܡܘܫܐ ܘܩܒܠ ܗܘ .

(iii) At 3:13 the one Syriac suffixed word ܘܣܚܝܗܝ is equivalent to the two Hebrew words ושחט אתו .

(f) Instances of other Syriac use of pronouns may be seen in their addition by way of idiom.

(i) At 14:51 Hebrew הבית gives clear definition with a definite article; the Syriac adds ܗܘ to ܒܝܬܐ to give an equivalent definition to the noun.

(ii) In such places as 18:4, where Hebrew use has one pronoun, אני יהוה , there is frequently the Syriac addition of a second ܐܢܐ to form such a phrase as ܐܢܐ ܐܢܐ ܡܪܝܐ . Neither Onq nor PsJ uses the pronoun as determinative or as an enclitic in a verbless noun clause as the Syriac does in this and the previous examples.

(g) There are some further additions made by the Syriac, with respect to verbs. 9:5 provides an instance of an added verb ܐܬܐ , although there is some change in sense as well as clarity. MT has "they took what Moses commanded in front of the tabernacle", Syriac has "they took everything that Moses commanded, and came to the tabernacle". Neither Onq nor PsJ makes this addition.

(h) There are some changes in word order, where emphasis may be as much at stake as idiom.

(i) At 9:3 ואל בני ישראל תדבר is rendered ܘܐܡܪ ܠܒܢܝ ܐܝܣܪܐܝܠ ; the verb comes first, and the indirect object follows. This instance draws attention to the fact that the word order is changed less frequently than might have been expected, given the Syriac preference for object to precede verb, as for example in the writings of Aphrahat. In 9:3 LXX interprets according to context, as does Sam, with γηρουσία.

(ii) At 8:35 MT יומם ולילה שבעת ימים is rendered ܥܒܕ
ܩܘܡ ܐܝܡܡܐ ܘܠܠܝܐ in the the Syriac. Onq and PsJ closely follow MT, and LXX has ἑπτὰ ἡμέρας ἡμέραν καὶ νύκτα.

While the convergences and divergences of idiom and syntax present both constraints and possibilities for the translator attempting to render Hebrew into Syriac, the more difficult elements of the task are those of interpretation and technical equivalent. The examples given above suggest that the Syriac translation is congruous with known Aramaic versions and LXX, but that a translator has been working from first principles of exegesis rather than plagiarism. It is not, however, a blind translation with nothing but the Hebrew text to go upon. The next stage of the discussion takes into account equivalents and technical terms to provide further evidence for these conclusions.

3. Influences internal and external

In the selection of passages which follow, three tendencies may be seen. The first is that a need for clarification requires an approach which owes as much to common sense as to anything else. The second is that other biblical passages influence the interpretation of particular phrases, and that stylisation, or internal harmonising of passages is evident. The text itself has suggested its own interpretation. The third is that interpretations known in Targumic and Rabbinic literature appear, as do instances which came to be rejected as unacceptable. In consequence they are either ignored, as in Targums; or forbidden, as in Mishnah, Sifra, or Talmud. No distinction can realistically be attempted between examples of phrases where an interpretative element can be seen and must be recognised as a matter of choice, and those technical terms where interpretative equivalents were found

necessary because the meaning or significance was unknown
or irrelevant. The whole purpose of this, or any other
version, is that it is comprehensible to its users.

(1) Passages where clarification is required.

(a) The Hebrew in 25:34, ושדה מגרש עריהם is not self-
explanatory (RSV "fields of common lands belonging to the
city") and is rendered ܡܬܠܐ ܕܚܩܠܐ, ܩܡܝܘܗܝ "the open
country on the borders of their cities", which understands
מגרש , probably originally pasture land or land to which
cattle were driven out from town or city, as "common land
adjoining settlements". Onq renders וחקל רוח קרויהון , PsJ וברם
חקיל פרוילי קירוייהון , LXX has οἱ ἀγροὶ οἱ ἀφωρισμένοι ταῖς
πόλεσιν, "fields set apart for the cities".

(b) At 11:3 there is a Hebrew construct phrase, which
does not lend itself to mechanical equivalence, and which is
rendered by the denominative verb, as a technical usage: MT
מעלת גרה , "bring up the cud" is rendered ܦܬܠܐ ܓܘܪܬܐ . Onq
and (PsJ) provide as MT, מסקא פ(י)שרא , LXX has ἀνάγον
μηρυκισμόν.

(c) At 10:3 the addition of the enclitic pronoun clarifies
the Hebrew: הוא אשר דבר יהוה is ambiguous as to its point of
reference. The Syriac adds a word to make it clear "This is
what the Lord said" ܗܢܐ ܗܘ, ܕܐܡܪ ܡܪܝܐ . LXX has τοῦτό
ἐστιν, ὃ εἶπεν κύριος. Onq and PsJ resemble the Syriac.

(d) There seems to be a reluctance on the part of the
Syriac to use cognate or denominative verbs where they
appear in the Hebrew.

(i) At 16:4 Hebrew has ובמצנפת בד יצנף ; יצנף is
rendered by ܢܣܝܡ ܟܘܪܬܐ , Onq using יחית ברישה and PsJ יטכס
ברישה : LXX has περιθήσεται.

(ii) At 7:35 לכהן is represented by ܠܟܗܢܘܬܐ (this
pattern of equivalent is also used by Onq and PsJ), LXX has
ἱερατεύειν.

(e) There are examples of a one word change which alters the character of a passage in order to clarify an understanding of a larger passage.

(i) At 8:34 for the Hebrew כאשר עשה "As the Lord did this day . . . ", Syriac has "As I did this day . . .", that is ܐܝܟ ܕܥܒܕܬ. Neither Onq nor PsJ concurs.

(ii) At 7:21, 25; 22:3 MT ונכרתה הנפש ההוא מעמיה (which Onq and PsJ follow, וישתיצי בר and וישתיצי אנשא ההוא מעמיה נשא ההוא מעמיה) is given Syriac ܘܐܒܕ ܢܦܫܐ ܗܝ, ܡܢ ܥܡܗ as equivalent. The Hebrew term is perhaps taken to refer to the premature, inexplicable and childless death of the individual concerned, with the consequent dying out of the family, see Neofiti and Rashi on 18:29; 20:6. Neofiti is cited in Chapter 5, p. 95.

(iii) At 25:35 there is the addition of a negative particle in the Syriac. The MT והחזקת בו גר ותושב וחי עמך "and you are to support him as a stranger and a temporary resident and he is to live with you" is rendered ܠܐ ܬܐܚܕܝܘܗܝ, ܐܝܟ ܥܡܘܪܐ ܘܐܝܟ ܬܘܬܒܐ. ܘܚܝܐ ܥܡܟ "you are not to regard him as a stranger and a temporary resident, but he is to live with you". That is, the impoverished neighbour is not to be regarded as an outsider to be helped, but is to be helped in exactly the same way that an outsider is helped.

(f) To conclude this section two examples illustrate the way in which explanation and equivalent blend together in order to clarify matters for Syriac users of the version.

(i) At 19:16 the Hebrew לא תלך רכיל בעמיך "you are not to go around as a tale-bearer among your people" is rendered by the idiomatic Syriac " you are not to slander your people" (indeed the same idiom appears also in Onq and PsJ, though much expanded in the latter), ܠܐ ܬܐܟܘܠ ܩܪܨܐ ܕܥܡܟ.

(ii) At 19:18 the use of a noun and a verb gives an equivalent for the two verbs of the Hebrew. For לא תקם ולא חטר את בני עמך the equivalent is ܠܐ ܬܗܘܐ ܢܩܡ ܘܢܛܪ ܠܒܢܝ ܥܡܟ

ܠܒܒܝ , making plain "you are not to persevere in enmity
against those who are of your people" for the elliptical
Hebrew "confront; keep". LXX gives οὐκ ἐκδικᾶταί σου ἡ
χείρ καὶ οὐ μηνιεῖς τοις υἱοῖς , "your hand shall not
avenge you, nor shall you be angry with a member of . . . ".

(2) There are passages where other scripture, sometimes a
neighbouring passage, has suggested an interpretation which
has been taken as preferable to others.

(a) At 25:9 MT והעברת שופר may suggest either
"proclaim here by a trumpet blast which may be heard
through the land", or "proclaim by sending a trumpet by
which may be proclaimed . . . ". The Syriac ܘܡܚ ܟܪܘܙ ܘܐܟܪܙ
understood the phrase as a proclamation through the land, cf
Exod 36:6 MT ויעבירו קול , Pesh ܘܡܚ ܐܟܪܘܙܘ . Onq and PsJ
render Lev 25:9 ותעבר (קל+) שופר יבבא , and LXX gives καὶ
διαγγελεῖτε σάλπιγγος φωνῇ, "make a proclamation with
a sound of a trumpet . . . ".

(b) At 17:10 and 20:5 an ambiguity has been resolved in
a similar way. The Hebrew ונתתי פני and ושמתי אני את פני
might be expected to indicate the showing of the divine face
in favour, but the opposite is intended. So the passages have
been rendered ܐܬܠ ܐܦܝ ܒܗ, and ܟܚܒܬ ܐܢܐ ܐܦܝ ܒܗ, (cf also
20:3,6; 26:17), in the sense found in such a passage as Jer
21:10, that is, "to set the face for evil and not for good", as if
the noun were אנף rather than פנים . See also the use of the
verb ואנפת in 1 Kings 8:46, and Deut 31:17 where Hebrew
והרה אפי בו is rendered by the Syriac ܘܢܬܚܡܬ ܐܦܝ ܒܗ. In
Leviticus, Onq gives ואיתין רוגזי , PsJ gives ואתן פנייתא למעסוק ,
Neofiti has "set the face of may anger against . . . ", and LXX
has ἐπιστήσω τὸ πρόσωπόν μου ἐπὶ . . . .

(c) At 24:22 the term אזרח is rendered by the Syriac as
ܟ ܐܙܪܚܝ , Onq and PsJ have יציבא , "native born", LXX
has the expected τῷ ἐγχωρίῳ. The word supplied for אדם in

24:20 is ܐܢܫܐ and LXX has the expected ἀνθρώπῳ. Yet in 16:29 there is expansion: the Hebrew האזרח והגר בתוככם "the native-born and the stranger residing among you" is rendered ܐܢܬܘܢ ܘܐܝܠܝܢ ܕܡܬܦܢܝܢ ܠܘܬܝ ܕܥܡܪܝܢ ܒܝܢܬܟܘܢ, "you and those who are turned to me who live among you". Onq has יציבא וגיורא דיתגירון ביניכון, and PsJ follows suit. The LXX gives ὁ αὐτόχθων καὶ ὁ προσήλυτος ὁ προσκείμενος ἐν ὑμῖν, "the indigenous and the proselyte/stranger who dwells . . . ". As has been noted already, the equivalent to גר is ܥܡܘܪܐ, but more is involved here. For cultic participation, as for accepting responsibility for living as a member of the community, a turning towards the Lord as well as residence is necessary. At 20:2, Hebrew הגר הגר has the usual Syriac rendering, ܘܡܢ ܐܝܠܝܢ ܕܡܬܦܢܝܢ ܠܘܬܝ ܕܥܡܪܝܢ ܒܐܝܣܪܐܝܠ, but the interesting equivalent in LXX ἢ ἀπὸ τῶν προσγεγενημένων προσηλύτων ἐν Ισραηλ, "those who have come as proselytes/strangers . . . " makes this point sharply in its own way. Clearly some scriptural passage, such as Isa 45:22 underlies these interpretations: MT פנו עלי והושעו whereas Syriac has ܐܬܦܢܘ ܠܘܬܝ --- ܕܬܬܦܪܩܘܢ, and LXX has ἐπιστράφητε πρός με; but the relationship between MT and the equivalents is far from clear, and the scriptural basis indirect.

(3) Hence the next sub-section turns to interpretations which are grounded in contemporary society, and which reflect a social rather than a scriptural context.

(a) At 25:45 the Hebrew התושבים הגרים is rendered ܡܢ ܒܢܝ ܬܘܬܒܐ ܕܥܡܪܝܢ ܥܡܟܘܢ, the Hebrew being a general statement about resident inhabitants, whereas the Syriac, with its use of ܒܢܝ, seems to consider that a specific class of persons is meant. It is here that Onq and (PsJ) use the term תותביא ער(י)ליא, "uncircumcised resident", and LXX has τῶν παροίκων τῶν ὄντων ἐν ὑμῖν, "the dwellers who are among you ... ". The question of the root גור comes up here also, and can be discussed from the view of social context, when it may even be the case that it is primarily the context for which the equivalent is needed.

The background to the Syriac version is to be found in discussions of Jewish-Gentile relations in the Second Temple period and later, a summary of which can be found in the revised Schürer, vol III,1 pp. 169-176, and especially n. 78 on p. 170. The matter is also discussed by Ohana in "Proselytisme et Targum palestinienne: Données nouvelles pour la datation de Neofiti I", and by Goodman, "Proselytising in Rabbinic Judaism".

The concept of the proselyte was established before the fall of the Second Temple, and the Greek term occurs at Matt 23:15 and Acts 2:10 and in Philo, e.g. Ant. 18,3,5; and the semitic equivalent in the Cairo manuscripts of the Damascus document, CD 12:10-11. PsJ uses יתגיר in the sense of becoming a convert; Onq represents Moses' father-in-law requesting to be accepted as a convert. Rashi finds in Exod 18:1-11 the instance of Jethro providing a classic instance of conversion: to God, to Moses, to Israel, to the Law. "Jethro, so was he called when he became a proselyte and fulfilled the divine precepts." The Peshiṭta suggests that the turning involved is a turning towards God; Philo, in the passage mentioned, regards it as a turning to the Law and to a way of life. Onq and PsJ translate גר variously, according to the context a resident, an uncircumcised individual, or a resident who is uncircumcised: this usage may reflect more or less approved usage in rabbinic circles. The equivalents are evidence that interpretation is as likely (probably more likely) to be a response to circumstance, which then finds suitable expression in exegesis.

(b) At 22:13, the Hebrew וזרע אין לה is rendered ܘܒܪܐ
ܠܝܬ ܠܗ to confirm that "offspring" is intended, (LXX
σπέρμα δὲ μὴ ἦν αὐτῇ). At 11:37 ܙܪܥܐ ܘܕܪܥ is the
equivalent for זרע זרוע , and LXX has σπέρμα σπόριμον, to
establish that a single seed is understood. Hence it is clear
what meaning is to be given to the Hebrew term in each
case. In the former verse both Onq and PsJ make the
further clarification, Onq ובר לית לה , PsJ וולד לית לה ; in the
latter verse only Onq inserts the idiomatic בר to make the
point. For the word זרע is inherently ambiguous, especially
in such passages as 18:20. Other passages, also, need to be
discussed in order to have a picture of the exegetical
opportunity. The Hebrew at 18:20 is לא תתן שכבתך לזרע ,
rendered ܠܐ ܬܬܠ ܘܐܬܐ ܕܡܬܕܡܝܐ , appropriately enough -
as also LXX οὐ δώσεις κοίτην σπέρματός σου ἐκμιανθῆναι
πρὸς αὐτήν. It is clear enough that by "seed" a third
possibility is presented, and understood straightforwardly
enough by the Syriac. At 20:2 the Hebrew אשר יתן מזרעו למלך
is patent of two meanings: "seed" as "offspring" and "seed" as
semen virilis. An addition to this second interpretation is
provided by the Syriac ܕܢܬܠ ܡܢ ܙܪܥܗ ܠܟܢܘܬܐ whereas
LXX has ὃς ἂν δῷ τοῦ σπέρματος αὐτοῦ ἄρχοντι.

There is a near repetition in the following verse, where the
root טמא provides another link with 18:20. Two things have
happened here. First, "seed" is understood, not as "offspring",
but as *semen virilis*, emphasised in vs. 21 where "in order to
conceive" (ܠܡܒܛܢ) is added. Second, the term מלך is not
taken to be a male deity, but a non-Israelite woman. There
is a cultic background, and the prohibition applies to native
Israelite and to converted Gentile. The term ܢܘܟܪܝܬܐ also
has a cultic overtone: it is added in 16:1, where MT has
בקרבתם and Syriac expands to give ܟܕ ܩܪܒܘ ܢܘܪܐ ܢܘܟܪܝܬܐ .
This is the Syriac equivalent also to בהקרבם אש זרה in Num
3:4. LXX has fastened upon the general cultic context and

the component of sexuality in its rendering of 18:21: ἀπὸ τοῦ σπέρματός σου οὐ δώσεις λατρεύειν ἄρχοντι. Further evidence of the same kind interpretation comes in 20:5, where Hebrew כל הזנים אחריו לזנות אחרי המלך מקרב עמם is rendered ܘܠܟܠ ܕܢܛܥܘܢ ܒܬܪܗ. ܠܡܛܥܝܘ ܒܬܪ ܡܠܟܐ ܡܢ ܓܘ ܥܡܗܘܢ . The Peshiṭta interpretation, not made by Onq or PsJ, was well enough known to be forbidden in *mMeg* 4:9, and appears also in Sifre to Deut 18:10: "Who passes his son or his daughter through the fire: that is he who marries an Aramaean and so sets up a son hostile to the place". The matter is discussed and further bibliography given in Day, *Molech: A god of human sacrifice in the Old Testament*, pp. 20-24, where valuable social background is given. This comment on the interpretative nature of the Peshiṭta and the setting of its exegesis is confirmed by Day's textual argument. The interpretation is generated by social context, with secondary reference to the text of scripture: it is not, in the writer's opinion, a matter of simple exegesis of scripture alone.

4. *Technical terms*

More difficult for a translator are the words which are technical terms whose elucidation depends upon exact knowledge, when either the passage of time or unfamiliarity make this a hazardous matter. Three possibilities present themselves. First, that the translator has knowledge, which the version conveys. Second, that the translator is guessing in a way that may be more or less informed. Or third, that the translator is imprecise, and the version reveals the imprecision.

(1) Probably knowledge led to the following equivalents.
    (a) At 23:36 MT עצרת הוא is translated ܘܟܢܘܫܝܐ ܗܘ ܚܢܢ

"be assembling" for "it is an assembly". Both Onq and PsJ render this כנישין תהון , while LXX uses a familiar formal phrase, κλητὴ ἁγία, which is usually used for מקרא קדש .

(b) At 15:26 there is a definition of uncleanness, where the point of comparison with another instance may be either the quality of the uncleanness, or the duration of the subsequent exclusion. The ambiguous MT כטמאת נדתה is rendered [Syriac] in the text, but [Syriac] in the variant. This second interpretation is ruled out by Sifra, and needless to say is not mentioned in Onq or PsJ: LXX has κατὰ τὴν ἀκαθαρσίαν τῆς ἀφέδρου. The translator of the main text acted on knowledge.

(c) At 15:3 MT טמאתו הוא is ambiguous, in that it can be either the person or the issue which is contagious. Syriac [Syriac] indicates that it is the issue, not the individual, which is contagious; this is an interpretation given by Onq and PsJ; but LXX has ἀκαθαρσίας αὐτοῦ.

(d) At 17:15 the Hebrew טרפה "torn" is interpreted by the rendering [Syriac] "torn by a wild animal" and elsewhere by the phrase [Syriac] "eaten by a wild animal". This too indicates knowledge of the matter.

(e) At 19:23 the consecration of the fruit is similarly given explanation: ורעלתם ערלתו את פריו שלש שנים יהיה לכם ערלים לא יאכל "you shall leave uncircumcised in its circumcision its produce; for three years it shall be uncircumcised to you; it is not to be eaten" becomes [Syriac] "leave them alone for three years, and you are not to eat any of their fruits". This too shows knowledge. Onq has ותרחקון רחקא , and PsJ stays close to the Hebrew. LXX has ἀπερικάθαρτος οὐ βρωθήσεται.

(f) The present writer's article "The best words in the best order" has discussed the matter of trees and fruit in 23:40, where the translator shows knowledge of possibilities found also in Onq, PsJ and Sifra.

(g) At 23:11, 15 there seems an attempt at precision based on knowledge: the Hebrew is ambiguous as to whether it means "the day after the Sabbath" or "the day after the festival". MT ממחרת השבת is rendered by the Syriac ܘܡܚܪ ܝܘܡܐ ܐܚܪܢܐ , thus leaving out the word "Sabbath", as does the interpretation in Onq and PsJ, and indeed Sifra *'Emor* 10, Neusner, vol. 3. p. 239. "Sabbath" is understood as "festival", as in LXX which has τῇ ἐπαύριον τῆς πρώτης. In a similar approach in vs. 15 the Syriac translated "seven weeks", not "seven Sabbaths"; Onq and PsJ also note that references to Sabbath days are not appropriate or relevant.

(2) This sub-section examines examples of passages where the translator guessed meanings rather than acted on knowledge.

(a) at 11:21 MT כרעים "shanks" is rendered ܛܦܪܐ "horny claw, talon" with reference to the locust's long legs used for jumping. There is a general uncertainty in this passage (shared at this point even by Rashi) which led the translator to provide only two terms, ܩܡܨ ܐ and ܚܓܠܐ for the four Hebrew terms חגב , חרגל , סלעם , ארבה . חגב is rendered in vs. 22 by ܩܡܨܐ , and the second term of the Syriac pair is a cognate of the MT equivalent. This might indicate that the list used by the translator was defective, rather than that the translator lacked nerve. Onq and PsJ both provide four terms here.

(b) Emerton's article "Unclean Birds and the Origin of the Peshiṭta", has discussed the list of unclean birds in 11:13-19, though 6b1's variant ܦܪܚܕܘܕܐ , "bat", for ܛܘܣܐ , "peacock", was treated there only in a footnote, with the comment that it could be either a correction to accord with the Hebrew, or original. Another possibility remains, that a participle ܛܝܣܐ was intended as a general term for a flying creature which was not precisely known, and that resemblance to the transcribed Greek ταώς is fortuitous. See also the discussion of 6b1's "variants" above. It must be admitted that guess may have been the basis of the rendering.

(b) At 18:14 the Hebrew reads ערות אחי אביך לא תגלה אל אשתו לא תקרב דדתך הוא and is closely followed by Onq and PsJ. In Syriac this is rendered ܦܘܪܣܘܡܗ ܕܐܢܬܬ ܕܕܟ ܠܐ ܬܓܠܐ. ܘܠܐܢܬܬܗ ܠܐ ܬܬܩܪܒ. ܡܛܠ ܕܐܢܬܬ ܕܕܟ ܗܝ. ܠܐ ܬܓܠܐ ܦܘܪܣܘܡܗ. A paraphrase and expansion have been used to show an equivalent to the Hebrew, understanding the second part of the Hebrew verse as an explication of the first.

(c) There are some instances of a desire for clarity of interpretation that has led to the expansion of a compact Hebrew phrase.

(i) At 18:9 MT מולדת בית או מולדת חוץ has an ambiguity as to whether the reference is to an outside mother or father. This phrase becomes in Syriac ܕܝܠܝܕܐ ܡܢ ܐܒܘܟ ܐܘ ܡܢ ܓܒܪܐ ܐܚܪܢ. "From your father or another man" is an interpretation which could be either from knowledge or from theory. LXX well renders this phrase ἐνδογενοῦς ἢ γεγεννημένης ἔξω, "born at home or elsewhere".

(ii) At 7:16, 18 two MT one-word participles, or a two-word phrase, הנותר , המקריב , הנפש האכלת , all become subordinate clauses. Peshiṭta gives ܡܕܡ ܕܡܫܬܪ ܡܢܗ and ܘܡܢ ܕܡܩܪܒ ܠܗ and ܘܢܦܫܐ ܕܬܐܟܘܠ ܡܢܗ respectively (from left to right). The Syriac translator avoided such single-word constructions, unlike LXX as at 18:9.

(iii) At 22:23 שׂרוע וקלוט (some kinds of deformity) is expanded and given a clear reference by the Syriac translator ܕܦܣܝܩܐ ܐܕܢܗ ܐܘ ܕܟܪܝܐ ܐܠܝܬܗ "with a notched ear or short tail" : Onq and PsJ also explicate the Hebrew idiom in something of the same way; LXX, to the writer's mind most happily in single words, ὠτότμητον and κολοβόκερκον "crop-eared and stumpy-tailed".

(d) It was not always possible or desired for distinctions to be drawn consistently.

(i) At 4:13 it can be seen that ܟܢܘܫܬܐ serves for עדה as well as for קהל ; though Onq and PsJ preserve the distinction between the two Hebrew words LXX uses συναγωγὴ both times.
Nor was precision apparently always thought necessary.

(ii) At 16:12 ܛܒܐ is given as the equivalent for דקה ; a more precise term than "good" for "pure" would be a closer equivalent.

(iii) At 23:3, שבת שבתון is also paraphrased ܫܒܬܐ ܕܢܘܚܐ , Onq שבא שבתא ; PsJ שבא ונייחא ; LXX σάββατα ἀνάπαυσις. But where the word שבתון is used twice in 23:39 it is given different equivalents: the first, ܒܛܘܠܝܐ , and the second ܢܘܚܐ . Onq and PsJ use ניחא twice, and LXX ἀνάπαυσις twice. Yet at 25:4 it is rendered simply ܢܘܚܐ , where Onq uses שמיטתא ; PsJ נייח דשמיטיתא ; LXX σάββατα ἀνάπαυσις.

(iv) A similar paraphrase occurs in 19:24 קדש הלולים rendered as ܩܘܕܫܐ ܘܬܫܒܚܬܐ , Onq supplying קודש תושבחן and PsJ virtually the same; LXX ἅγιος αἰνετὸς, "a holy subject of praise".

(3) A separate group of equivalents is provided by instances of uncertainty of the meaning of the text to be translated, or by a use of familiar Syriac terms for Hebrew terms which are opaque.

(a) at 22:24 three Syriac terms are used to express four Hebrew terms, presumably because the first Syriac term, ܪܥܝܥ , covers the first two Hebrew, מעוך , "squeezed", and כתות , "crushed", while ܦܣܝܩ , "castrated", and ܡܚܒܠ , "mutilated", are equivalents of נתוק and כרות . Onq uses four terms, the first two related, מריץ , רציץ , צליף , and גזיר ,

"bruised, cut, torn, or cut"; while PsJ here makes two phrases: ובמעיך ודכטיסן פחדוהי ודסחית ודמסרס גידוי . The first two words are related to testicles, the other two to limbs. LXX uses four words, θλαδίαν, ἐκτεθλιμμένον, ἐκτομίαν, ἀπεσπασμένον, "broken, crushed, gelded, mutilated".

(b) At 26:30, *per contra*, the definition has been blunted, as a general term is used for the specific, in a passage concerning the overthrow of sanctuaries and idols. במתיכם becomes ܒܝܬ̈ܐ "temples", LXX στήλας; but ܕ̈ܚܠܬܗܘܢ "objects of worship" is used as equivalent both for חמניכם "pillars of the sun", and גלוליכם "divine images". LXX supplies two terms ξύλινα χειροποίητα, "wooden artifacts" for the first, εἰδώλων for the second. For this last Onq and PsJ give טעותכון "abominations".

(c) Finally there are two examples of the use of words which appear to be familiar terms which are used to represent infrequent or opaque Hebrew terms.

(i) At 13:39 the Syriac prefers a familiar term ܩܠܦܝܬܐ ܓܪܒܐ as equivalent for a Hebrew term not previously used, בהק הוא פרח , (Onq בוהקא הוא סגי ; PsJ צהר הוא סגי) in describing an eruption on the flesh.

(ii) At 19:31 the terms ܘܙܟ̈ܘܪܐ ܘܩܨ̈ܘܡܐ "users of magic arts and sooth-sayers" are used as equivalents of Hebrew האבת and ידענים "utterers of noise and oracle-givers"; the LXX uses, to the writer's mind happily, ἐγγαστριμύθοις and ἐπαοιδοῖς "ventriloquists and charmers". Onq supplies בדין and זכורו , and PsJ has תבעי גרם , משקי זכורו , שאלי בידין , ידוע.

5. *Some cultic terms*

The present writer's "The best words in the best order" discusses the logic which has influenced the Peshitta rendering in cultic and cultural sections of Leviticus.

(1) A similar logic can be seen in the following instances in cultic sections.

(a) There is one root in Syriac, ܦܪܫ , which does duty for no less than four Hebrew roots. On the face of it, this suggests ignorance or incompetence, and it calls into question the ability or willingness of the translator to provide responsible terms for the cultic material. A closer look shows otherwise. In 10:10 the root is used to render בדל "to make a distinction between", LXX διαστεῖλαι; in 10:15 its noun ܦܘܪܫܐ is used for both "wave offering" and "heave offering", LXX ἀφαιρέματος, ἀφορίσματος; and again in 14:57 the Hebrew להורת ביום הטמא וביום הטהר is translated ܘܠܡܦܪܫܘ ܒܝܬ ܛܡܐܐ ܠܕܟܝܐ , LXX ἐξηγήσασθαι. In 10:10 Onq and PsJ, however, give ולאפרשא ; in 10:15, where MT has שוק התרומה וחזה התנופה , Onq and PsJ both have שקא דאפרשותא וחדיא דארמותא . At 14:57 Onq supplies לאלפא , "instruct", as the equivalent. The Syriac recognises the underlying unity in these Hebrew words, in that they all involve separateness: hence the single root ܦܪܫ is the most appropriate equivalent.

(b) Some other words clearly caused difficulty. In 13:42, 43, 55 MT has בקרחתו and בגבחתו (areas on the head without skin, either a bald crown or a forehead). In vv. 42, 43 these are transliterated ܩܪܚܘܬܗ and ܓܒܚܘܬܗ ; in vs 55, however, they are rendered "on the new part or the old", ܒܚܕܬܘܬܗ or ܒܥܬܩܘܬܗ , thus making a distinction between patches which are on persons and patches which are not on persons. LXX renders φαλακρώματι and ἀναφαλαντώματι, "baldheadedness", "without eyebrows, baldness".

(c) Problems of equivalents were encountered in the passage on clean and unclean. The four animals of 11:4-7 have cognates as equivalents, . . . ܘܠܚܡܐ . . . ܠܓܡܠܐ ܘܐܪܢܒܐ ܘܚܙܝܪܐ, though the longer list in 11:29, 30 is more problematic, as also are the lists of 21:20 and 26:16. The Hebrew list, 11:29,30, is החלד והעכבר והצב . . . והאנקה והכח והלטאה והחמט והתנשמת ; the Syriac list ܚܘܠܕܐ ܘܥܘܩܒܪܐ . . . ܘܐܢܩܬܐ ܘܐܟܡܐ ܘܥܠܝܐ ܘܝܪܘܪܐ ܘܣܠܡܢܕܪܐ . The English equivalents are by no means certain. The *New English Bible* may well be right in seeing the first as, not "weasel", (though *sic* Neofiti) nor "ghecko", but "mole-rat", and the second as neither "sand ghecko" or "mouse" (*sic* Neofiti) but (as Syriac) "jerboa". תנשמת is taken as "chameleon". In the other list of flying creatures, 11:18, it might be rendered "bat", and is taken by Neofiti as "mole".

(d) Similar problems were met in the classification of disqualifications from the priesthood. At 21:20 the Hebrew list of disqualifications is או גבן או דק או תבלל בעינו או גרב או ילפת או מרוח אשך . The Syriac does not follow the same order or indeed give the same sense. It reads: ܐܘ ܚܒܝܨܐ ܐܘ ܙܥܘܪܐ. ܐܘ ܥܠܝܒ ܨܝܢ̈ܘܗܝ, ܐܘ ܓܪܒܢܐ ܐܘ ܫܘܚܢܐ ܐܘ ܐܝܬ ܠܗ ܫܘܚܢܐ ܒܟ̈ܘܒܘܗܝ, ܐܘ ܐܝܬ ܒܗ ܓܠܝܕܐ. ܐܘ ܚܒܝܨܐ. ܐܘ ܚܘܫ ܐܘ ܐܬܪܥܐ. The Syriac rightly takes גבן as "crook-backed", and דק as "small", but then provides a doublet, which accords with PsJ and Rashi whose understanding of גבן is: "eyebrows so long that they cover the eye"; of דק : "a membrane in the eye"; and of תבלל : "a white line running into the black of the pupil". These two terms have been taken with תבלל , and all three taken as dependent upon עינו : hence "who has long eyebrows, or a hair, or a milkiness in the eye". But ילפת should have been rendered, as it is elsewhere, by ܩܠܦܝܬܐ or some such term for a skin eruption, but instead has the equivalent ܚܒܝܨ , a reversion to "hunchback". The last two words in the sentence have been discussed above, and also under 9a1's variant ܫܒܝܠ . LXX is similarly confused about the relationship between the words: ἢ κυρτός ἢ ἔφηλος ἢ πτίλος τους ὀφθαλμοὺς ἢ ἄνθρωπος ᾧ ἂν ᾖ ἐν αὐτῷ ψώρα ἀγρία ἢ λιχήν, ἢ μόνορχις, "hump-backed, blear-eyed, without eyelashes, having a malignant ulcer, a skin eruption, monotesticular".

(e) Of a similar order is the finding of equivalents in passages on disease. At 26:16 the Hebrew reads והפקדתי עליכם בהלה את השחפת ואת הקדחת מכלות עינים ומדיבת נפש , which Syriac renders ܐܦܩܘܕ ܥܠܝܟܘܢ ܒܗܠܬܐ ܘܓܪܒܐ ܘܫܘܚܢܐ . ܘܐܪܐ ܗܕܐ ܕܬܟܠܐ ܥܝܢܐ ܘܡܕܝܒܐ ܢܦܫܐ . Thus the context of leprosy is maintained, rather than wasting fever, although the latter is required for the reference to perspiration at the close.

(f) Interpretation was considered necessary in the passage concerning the breastplate and ephod. At 8:8 the Hebrew האורים and התמים (PsJ, Onq אוריא , תומיא) are rendered ܢܗܝܪܐ ܘܫܘܡܠܝܐ . The first has been understood as "intellectual light", relating the word to אור , perhaps with an overtone of ܐܘܪܝܬܐ for תורה ; תמים from the understanding that the root תמם signifies "true", in the sense that the promises of the Lord, or Torah, are true. Onq and PsJ do not interpret. It is worth consulting Rashi on Exod 28:30. The Peshiṭta at that verse reads: ܥܠ ܚܘܫܒܐ ܕܕܝܢܐ ܢܗܝܪܐ ܘܫܘܡܠܝܐ . Rashi comments that the inscription of the divine name on the breastplate enabled it to be a means of giving judgment, citing Num 27:21. There the Syriac version again interprets, for במשפט האורים , "by the judgment of the Urim", it supplies ܒܕܘܡܣܐ ܕܫܐܠܬܐ . These then are different possibilities from a tradition of translation known to Rashi, who also cites bYoma 73b. LXX uses δήλωσιν and ἀλήθειαν , "explanation" and "truth" in Exod 28:30 and Leviticus.

(g) At 6:14 there is the Hebrew word תפיני in a passage on the meal offerings and their preparation. The Syriac seems to understand this as a derivation from the root פתח "to break up", possibly cognate with the Syriac root ܦܬ . Onq and Rashi seem to relate the word to the root אפה "to bake", hence "thoroughly baked". LXX inclines to this also, using ἑλικτά in the sense "baked over again".

(2) Two instances have cultural as much as cultic background, as they may reflect custom and comment on it.

(a) At 10:6 the phrase ראשיכם אל תפרעו is translated ܪܫܝܟܘܢ ܠܐ ܬܦܪܥܘܢ , in the sense "shave the head": the opposite sense to that of the Hebrew, which would seem to be related to the Assyrian *pirw* "to sprout long hair, as in Sifra *Shemini Mekhilta de Miluim*, Neusner, vol. 2, p. 132. LXX seems to think of an Arabic word, *frgh*, "to let go, be vacant", hence τὴν κεφαλὴν ὑμῶν οὐκ ἀποκιδαρώσετε, "do not remove your headdress". This appears to be an instance of the Syriac root having the opposite sense to the Hebrew, or the change between *aph'el* and *pi'el* making such a difference. The last example is also concerned with hair.

(b) At 19:27 the Hebrew לא תקפו פאת ראשכם ולא תשחית את פאת זקנך is rendered ܠܐ ܬܩܦܘܢ ܣܥܪܐ ܕܪܫܝܟܘܢ ܘܠܐ. ܬܚܒܠܘܢ ܦܐܬܐ ܕܕܩܢܝܟܘܢ and by LXX οὐ ποιήσετε σισόην ἐκ τῆς κόμης τῆς κεφαλῆς ὑμῶν οὐδὲ φθερεῖτε τὴν ὄψιν τοῦ πώγωνος ὑμῶν. It is possible that this is couched as an antithesis to the previous passage; but probably there are two understandings of the Hebrew root involved. נקף has the sense of "strike off, mutilate", whereas another root נקף has the sense of "go round", which is the traditional interpretation and is that of Rashi. LXX might have followed this second interpretation, too, if σισόην means a "roll of hair". Syriac has possibly thought of the root קפא , "thicken, heap up" (*cf* Job 10:10), or considered the Syriac root ܩܦܐ "to heap up".

All these examples well illustrate the difficulties which faced a translator from Hebrew into Syriac, and give some idea of the way in which the Syriac translators worked, with some indication of the way in which some Aramaic and Greek translators made their versions. Clearly, the author of the Peshiṭta of Leviticus was working with some knowledge of a general kind, and within the pattern of interpretation found within the tradition and method regarded as targumic. But the Peshiṭta version was made before certain accredited interpretations became as definitive in exegesis as the text was for exegesis.

CHAPTER SEVEN

THE EDITORS OF THE PRINTED EDITIONS

The Leiden edition combines typological and historical interests. Its text inclines to the standard one of the majority of manuscripts, while its apparatus makes possible a study of the version's history and typology. Critical work has gone into all printed texts of the Peshiṭta, even if their ecclesiastical significance required that this be unacknowledged. But in all cases editorial judgments as well as manuscript availability have determined the nature of the text printed.

1. *The background of the Leiden edition*

The work of the editors of the printed editions deserves comment, as they were working within two constraints. In the first place there was a need which they had identified, or which had been identified for them, for a Syriac text. They responded to this need. In the second place, the availability of material was fortuitous: both with respect to the quantity which had survived, and the time and circumstance of its becoming available. The number of manuscripts available was not unlimited; such as were available had survived more by chance than by design. In addition, the editors (often reluctant editors) were influenced in the manner of editing texts by the thought and expectations of their contemporaries: they were not free agents. All too often there was an understandable pre-judgment concerning the value of manuscripts: *prima facie* the older or the more unusual was considered the more valuable. It had not been adequately understood that the search for the "better" manuscript, like that for the "better" reading, is a subjective thing. Granted, the exemplar of a manuscript presumes the existence of a manuscript older than itself; but that is a statement of fact and not of value. Only the systematic and critical collection and collation of manuscripts, made possible by the Peshiṭta edition, has brought recognition that the term Peshiṭta refers to a text tradition which has a life of its own, and the corollary that the apparatus is as important as the text selected for an edition. The work of an editor is therefore primarily concerned with what should be excluded from the text, whether relegated to an apparatus if there should be one, or passed over in silence if there should not be one. In contrast, the editors of earlier printed material were under the constraint that the revealing of critical matters, and therefore the provision of an apparatus, was out of the question.

The Leiden edition of the Peshiṭta version of the Old Testament in Syriac provides for the first time a complete and acknowledged critical edition of a kind to satisfy the plea made as long ago as 1849 by Canon John Rogers of Exeter. In his pamphlet, *Reasons why a New Edition of the Peschito, or Ancient Syriac Version of the Old Testament, should be Published, with Variae Lectiones from Ancient MSS and Editions*, he regretted the lack of a critical edition, and noted the then recent manuscript acquisitions of the British Museum which might provide a base for one. In fact, however, there have been unacknowledged critical editions based on the kind of evidence required by Canon Rogers. But the delay until the 1960s in meeting the plea for an acknowledged soundly based critical edition may be attributed to three factors. First, a doubt as to the advisability of making known the concerns of orientalists to a readership within oriental churches. It is not in church history alone that the clash between the interests of "les orientalistes" and "les Orientaux", to use the terms of Fiey,

Jalons pour une Histoire, p. 1, has been of moment.
Secondly, the magnitude of the task of ensuring that all
appropriate manuscripts, whether in the British Museum or
elsewhere, had been consulted. Thirdly, a doubt of the
value of work on a text whose worth was considered to be
only that of a witness to a Hebrew original, and which had
further come to be discounted as being the deposit of non-
Chalcedonian churches.

2. *Leiden and the "real" Peshiṭta*

However, mention of "the Peshiṭta" once more raises
questions about criteria for defining an authoritative and
authentic text. The questions which now need to be
answered are firstly, the extent to which the Leiden Peshiṭta
has replaced its predecessors as a text in some way authentic
and definitive; and secondly, the way in which its arrival coincides with a change in intellectual climate. After all,
different times make different demands on those who work
on the Hebrew biblical text and its dependent versions.
Previous chapters have shown that methods of translation,
concern with language, matters of exegesis, and church
history all broaden the current approach to versions: in much
the same way as Qumran material has broadened the
approach to text and the communities which produce it.
Hence the nature of the Leiden Peshiṭta will determine the
usefulness of its text and its critical apparatus. The value of
its critical apparatus will be judged by the extent to which it
makes possible an assessment of the typological changes in
the Peshiṭta tradition, and sheds light on varieties of
interpretation of the presumed Hebrew exemplar. In so far
as its text is used for work with MT, then it has to be shown
that its text is superior (or at least preferable) to those
available for the preparation of *Biblia Hebraica
Stuttgartensia*. Only in Samuel is there a listing of the

editions consulted, which are as follows:

S^A Codex Ambrosianus (7a1) ed. A.M. Ceriani, 1876sqq;
S^L Lee's *Pentateuchus Syriace* 1821;
S^M Mosul edition, 1887sqq, reprinted 1951;
S^U Urmia edition 1852, reprinted 1952;
S^W Walton's Polyglot, London 1654sqq.

In respect of Leviticus it may be noted that Le Jay seems to have used four manuscripts (13a1, 17a5-7). Walton used Le Jay and three other manuscripts (12b1, 17a3, 4: see Thorndike's introduction to Vol VI). Lee used five manuscripts (12a1; 12b2; 17a1, 3, 4: see John Rogers' "Professor Lee's Remarks on the Collation of Syriac MSS". Barnes used ten manuscripts (6b1; 7a1; 8b1; 9a1; 9m1; 12a1; 12b2; 13b3; 18b3, see Barnes, "A New Edition of the Pentateuch in Syriac". The Leiden Peshiṭta, however, can call on 70 manuscripts from which collations can be (though not necessarily have been) made, see *List*. The early years of preparation for the edition were taken up with the search for appropriate manuscripts in such collections as London, Oxford, Milan, Cambridge, Rome, Birmingham (Selly Oak), the Library of the Chaldean Patriarchate in Mosul and Vassar College, Poughkeepsie. Appropriately, the first publication of the Peshiṭta Institute was the Preliminary *List* in 1961. This enterprise could well be described in Haefeli's phrase on p. 113 of *Die Peshitta des Alten Testamentes*: ". . . eine kostspielige, zeitraubende und schwierige Arbeit . . . ". The phrase comes in a disquisition on the need for more and better manuscripts, together with a suggestion as to what kind of manuscript the word "better" might suggest: he seems to have intimidated not only himself but all others between his remarks in 1927 and the Leiden undertaking 30 years later.

The drawback to the Leiden edition is the obverse of its strength: namely, the possibility of a large number of variants. Some criterion has to be established for determining the text readings and the apparatus readings: the one of selecting the majority reading of pre-tenth-century manuscripts was adopted. Gelston comments on this, p. 87, in his 1988 Symposium article:

> The distribution of significant variant readings between text and apparatus was determined by the accident of the degree of attestation available for the distinctive readings of the oldest MSS.

Other possibilities might have included the taking of a printed text, for example the Mosul edition, as a starting point and to have worked backwards from that. But the Mosul edition comes at the end of a period of growth, and its antecedents are not always identifiable. There is something of the mongrel in its make-up, and in any case it was not intended to be a critical edition. Rather, it was intended to be a definitive stabilising of a traditional text fed by different sources. Alternatively, the oldest text of all might have been chosen as a starting point for an edition. But 7a1 is the oldest complete text: there are indeed older manuscripts, but they are of single books, or single groups of books; in some cases they are only fragments of text.

Such a choice on the grounds of age raises again basic questions as to which the "real" Peshitta might be: whether it is the closest mechanical equivalent to the Massoretic Text, or the one removed furthest from it, taken as evidence of independence from referral to it. Further to confuse the issue, Tov comments, in "Hebrew Biblical Manuscripts from the Judaean Desert", p. 7:

The texts have thus taught us no longer to posit MT at the center of our textual thinking. If, in spite of this, they are still compared with MT, this merely represents a scholarly convention derived from the central status of the text in Judaism and the availability of good editions of MT.

In the light of that comment, the central role of MT as a point of referral can no longer hold good, without qualification, in attempting to discover the "real" Peshiṭta. If the "real" Hebrew turns out to be merely a "scholarly convention" there is no objective unit against which Versions can be measured. Perhaps that emphasises the importance of establishing the Peshiṭta on its own recognisances. The combination of text and apparatus in the Leiden edition draw attention to the synchronic and diachronic nature of Syriac text traditions. It further suggests that a manuscript is the result of influences outside and inside itself, and cannot be assessed independently of them. Yet at the end of the day, the Peshiṭta is a version: its life has an independence, while its origin lies with its parent.

This chapter, which is followed in Chapter 8 by a table setting out the readings of the earlier printed editions against those of the Leiden edition, is built on the foundation of Emerton's "The Printed Editions of the Song of Songs in the Peshiṭta Version". The table is not intended to repeat the details of the edition's Apparatus, merely to suggest the likely sources from which the editors drew individual readings. On this basis it is possible to comment on the aims of the editors and to draw attention to the cumulative consequences of their editorial decisions. The relation between personalities of editors, texts and churches has been given some attention in the present writer's "Text, Scholar and Church", showing that the printed editions can be correlated with the manuscript traditions, and that there is a relation between ecclesiastical convention and critical endeavour.

3. *The first editions*

For the Peshiṭta the *editio princeps* is that of Guido le Jay and others, Paris 1645, and it is sufficiently established that the Syriac version (Pentateuch in vol VI, remainder in vols VII-IX) was the work of Gabriel Sionita. Now this puts the work in the range of the Maronites, the scholarly activity of the Assemanis, the textual studies of Sergius Risius, the patronage of Clement XI and a seventeenth-century concern for an authoritative and complete text of the Old Testament. The manuscript underlying the Syriac text of this Polyglot is 17a5; but this itself is the result of textual work on the part of Abraham Ecchellensis and Gabriel Sionita, in which selection and accident played their part- convenience as much as acumen suggesting the underlying manuscript. The manuscript is one of that group of manuscripts which Barnes described as "poor relations", if not descendants of 12a1, or transcriptions of 9a1: *Chronicles* p. vii. Traditionally, poor relations are cousins, and so it is here. The exemplar of 17a5 is 15a2, which mediated the text of 12a1 to other seventeenth-century manuscripts, and which itself was corrected, or perhaps it is fairer to say, modified, by recourse to 10m3. 17a5 itself shows modifications, sometimes with reference to 13a1. The evidence of the Leviticus manuscripts bears out what has been found and stated by others, notably by Koster in his *Exodus*. There is discussion on the grouping and relationship of Leviticus manuscripts in the Leiden volume, pp. vii-xxvii.

Before turning to compare the Paris Polyglot with the Leiden edition, it is worth looking briefly at the London Polyglot, 6 vols, London 1657, the work chiefly of Brian Walton. In fact it reproduces the text of the Paris Polyglot of Le Jay, with only a few minor errors. This London Polyglot has set the terms of all the other printed versions, including even those of Urmia and Mosul. So it is pertinent to enquire what advantage the Leiden Peshiṭta might have over the Walton edition. In short, the Leiden Peshiṭta represents a text (the emended 7a1) earlier than that of the base (12a1) of the underlying text (17a5) of the exemplar (17a5) of the Paris edition. The Leiden edition therefore has as its foundation a text which has been less affected by the organic changes of assimilation, accretion and loss which are inevitable when manuscripts interbreed, whether inside or outside their immediate families.

Something can be said of the history of the manuscript 12a1, which lies behind the printed editions previous to Leiden. As it is the exemplar of 15a2, it is reasonable to suppose that it was with that manuscript in Jerusalem in the fifteenth century; it was later taken to Travancore, and given in the nineteenth century to Claudius Buchanan. Burkitt described it in *Kerala Society Papers* 1, p. 42 as being written in "the Estrangela of *Tur-'Abdin"*, and on p. 41 considered that it had come with the metropolitan Gregorius, sent from the Patriarch of Antioch whose residence was in Amid (Diyarbakir) or in the mountains of Tur-'Abdin between the Euphrates and the Tigris. He records that it may safely be dated to the twelfth century A.D., noting that on fol. 141, in the margin, the Patriarch Michael is mentioned, to be understood as Michael the Great, who died in 1199 A.D.

The origin and early history of the manuscript has most recently been studied by Hunt, "The Syriac Buchanan Bible in Cambridge". The writing and illuminations show that the manuscript had its origin in Edessa, and that its subsequent history belongs to the life of centres of religious life which were to be found in the Latin dominated Syriac Near East.

Her findings, based on iconography, are in accord with the present writer's conclusions, see Chapter 9, based on textual study. The textual character of this manuscript is similar to 7a1 and 8a1, but it has developed away from the mainstream of the ancient manuscripts, and has therefore diverged from that pattern of text which is shown most clearly in 10b1 and the other examples of the standard text. It is evidence for the development of related but differing texts, associated with geographical areas whose history and culture were separate.

The Paris and London Polyglots, which ultimately rest upon this text, need to be examined for the presence of errors, and the discovery of the stage at which they might have been incurred. The errors could be made either by Le Jay or by Walton, or could have been made earlier, in the copying of 17a5 if not its exemplars. There is no doubt of the importance of 12a1, as a link between the older and some later Peshiṭta manuscript traditions; its position as a chief influence on the printed editions depends, at least to some degree, on the care shown by Sionita in his handling of material derived from it through 15a2. It should be remembered that both 15a2 and 17a5 are eclectic texts, since each takes into account readings from other manuscripts.

(a) The following verses contain errors, present in the Paris Polyglot, which are followed by Walton, and (where marked +L) also by Lee:

7:12, 19; 11:40+L, 42; 13:32; $18:30_2$o; 20:11+L; $21:14_2$o+LM, 21/22; 22:19+L; 23:14, 16, 22; 24:6; 26:16.

(b) Errors made by Walton alone are at :

1:8; $22:14_2$o; 22:27; 25:8; 26:6; 27:30.

4. *Samuel Lee*

The next edition which attracts attention is that of Lee. It is, like Le Jay and Walton, a complete text of the bible. The noticeable factor in this edition is the extent to which readings in Walton are rejected, and the basis on which the rejection is done. What Lee considered to be error is corrected, and, for the rest, the main tradition which was followed, through 12b1.2, was that which resembled (9b1) 10b1. Hence there is a modest move towards the standard text: a move which demonstrates that the work of the editor is to exercise judgment. The result of this exercise of judgment by Lee is the production of a text which is closer to that of the Polyglots than the Leiden text is, but which has modified the Polyglots where an older manuscript was judged to give a reading whose superiority lay, as it turned out, simply to be one of date rather than inherent value. How this came to be is instructive, and can be determined by the study of Lee's text in the table below, and by consideration of an article giving the sources he claimed to use.

The article is a communication, "Professor Lee's Remarks on the Collation of Syriac MSS", *The Classical Journal,* 1821. It is signed only by the initials JR, which may safely be taken to be those of Canon John Rogers. It is also worthwhile considering Barnes, "The Printed Editions of the Peshitta of the Old Testament". Lee's edition was under the auspices of the British and Foreign Bible Society, and could therefore itself have no indication of critical method. The same was true of Barnes' own edition of the Pentateuch in the next century. Now Lee's edition of 1823 was based upon the London Polyglot of Brian Walton: for Leviticus this included both the main text and also the further collations made by Thorndike. Lee had access to the manuscripts used by Thorndike (12b1, 17a3,4). He also had access to Gloster Ridley's twelfth-century Pentateuch (12b2, one of four manuscripts sent from Amid) and also to the Travancore manuscript, 12a1.

In fact, though Canon Rogers did not know it, Lee's edition included, in these last two manuscripts alone, representatives of two of the classic manuscript traditions, usually described as Eastern (i.e. Nestorian) and Western (i.e. Maronite). For 12b2 normally accompanies the 9b1, 10b1 kind of text; and 12a1 lies behind the 15a2 family. It is an irony, not entirely surprising, that both these manuscripts are associated with the same area, Amid (Diyarbakir) or Tur-'Abdin, close to the old Syriac area of Osrhoene, and what later became the centre of Monophysite monasticism. Lee's edition conflated the two divergent traditions, though giving preference to that of 12b2 at the expense of 12a1. He judged, it may be presumed, that the text from a twelfth-century manuscript took precedence over that from a seventeenth-century print, even when there was testimony from another twelfth-century manuscript which colluded with the seventeenth-century manuscripts.

Excluding orthographic matters, in Leviticus Lee made about 90 changes to the Walton text. About 70 of these are rejections of readings found in Le Jay and Walton. Nearly 20 are a matter of preference, sometimes of error. About 30 of Lee's readings (no doubt based upon the presumed superiority of 12b1.2) have the effect of being a preference for the Eastern as against the Western text. But, then, Lee did not have exact knowledge of the textual antecedents of Walton, and was under the necessity of assessing his material *prima facie*. Not surprisingly, though, where evidence from different manuscripts concurred, this factor determined the preference. The alterations to text can be set out as follows:

1. The correction of an error or unique reading originating in 12a1, 15a2, 15a2[1], 17a5, 17a5[1], P or W, compared with 12b1, 2.

1:8; 2:12; 4:4, 21; 5:8, 13, 22(*bis*), 25; 6:3; 7:12$_3$0, 14, 19, 25$_2$0; 8:24; 11:11, 32$_2$0, 42/43; 13:5, 6, 7, 8, 32$_2$0, 49, 51(*bis*), 58; 14:13, 16, 17, 21, 42, 47(*bis*); 15:3, 25, 30$_1$0 ,33(*bis*); 16:28, 34; 17:2; 18:30$_2$0; 19:10, 36; 20:3, 18, 19(*bis*), 21; 21:21/22; 22:13(*bis*), 14, 20, 21$_1$0, 22, 27; 23:6$_1$0, 8, 14, 16, 22, 37$_3$0; 24:6, 11; 25:49$_2$0, 52; 26:1, 16, 36; 27:5, 30.

2. There are however other readings initiated by Lee:
4:32=12b1; 5:6=?12a1,12b2; 7:12$_4$0(faulty correction), 14; 11:20, 42(*err*); 13:21(*err*)=12b1, 32=12b1, 34, 58(*err*); 16:20=12b1; 18:17, 21(*err*), 30$_1$0+UM=12b1; 20:26+UM=12b1.2; 21:12; 25:4=12b2.

12b2 requires some comment: in Leviticus it is within the pattern of (9b1) 10b1 and the standard text, being found within this pattern some 96 times. It has readings peculiar to itself (other than INSCR) only at 1:9; 3:5; 4:27; 7:2(*sey*), 12; 10:9; 20:16; 22:32; 25:21; 26:36. None of these readings is followed by Lee, who seems to prefer a consensus of witnesses. This behaviour of 12b2 shows a different pattern from other books, as Koster comments, *Exodus* p. 330, 331: "Already these last variants show that 12b2 has a certain independence in the P tradition".

The general effect, then, of Lee's text is that it is a conflation, with a tendency towards the standard text. The distinctiveness of 12a1*fam* has been moderated, in addition to the correction of errors in the printed texts. Lee seems to have followed the custom of editors, and examined individual words only, except where mechanical errors involved longer units.

5. *William Emery Barnes*

Barnes presents a text which is much more scholarly, in that the readings seem to have been pondered as well as weighed. But here again the age of the manuscript seems to have played a large part in assessing worth. The only indication to the text critical nature of the work lies in the title page:

Pentateuchus Syriace post Samuelem Lee Recognavit Emendavit Edidit Guilelmus Emery Barnes adiuvantibus Carolo W. Mitchell Iohanne Pinkerton. Further understanding of the text's production is gleaned from other sources and internal evidence. Barnes had the advantage of having to hand a wider range of manuscripts than his predecessors, but like Lee, had the disadvantage of working under the aegis of the British and Foreign Bible Society. The edition was ecclesiastical rather than scholarly; neither apparatus nor accompanying rationale could be supplied. It is further to be regretted that the project included the Pentateuch only.

Presumably the manuscripts that Rogers had in mind when he urged a new critical edition taking into account newly-found manuscripts were those in the British Museum's Tattam acquisitions. The first series arrived in 1838 (Additional Manuscripts 12,133-12,181), to be followed by the second series (Add Mss 14,425-14,739). The two lots of acquisitions negotiated by M. Auguste Pacho (Add Mss 17,102-17,274 and 18,812-18,821) arrived too late for Rogers to have taken note of them. These collections included manuscripts which Barnes used, for present purposes the most important being Add Ms 14,425 (5b1) and Add Ms 14,427 (6b1). He was able to include also two further manuscripts which have occupied much attention, and which are in all probability from the same source: the Ambrosian Library 7a1 and the Florentine 9a1 (Oriental manuscript 58 in the Laurentian Library). Barnes' judgment inclined him to revise Lee in the light of a preference for the earlier manuscripts; but there is also a significant dependence upon the Urmia edition (which he admitted to referring to freely) for changes, some 24 of them. Presumably the provenance of that printed edition, or the anticipated usage of his own edition, led to this curiosity. In the event he

made some 130 changes, resulting in a text which shows a
rejection of later, for the most part Eastern, manuscripts: his
preference was for 6b1, and for the manuscript 8b1 which
was already in the British Museum, catalogued Ms Or 4400.
Neither of these fall firmly within the (9b1) 10b1 pattern of
text. The information concerning the manuscripts used (for
Leviticus, it will be recalled, 6b1 7a1 8b1 9a1 12a1 12b2 are
the ones which concern present discussion), is in Barnes' own
article, "A New Edition of the Pentateuch in Syriac", but the
method he employed can best be seen in an examination of
the list of readings in the table in Chapter 8. Further
information and assessment of the material used is given by
one of his assistants in the project, J. Pinkerton, "The Origin
and Early History of the Syriac Pentateuch". This is an
article which is a classic in text studies, and, regrettably, a
memorial to its writer killed in the Great War.

Barnes gives priority to 8b1, and to 6b1 where that is
available. Where Barnes concurs with Lee, these
manuscripts usually provide the reason; where he departs
from Lee, it is usually with their encouragement. The
readings where Barnes goes against Lee are:

> 2:5, 8, 12$_2$0; 3:5, 14; 4:12, 13, 22, 31, 32, 35; 5:6, 16(*bis*); 6:11, 22; 7:6,
> 12, 14, 25, 36; 8:19; 9:5, 24; 10:6, 12, 14, 19; 11:10, 20, 26, 27, 29, 32,
> 40, 41, 42, 46; 12:7; 13:3(*bis*), 4$_2$0, 13, 15, 17, 20, 21, 25, 29, 32(*bis*),
> 34, 38, 44, 52, 55$_3$0, 56, 58; 14:21, 36, 38, 48(*bis*); 15:10, 12, 24, 26,
> 30, 33; 16:14, 20, 27; 17:3, 8, 7, 10, 11; 18:11$_2$0, 17, 21, 27(*bis*), 28,
> 30(*bis*); 19:28(*bis*), 34; 20:8, 11, 16, 19, 23, 26; 21:12, 14, 18; 22:6,
> 14, 18(*bis*), 19, 21, 23, 25; 23:3, 4, 6, 8, 15, 27, 30, 37, 39; 25:4, 7,
> 8, 16(*bis*), 25, 30, 32, 33, 46, 49; 26:5, 6, 18, 25, 27, 28, 40, 41;
> 27:3, 8$_2$0, 9, 25.

The overall effect of this is to pull the text into that of the
7a1/8b1 kind of text away from Lee's tendency to modify
Walton with 12b1.2. For as well as the places where 8b1
can be seen as a controlling influence, these 130 divergences
from Lee result in a text resembling that of 7a1.

6. *Urmia*

However tantalising these small glimpses of editorial preparation may be, the glimpses given of the editing of the Urmia and Mosul editions tantalise yet more. Of the 78 changes made in the Urmia edition none, either alone or in conjunction with others, provides any clear evidence of system or consistency. There seems no reason to consider it as more than a minor modification of Lee.

Like Lee's edition, the Urmia is an ecclesiastical version, and no suggestion of critical activity could be set out. Dr Isaac Hall was in correspondence with the Rev'd H.M. Perkins, son of the Rev'd Justin Perkins, D.D., who was responsible for this Urmia edition, see Gwilliam in "The Materials for the Criticism of the Peshitto New Testament", pp. 55, 56. For the Urmia edition, Hall was told, sources not in print were consulted. But while it was absolutely certain that the editors had used not one, but many, manuscripts found by them in the district of Urmia as the control in establishing the text, no specific information on sources was given. It was necessary to balance purity of scholarship against unwise notions of progress and to take into account the innate conservatism of native custom. There is a tantalising reference to manuscripts "as old as the twelfth century . . . and here and there one very much older", yet the final comment, p. 56, is:

> It is easy to account for Dr Perkins' silence as to the particular sources of his text, as also with respect to its peculiarities. It would not have done, at that time, for a man to have given any public prominence to text-critical matters.

A comment of a similar kind from Moore's remarks on the edition in *Andover Review*, 7, 1887, p. 101, is reported in Bloch's "The Printed Texts of the Peshitta Old Testament", p. 141. So it is not easy to comment on the basis of firm

external evidence on the Urmia edition: yet again, internal
evidence must be the guide. In some 130 places it provides
readings which differ from the Leiden text; it disagrees with
Lee in about 45. There are unique readings in:

> 4:3; 6:4(*bis*); 7:6, 12; 11:23; 13:39; 14:6, 11, 44; 17:14; 18:25; 19:36;
> 22:16.

These have, however, the impression of being mechanical
matters of single letters, for the most part *waw*. Any
connection with manuscript exemplars seems absent, or at
best, fortuitous. 21:9 is a broken letter rather than a scribal
error. Yet the edition is not a slavish copy of an earlier
printed one; it is not demonstrably dependent upon Le Jay or
Walton, or even solely upon Lee. Lee's pattern of text,
however, is followed at:

> 4:22, 35; 5:6*, 16; 6:11, 22; 7:6, 16, 36; 8:19; 10:6, 8, 14; 11:10,
> 20*(*bis*), 27, 29, 32, 35, 38, 40(*bis*), 46; 13:3(*ter*), 4(*bis*), 13, 15, 20,
> 25, 32*, 34*, 38, 43, 44, 52(*bis*), 55(*bis*), 57; 14:21, 32, 36, 38, 48$_2$0,
> 51$_2$0; 15:10, 12, 19, 26, 30$_2$0; 16:20*, 27; 17:7, 10(*bis*), 11, 12; 18:10,
> 11(*bis*), 14, 16, 28, 30*(*bis*), 32, 19:8, 28, 32; 20:19, 23, 26*; 21:10,
> 20; 22:6, 23, 25; 23:4, 15$_2$0, 30, 37, 39; 24:2; 25:7, 16, 25, 30, 32, 33,
> 41, 49; 26:5, 6, 18, 22, 25, 27, 39, 40; 27:3, 6, 8(*bis*), 9, 10, 25.
> 27:25 has no manuscript correlation other than 17a5[1], and may be
> taken as a shared error; as indeed 2:13(+ 15a2); 25:4(+M 19b1.5),
> 25:8(+M 9b1*etc*). The verses marked * are suggestive for the part
> played by Lee, although Lee's unique readings are not reproduced.

The list of readings set out above shows that the majority
of instances (some 75) are where elements from both (9b1)
10b1*etc* and 12a1*etc* concur; in 14 cases there seems to be
no manuscript support. The noticeable feature is that there
is little relation to 6b1 and 8b1. Hence the pattern is one of
increasing movement towards the standard text, but with
some retention of the 12a1 type. The material prepared for,
but not used in, the Leiden edition does not suggest any
consistent use by Perkins of manuscript material. If that
were the case, such manuscripts as were used conformed to

material already within the existing patterns of text, and did not obtrude.

7. *Mosul*

The Mosul edition is perhaps the easiest and most attractive Syriac edition to use, despite the clarity of Lee's Serta fount. The difficulties in the preparation again relate to ecclesiastical constraints: only after considerable debate was it possible to prepare an edition based on a text other than the Vulgate. The episode instances a clash between the interests of "authoritative" against "authentic" texts, the concerns of "les Orientaux" over against "les orientalistes". It needs to be set against the background of the abortive Lazarist attempts (albeit for a New Testament edition) which foundered on the current convictions about "préjugés latinisants et . . . idées erronées au sujet de l'authenticité de la Vulgate", see Vosté, "La Pešitta de Mossoul et la révision catholique des anciennes versions orientales de la Bible".

Happily, though there was still to be a silence concerning manuscript sources, when it came to Mgr Joseph David's edition of a Syriac bible published in Mosul, a solution to the problem of the last paragraph was found on grounds that were juridical as well as scientific. The Peshiṭta was agreed to be "le texte sacré officiel des Maronites, Syriens et Chaldéens", and hence accorded an authority independent of the Holy See. The editor, the future Mgr David, was ordered "d'acquérir les livres bibliques et liturgiques des Chaldéens dans le but d'en faire une édition exempte de toute erreur". However, while manuscripts were undoubtedly consulted for the Mosul edition, as for the Urmia, it cannot be demonstrated that it rested upon ancient manuscript traditions alone. It is far more the case that it, too, relied upon a tradition of the printed text. Yet there was modest if

deliberate critical activity. It is disappointing to record that
the text is very closely related to Urmia, and hence to Lee:
while 19g5.7 and 19<?a1-5 may show evidence of
preparations for the edition, little in the Leiden apparatus
suggests which manuscripts were peculiarly in the confidence
of the Mosul editor.

So again, other than from internal evidence, there is little
that can be said about the basis on which the Mosul edition
was constructed. It varies some 100 times from the Leiden
edition, and provides unique readings at

> 6:21; 17:8; 18:15; 19:23; 25:5. It accompanies Urmia at 5:6(+L);
> 8:11(+18b4), 26; 11:20(+L1); 13:32, 34(both+L 12b1); 14:6(+18b4);
> 16:20(+L 12b1); 18:19(+15b1), 30(+L9a1 12b1); 20:6, 26(+L 9b1*etc*);
> 25:4(+19b1.5), 8(+9b1*etc*); 26:14(+7a1).

The edition is normally found in the grouping PWLUM,
indicating that, as Urmia, it is a modification of the 12a1*fam*
text, influenced by the Eastern, or Mosul type of text, and to
a lesser extent by that of the Median (7a1) type. It is to the
significance of these terms and to the relationship of text
and circumstance that the discussion now moves, after the
table of readings given by the printed editions over against
the Leiden text. But it can be said in summary that the
Leiden text is the only truly critical text, in that evidence is
set out, and that clear indications are given of the method of
working and of priorities followed in selecting readings to be
placed in the text or relegated to the Apparatus. The
combination of disparate aims, the search for text history
and transmission history, results in this allocation of readings
either to the text or to the apparatus. But at the end of the
day, a text edition initiates text debate, it does not terminate
it. In that sense the Leiden edition is for "les orientalistes"
rather than for "les Orientaux".

CHAPTER EIGHT

PRINTED EDITIONS AND LEIDEN EDITION

The list below sets out first the *lemma* of the Leiden edition, then the variant(s) from the earlier printed editions, and adds in the third column the possible source of the variant adopted by the relevant editor(s). The list of manuscripts is not, therefore, a complete list, but provides only enough evidence to support the arguments of the previous chapter. That is, that P depends on 15a2 derived through 17a5; W depends on P; L depends on W modified by 12b1.2; B depends on L modified by 6b1, 8b1; U and M depend on L with some modification by 9b1*etc*; Leiden depends on 7a1 modified by majority of 6b1-10b2.

The following abbreviations and signs are found in this chapter:
B = Barnes' Pentateuch; L = Lee's Old Testament; M = Mosul edition; P = Le Jay's Paris Polyglot; U = Urmia edition; W = Walton's London Polyglot.
 > = leading to; 12a1 *fam* = 12a1 15a2 17a1-5.10.
etc = also other manuscripts, usually of that same type .
majority = the majority of *all* the manuscripts listed on pp. vii-xxvii of the Leviticus volume, and summarised there on p. vii, II-2.

Text	Leiden] Other printed texts	? Source of variant
1:8	ܪܚܡܐ] ܪܚܡܐ W	Error in W
1:11	ܩܪܒܝܢ] ܩܪܒܝܢ PWLBUM	From P
2:5	ܠܒܪ] om dalath PWL	15a2[1]>17a5
2:8	ܐܝܬܝ 2°] om B	?
2:12	ܐܝܬܝܟ] pr waw PW	17a5 alone
	ܐܠܗܐ] ܚܝܘ B	7a1 8b1
2:13	ܘܠܐ] om waw U	15a2

3:5	ܚܝܐ] *om* B	7a1 8b1
3:8	ܘܡܝܐ] *add* ܚܝܐ M	8b1 13a1 13b3 17b2 19b1.5
3:14	ܐܡܝܪܝܡ] *om* PWL	12a1*fam>*P
4:3	ܐ ܢ] *pr waw* U	?
4:4	ܐܬܝܐ] *om* PW	12a1*fam>*P
4:12	ܘܡܝܐ,ܘܡܝܐ] PWL	*waw init del* 17a5
4:13	ܠܚ ܐܡܠܚ] PWL	12a1*fam>*P
4:21	ܘܡܝܐ,ܘܡܝܐ PW	12a1*fam >*P
4:22	ܠܚ ܐܡܠܚ PWLUM	12a1*fam>*P
4:31	ܐܡܪܝܐ] *om* B	6b1 8a1* 8b1
4:32	ܐܪܡܝܐ ܐܪܡܝܐ PW; *s.sey* LM	12a1*fam>*P c.sey 12b1*s.sey*
4:35	ܠܚ 2⁰] ܩ PWLUM	8a1ᶜ 9b1 10b2*etc* 12a1*fam*
5:6	ܡܠܝܐ ܐܠܝܐ LUM	9b1 *etc*
5:8	ܘܡܝܐ ܠܚܐ PW	12a1*fam>*P
5:13	ܐܟܪܝܐ ܡܟܪܝܐ PW	15a2 17a5>P
5:16	ܐܡܝܐ] *c. sey* PWL	17a5>P
	,ܘܡܝܐ] ,ܘܡܝܐ PWLUM	9b1*etc* 12a1*fam>*P
5:22	ܠܚ ܠܚ *or* ܠܚ ܠܚ PW	12a1*fam>*P
	ܡܠܝܐ ܠܚ] PW	12a1*fam>*P
5:25	ܐܚܝܐ ܐܚܝܠܚ PW	12a1*fam>*P
6:3	,ܡܝܐ] ,ܡܝܐ PW	12a1*fam>*P
6:4	ܐܠܝܐ] *om waw* U	?
	ܐܪܚܝܐ] *om* U	?
6:11	ܐܚܝܐ] *s. sey* PWLUM	12a1*fam>*P
6:21	ܐܝܢܐ] *om* M	?
6:22	ܐܚܝܐ] *s. sey* PWLUM	?
7:6	ܐܚܝܐ] *s. sey* PWLUM	6b1 12a1*fam>*P

	ܢܬܟܠܘܢܗ] ܢܬܟܠܘܢ U	?
7:12	ܘܠܓܢܒܪ̈ܐ] *om waw* U	?
	ܕܡܫܝܚܝܢ] ܕܡܫܝ̈ܚܝܢ PWL	*err* 17a5>P
	ܒܡܫܝܚܐ 2⁰ --- ܢܦܫܐ] *om* PW, *tr post* ܒܡܫܝܚܐ 1⁰ L	17a5>P
7:14	ܦܘܪ̈ܫܢܐ] *pr dalath, s. sey* PW *s. sey* LM	? 6b1 6k2 10b1 12a1*etc*
7:16	ܐܦ] *pr waw* PWLBUM	majority
7:19	ܒܥܘܪܐ] ܒܣܘܪܐ PW	*err* 17a5>P
7:25	ܕܐܬܟܠܘܠ] ܕܐܬܟܠ B	6b1
	ܗܝ] *om* PW	17a5>P
7:36	ܕܦܫܛ] *pr* ܐܝܟ PWLUM	majority, not 6b1 8b1
8:11	ܡܫܝܚ] *add* ܐܢܘܢ UM	18b4
8:19	ܡܢ] *om* PWLUM	15a2 17a5>P (Not 8b1)
8:24	ܕܡܐ 2⁰] *om* PW	15a2 17a5>P
8:26	ܘܫܘܪܬܐ] ܫܘܪܬܐ UM	?
9:5	ܐܢܘܢ] ܠܗܘܢ PWL	12a1*fam*>P
9:24	ܘܦܓܪܐ] ܕܦܓܪܐ PWL	12a1*fam*>P
10:6	ܒܢ̈ܘܗܝ] *add* ܕܐܗܪܘܢ PWLUM	9b1*etc* 12a1*fam*>P
10:8	ܘܡܠܠ ܡܪܝܐ] ܘܐܡܪ - ܠܐܗܪܘܢ ܥܡ ܐܗܪܘܢ ܘܐܡܪ ܠܗ PWLBUM	majority, not 8b1
10:12	ܒܢ̈ܘܗܝ] *add* ܕܐܗܪܘܢ PWL	9b1*etc* 12a1*fam*
10:14	ܐܟܘܠ] ܐܟܘܠܗ PWLUM	12a1*fam*>P
10:19	ܘܐܟܠܗ] ܐܟܠܗ BU	?
11:10	ܒܟܠܗ̇] *pr waw* PWLUM	9b1*etc* 12a1*fam*>P
11:11	ܡܢ] *pr waw* PW	15a2 17a5>P
11:20	ܕܡܗܠܟܐ] ܕܡܗܠܟܝܢ LUM	9b1*etc*
	ܦܓܪܐ ܐ ܗܝ] ܦܓܪܐ ܗܘ PWLUM	12a1*fam*>P 9b1*etc*

11:23	ܐܝܪܒܐ] ܐܝܪܒܐ U	?
11:26	ܠܗܘܢ] ܠܗܘܢ B	6b1 7a1
11:27	ܠܚܝ] *pr waw* PWLUM	15a2 17a5>P
11:29	ܠܚܡܐ] *pr dalath* PWLUM	12a1*fam*>P
11:32	ܠܚܡܐ] ܠܚܡܐ PWLUM	15a2 17a5>P 17a6 17g4
	ܐܘ ܗܘ] *om* PW	12a1*fam err* >P
11:35	ܠܗܬ̈ܐ] *s.sey* PWLBUM	6b1 8b1*etc* 15a2 17a5>P
11:38	ܠܥܠܐ] ܥܠܘ PWLBUM	6b1 8b1*etc* 12a1*fam*>P
11:40	ܫܢ ܕܟܪܒܐܠ] ܠܟܪܘܣܐܠ PWLUM	*err in* P
	ܠܝܪܟܐ] *add* ܡ ܠܟܪܘܣܐܠ, ܕܟܪܘܣ ܐܠܠܣ ܡ̈ܪܝܐܡ, ܠܡܘܣܐ ܠܐ ܠܐ.ܪ ܠܝܪܟܐ PWLUM	*err in* P
11:41	ܠܝܐ] ܠܝܐ PWL	15a2 17a5>P
11:42	ܐܠ] -------- (43) ----- ܟܡܐ] *om* PW	*err* 17a5>P
	ܐܪܟܐܠ] ܐܪܟܠܐ L	*err*
11:46	ܡܢ] ܡܢ PWLUM	6b1 9b1*etc* 15a2 17a5>P
12:7	ܠܚܝ] *add* ܡܢ PWL	17a5>P
13:3	ܠܘܣܐ] ܠܘܣܐ PWLBUM	15a2 17a5>P
	ܕܪܡܝܡ 2⁰--- ܟܐ] *om* PWLUM	6b1 15a2 17a5>P
	ܠܒܘܣܗ 1⁰] ܠܒܘܣܗ.ܪ B	6b1 7a1
	ܠܚܒܘܐ] ܠܚܒܘܐ PWLB	15a2 17a5>P
	ܠܒܘܣ] *pr waw* PWLBUM	15a2[1] 17a5>P 17g4
13:4	ܠܚܒܘܐ] *add* ܡ, PWLBUM	9b1*etc* 12a1*fam*>P
	ܠܒܘܣ.ܪ] ܠܒܘܣ PWLUM	9b1*etc* 12a1*fam*>P
13:5	ܠܝܪܟ] ܝ ܠܝܪܟ PW	12a1*fam*>P
13:6	ܠܚܡ.ܪ] ܠܚܡ PW	12a1*fam*>P

13:7	ܟܬܘܡܠܐ] ܟܬܘܫܢ PW	12a1*fam*>P
13:8	ܟܬܘܡܠܐ] ܟܬܘܫܢ PW	12a1*fam*>P
13:13	ܡܝܚܠܐ] *add* ܟܡܚ PWLUM	9b1*etc* 12a1*fam*>P
13:15	ܟܡܠܐ] *pr lamadh* PWLUM	9b1*etc* 12a1*fam*>P
13:17	,ܡ] ܐܡ PWL	12a1*fam*>P
13:20	ܟܫܐ] ܡܝܫܐ PWLUM	9b1*etc* 12a1*fam*>P
13:21	ܟܥܐ] ܟܫܥܐ L	12b1
13:25	ܟܚܠܐ] *pr waw* PWLUM	9b1*etc* 12a1*fam*>P
13:29	ܟܬܘܫܠܐ] ܟܬܥܥ PWL	12a1*fam*>P
13:32	ܡܝܫܐܠܐ] ܟܫܐ PWL	6b1 only
	,ܚ] *om* PW	*err; mis-correction in 17a5>P*
	ܟܚܥܝܠܐ] ܟܚܥ LUM	12b1
	ܚܥܝ B	?
13:34	ܟܚܥܝܠܐ] ܟܚܥ LUM	12b1
	ܚܥܝ B	?
13:38	ܟܝܐܚܠܐ] ܟܝܐܚ ܐܟ PWLUM	15a2[1] 17a5>P 18b6 19b4
13:39	ܟܐ] *om* U	
13:43	ܡܝܡܠܐ] ܟܝܡܠܐ PWLBUM	6b1 8b1*etc* 12a1*fam*>P
13:44	,ܡܘܟܠܠܐ] ܡܝܟܠܠ PWLUM	10b1*etc* 12a1*fam*>P
13:49	,ܡ] ܐܡ PW	12a1 15a2 17a5>P
13:51	ܟܚܚ ܠܚ ܐܟ] *om* PW	12a1*fam*>P
	,ܡ] ܐܡ PW	12a1*fam*>P
13:52	,ܡܘܝܡܠ 1°] *add* ܟܡܚ PWLUM	10b1*etc* 12a1*fam*>P
	,ܡܘܝܡܠ 2°] ܡܘܝܡܠ PWLBUM	majority
13:55	ܟܬܘܫܠ 2°] *om* PWLBUM	8b1*etc* 12a1*fam*>P
	ܚܠܡ ܟܐܠ] *om* PWLBUM	8b1*etc* 12a1*fam*>P
	,ܡܝܡܐܟ],ܡܝܡܐܟ PWLM	15a2 17a5>P
13:56	ܡܝܠܚܠܐ] *pr waw* PWL	12a1*fam*>P
13:57	ܡܝܡܠܐ],ܡܘܝܡܠ PWLBUM	10b1*etc* 12a1*fam*>P

13:58	ܢܘܡܪܐ [ܪܟܒܬܐ PW	15a2 17a5>P
	add ܪܟܒܬܐ L	add in L
14:6	ܠܣܡܐ] om waw U	?
	ܪܢܘܬܐ] om UM	18b4
14:11	ܠܐܡ ܠܐܡܗܐ U	?
14:13	ܪܚܣܒ [ܪܚܒܒ PW	12a1fam>P
14:16	ܚܒܚ ܚܒܝ [ܚܡܚ ܢܝ PW	15a2 17a5>P
14:17	ܪܟܒ ܪܟܢܝ [ܪܟܒܢ.ܡ PW	17a5>P
14:21	ܪܩܐܘܪܟܝ [ܪܩܘܪܟܝ PW	15a2¹ 17a5>P
	ܪܩܠܐܪܟ add ܣܡܢܐ PWLUM	15a2¹ 17a5>P 18b2¹ 19b1
14:32	ܪܠܐ] ܪܠܝ PWLBUM	6b1 9b1etc 12a1fam
14:36	ܣܡܚ ܣܡܠܒܣܐ] tr PWLUM	9b1etc 12a1fam>P
14:38	ܠܡ] pr ܪܚ ܠܚܐ PWLUM	9b1etc 12a1fam>P
14:42	ܣܡܡܐ ܠܒܣܐ] ܣܡܡܣ ܠ PW	17a3
14:44	ܪܘܡܐ] om waw U	?
14:47	ܪܟܒܢܝ 1⁰, 2⁰] ܪܟܒܢܝ.ܝ PW	17a5>P
14:48	ܗܠܟܡ] ܣܠܟܗ PWL	12a1fam>P
	ܪܟܣܚܒ 2⁰] ܣܟܣܚ PWLUM	9b1etc 12a1fam>P
14:51	ܪܩ ܗܦ ܠܣܝ ܪܩܦ ܝ U	9b1etc 18b4 19b2
	ܪܣܡܠܐ] ܪܡܣܩ PWLBUM	6b1etc 12a1fam>P
15:3	ܪܢܝ] pr ܪ ܠ PW	17a5¹>P
15:10	ܠ ܪܟ] ܪܟܢܝ PWLUM	12a1fam>P
15:12	ܒܦܢ] ܪܩܘܡܒܢ PWLUM	9b1etc 12a1fam>P
15:19	ܠܡ] om PWLBUM	majority
15:24	ܪܠܐܟܡ] ܣܚܒ PWL	12a1fam>P
15:25	ܪܢܝܪܟܒܐ] ܣܡܡ PW	12a1fam>P
15:26	ܪܟܠܪܟܐܗܪ] ܪܚܒܡܢ PWLUM	9a1 9b1etc 12a1fam>P
15:30	ܣܡܚ 1⁰] om PW	12a1fam
	ܪܢܝ ܪܟܒܢܝ] PWLUM	9b1etc 12a1fam>P
15:33	ܪܗܡܟܐ] pr dalath PW	17a5>P

	] *pr dalath* PWL	17a5>P
	] *add*	
	, PW	15a2[1] 17a5>P
16:14	PWL	17a1
16:20	] *pr waw* LUM	12b1
16:27	PWLUM	8b1*etc* 12a1*fam*>P
16:28	PW	12a1*fam*>P
16:34	PW	12a1*fam*>P
17:2	PW	15a2 17a5>P
17:3	PWLM	17a5[1] >P
17:7	PWLUM	9a1 9b1*etc* 12a1*fam*>P
17:8	2[0] *om* M	?
	] *pr dalath* PWL	7a1 12a1*fam*>P
17:10	] *pr* PWLUM	9a1 9b1*etc* 12a1*fam*>P
	PWLBUM	majority
17:11	PWLUM	9b1*etc* 12a1*fam*>P
17:12	] *pr dalath* PWLBUM	8b1*etc* 12a1*fam*>P
17:14	2[0]] *om dalath* U	?
18:10	PWLBUM	6b1*etc* 12a1*fam*>P
18:11	PWLBUM	6b1*etc* 12a1*fam*>P
	2[0]] *add* PWLUM	9b1*etc* 12a1*fam*>P
18:14	PWLBUM	6b1*etc* 12a1*fam*>P
18:15	M	?
18:16	PWLBUM	6b1*etc*12a1*fam*>P
18:17	L	?
18:19	UM	15b1
18:21		

	ܠܐ ܟܡܐ L	*err*
18:23	ܕܠܛܡܐܘܬܐ] ܕܠܛܡܐܬܐ PWLB	12a1*fam*>P
18:25	ܥܘܠܗ̇] ܥܘܠܐ U	?
18:27	ܕܗܠܝܢ ܟܠܗܘܢ] ܕܟܠܗܘܢ ܗܠܝܢ PWL	12a1*fam*>P
	ܘܐܬܛܢܦܬ] ܘܐܬܛܡܐܬ PWL	12a1*fam*>P
18:28	ܠܥܡܐ] ܠܥܡ̈ܡܐ PWLUM	10b1*etc* 12a1*fam*>P
18:30	ܛܪܘ] *pr* waw LUM	9a1 12b1
	ܢܛܘܪ̈ܬܝ] ܢܛܘܪ̈ܘܬܝ PW	*err* in P
	ܬܥܒܕܘܢ] *add* ܐܝܟ ܚܕ PWLUM	10b1*etc* 12a1*fam*>P
19:8	ܘܬܐܒܕ] *om waw* PWLBUM	6k2 8b1*etc* 12a1*fam* >P
19:10	ܠܘܬܝ] *add* ܕܥܡܪܝܢ ܒܝܢܬܟܘܢ PW	13a1
19:23	ܘܠܐ] *om waw* M	?
19:27	ܘܠܐ] *om waw* U	17a3
19:28	ܒܟܘܢ] ܠܟܘܢ PWLUM	9b1*etc* 12a1*fam*>P
	ܡܪܝܐ] *add* ܐܠܗܟܘܢ PWL	12a1*fam*>P
19:32	ܡܪܝܐ] *add* ܐܠܗܟ PWLBUM	9b1*etc* 12a1*fam*>P
19:34	ܕܥܡܪܝܢ] ܘܥܡܪܝܢ PWL	12a1*fam*>P
19:36	ܘܡܬܩܠܐ ܕܩܘܫܬܐ] *om* PW	17a5>P
	ܢܗܘܘܢ] ܢܗܘܐ U	?
20:3	ܡܢ 2°] *om* PW	12a1*fam*>P
20:4	ܕܠܐ] ܘܠܐ PWLB	8b1 12a1*fam*>P
20:6	ܘܬܛܥܐ] ܕܬܛܥܐ UM	?
20:8	ܐܢܐ 3°] *om* PWL	6b1*etc* 12a1*fam*>P
20:11	ܘܒܪܐ] *om waw* PWL	*err* in P
20:13	ܬܪ̈ܝܗܘܢ] *post* ܢܬܩܛܠܘܢ PW	17a5>P
20:16	ܘܐܦ] *om waw* PWL	12a1*fam*>P

20:18	ܘܕܘܒܐ] ܡܒܘܥܗ̇ ---- ܕܕܡܗ̇	
	ܕܡܒܘܥܗ̇ ܘܐܦ ܗܝ ܓܠܬ ܟܠܐ	
	ܡܒܘܥܐ ܕܕܡܗ̇ PW	15a2 17a5
		om vv. 18/19
20:19	ܦܘܪܣܢܐ] *pr waw* PWLUM	17a5^{1}
	ܕܚܬܗ ܕܐܒܘܟ] ܕܚܬܗ̇ -- ܕܐܒܘܟ	
	ܘܕܚܬܗ̇ ܕܐܡܟ PW	*cf* 9a1; 17a5^{1}>P
	ܘܚܒܠܐ] ܦܘܪܣܢܐ- ܢܩܒܠܘܢ	
	ܘܗ PW	17a5^{1} >P
20:21	ܢܗܘܘܢ] ܢܡܘܬܘܢ PW	12a1*fam*>P
20:23	ܒܢܡܘ̈ܣܐ] *s.sey* PWLUM	10b2 12a1*fam*>P
20:26	ܘܬܗܘܘܢ] *add* ܠܝ LUM	9b1*etc*
21:10	ܐܢܬܗ] ܐܢ̈ܬܘܗܝ PWLBUM	8b1*etc* 12a1*fam*>P
21:12	ܕܟܠܬܐ] *om dalath* L	?
21:14	ܘܕܡܛܠܩܐ] *om waw* BU	9a1 9b1*etc* 12a1*fam*>P
	ܘܡܛܠܩܐ PWLM	*err* in P
21:18	ܕܣܚܝܪ] *om dalath* PWL	17a5>P
21:20	ܚܘܪܘܪܐ] *c.sey* PWLBUM	8b1*etc* 12a1*fam*>
21:21	ܕܐܠܗܗ - (22) -- ܠܐ 2°] *om* PW	*err* 17a5>P
22:6	ܢܦܫܐ] *pr* ܟܠ PWLUM	9b1*etc* 12a1*fam*>P
22:13	ܠܒܝܬ] ܠܘܬ PW	12a1*fam*>P
	ܡܢܗ] ܘܡܕܫܐ PW	17a5>P
22:14	ܕܢܐܟܘܠ] ܢܐܟܘܠ ܒܗ PWL	17a5 *l.n.*
	ܢܦܫ] ܢܦܫܗ W	*err* W
22:16	ܘܢܩܒܠܘܢ] ܢܩܒܠܘܢ U	?
22:18	ܢܕܪ̈ܝܗܘܢ] ܢܕܪ̈ܝܟܘܢ PWL	12a1*fam*>P
	ܦܘܪ̈ܥܢܝܗܘܢ] ܦܘܪ̈ܥܢܝܟܘܢ PWL	15a2 17a5>P
22:19	ܘܡܢ 1° and 2°] ܐܘ ܡܢ PWL	*err* in P
22:20	ܟܠ] *pr waw* PW	17a2
22:21	ܠܡܦܪܫ] ܘܢܦܪܘܫ PW	12a1*fam*>P
	ܚܪ̈ܐ] ܚܐܪ̈ܐ PWL	17a5>P
22:22	ܡܢܗܘܢ 2°-- ܠܡܕܒܚܐ] *om* PW	17a5>P

22:23	ܚܣܝܪ] *add* ܕܡ PWLUM	9b1*etc* 12a1*fam*>P
22:25	ܠܐ 2°] *pr waw* PWLUM	9b1*etc* 12a1*fam*>P
22:27	ܩܘܪܒܢܗ] ܩܘܪܒܢܐ W	*err*
23:3	ܘܫܒܬܐ] ܘܒܫܒܬܐ PWL	12a1*fam*>P
23:4	ܬܩܪܘܢ] *pr dalath* PWLUM	17a5>P
23:6	ܘܒܚܡܫܥܣܪܐ] ܘܒܚܡܫܬܥܣܪ PW	12a1*fam*>P
	ܦܛܝܪܐ] *c.sey* PWLM	12a1*fam*>P
23:8	ܩܘܪܒܢܐ] *c.sey* PWL	12a1*fam*>P
23:14	ܠܚܡܐ 2° - ܗܢܐ] *om* PW	*err* 17a5>P
23:15	ܫ̈ܒܘܥܝܢ] ܫܒܘ̈ܥܝܢ PWLM	17a1.2.10
	ܝܘ̈ܡܝܢ] *add* ܠܟܘܢ PWLBUM	9b1*etc* 12a1*fam*>P
23:16	ܠܒܬܪ] ܠܒܝܬ PW	*err* 17a5>P
23:22	ܕܐܪܥܟܘܢ] ܕܙܪܥܟܘܢ PW	*err* in P
23:27	ܩܘܪܒܢܐ] *c.sey* PWL	6b1 12a1*fam* >P
23:30	ܐܘܒܕܢܗ ܠܢܦܫܐ] ܬܐܒܕ ܢܦܫܐ PWLUM	9b1*etc*12a1*fam*>P
23:37	ܩܘܪܒܢܐ] *c.sey* PWLBUM	8b1*etc* 12a1*fam*>P
	ܘܢܘ̈ܣܟܐ] *s.sey* PWL	15a2 17a5>P
	ܕܝܘܡܐ] ܠܝܘܡܐ PW	17a5>P
23:39	ܡܛܠܠܬܐ] ܡܛܠܠܬܗ PWLUM	9b1*etc* 12a1*fam*>P
	ܡܛܠܠܬܐ B	8b1 9a1
24:2	ܕܙܝܬܐ ܕܟܝܐ] ܕܟܝܐ ܕܙܝܬܐ PWLBUM	8b1*etc* 12a1*fam*>P
24:6	ܣܕ̈ܪܐ] *add* ܐܡܝܢܐܝܬ ܢܡܘܣܐ ܠܥܠܡ ܠܕ̈ܪܝܗܘܢ PW	*err* in P, *cf* vs. 9
24:11	ܐܢܬܬܐ] *om* PW	15a2 17a5>P
25:4	ܘܫܢܬܐ] ܒܫܢܬܐ L	12b2
	ܬܣܩܠܘܢ] *pr waw* UM	19b1.5
25:5	ܕܫܒܬܐ] *om* M	?
25:7	ܬܗܘܐ] *pr waw* PWLUM	9a1 9b1**etc* 12a1*fam*>P
25:8	ܫ̈ܒܥܐ ܕܫܢܝܐ] ܫ̈ܢܝܢ ܕܫ̈ܒܥܐ PWL	12a1*fam*>P

	ܫ̈ܢܝܐ ܕܫ̈ܢܝܐ UM	9b1*etc*
	ܕܫܢܝܢ] ܕܫ̈ܢܝܐ W	*err*
25:16	ܕܥܠܠܬܐ] ܕܫ̈ܢܝܐ *tr* PWLUM	9b1*etc*12a1*fam*>P
	ܕܥܠܠܬܐ B	6b1 8b1
	ܕܫ̈ܢܝܐ 3°] *om* B	6b1 8b1 9a1*
	ܡܢܟܘܢ] ܡܢܟܝܢ PWL	13a1[1]15a2 17a5>P
25:25	ܢܦܪܘܩ] *pr waw* PWLUM	9b1*etc* 12a1*fam*>P
25:28	ܥܪܝܪܐ] ܥܪܝܪܬܐ PWLB	17a5>P
25:30	ܕܒܡܪܬܐ] ܕܡܪܬܐ PWLUM	12a1*fam*>P
25:32	ܒ̈ܬܐ] *pr waw* PWLUM	9b1 12a1*fam*>P
25:33	ܕܒܩܘ̈ܪܝܐ] ܕܩܘ̈ܪܝܐ PWLUM	9b1*etc* 12a1*fam*>P
25:41	ܕܐܒܗܘܗܝ] ܕܐ̈ܒܗܘܗܝ PWLBUM	9a1 9b1*etc* 12a1*fam*>P
25:46	ܒܬܪܟܘܢ] *pr* ܡܢ PWLM	15a2 17a5>P
25:49	ܡܢ 1°] *om* PWLUM	9b1*etc* 12a1*fam*>P
	ܘܢܬܦܪܩ] ܕܢܬܦܪܩ PW	15a2 17a5
25:50	ܕܙܒܢܗ] *add* ܒܗܕܐ ܠܫܢܬܐ ܕܦܘܫܩܐ PW	15a2[1] 17a5>P
25:52	ܘܐܝܟ ܠܦܘܬ] ܘܠܦܘܬ PW	17a5[1]>P
26:1	ܘܡ̈ܢ ܠܚܡܐ] ܕܡ̈ܢ ܠܚܡܐ PW	12a1*fam*>P
26:5	ܠܣܒܥܟܘܢ] ܠܣܒܥܐ PWLUM	9b1*etc* 12a1*fam*>P
26:6	ܕܡܕܚܠ] *pr* ܡܢ PWLUM	9b1*etc* 12a1*fam*>P
	ܡܢ] *om* W	*err*
26:14	ܠܐ ܕܝܢ] *tr* UM	7a1
26:16	ܬܙܪܥܘܢ] ܘܙܪܥܘܢ PW	*err* in P
26:17	ܕܪܕܦ] *pr* ܡܢ PWL	12a1*fam*>P
26:18	ܬܘܒ ܒܗܠܝܢ] *tr* PWLUM	9b1*etc* 12a1*fam*>P
26:22	ܘܬܚܡܠܟܘܢ] ܘܬܚܒܠܟܘܢ PWLBUM	6b1*etc* 12a1*fam*>P
26:25	ܕܒ̈ܥܠܕܒܒܐ] ܕܒ̈ܥܠܕܒܒܟܘܢ PWLUM	9a1 9b1*etc* 12a1*fam*>P
26:27	ܒܗܠܝܢ ܬܘܒ] *tr* PWLUM	9b1*etc* 12a1*fam*>P
26:28	ܘܐܦ] *om waw* PWL	12a1*fam*>P
26:36	ܕܪܕܦ] *pr* ܡܢ PW	12a1*fam*>P
26:39	ܘܐܦ] *om waw* PWLBUM	9a1 10b2*etc* 12a1*fam*>P

26:40	ܟܠܗܘܢ‎] ܒܟܠܗܘܢ‎ PWLUM	9b1*etc* 12a1*fam*>P
26:41	ܐܦ‎] pr waw PWLM	8b1 12a1*fam*>P
27:3	ܘܛܠܠ‎] om PWLUM	8b1*etc* 12a1*fam*>P
	ܚܕܘܬ̈ܐ‎] om dalath PW	12a1*fam*>P
27:5	ܘܒܪ̈ܫܐ‎] om PW	17a5>P
27:6	ܕܚܘܪ‎ 2°] om PWLBUM	6b1*etc* 12a1*fam*>P
27:8	ܗܘܐܠ‎ ܘܒܚܝܛ‎,] tr PWLBUM	6b1*etc* 12a1*fam*>P
	ܐܝܕ‎] pr waw PWLUM	9b1*etc* 12a1*fam*>P
27:9	ܩܝܡ ܗܘܝ‎ ܠܒܝܪ̈ܐ‎ ܠܒܝܪ̈ܐ‎ 2°] ܩܝܡ‎ - ܠܒܝܪ̈ܐ‎ PWLUM	9b1*etc* 12a1*fam*>P
27:10	ܠܠܒܝܪ̈ܐ‎] om PWLBUM	6b1*etc* 12a1*fam*>P
27:25	ܒܚܝܛܠܬܐ‎] add ܕܥܩܘ̈ܒܐ‎ PWLUM	17a5[1]
27:30	ܠܚܘܡ̈ܝ‎] ܟܘܡ̈ܝ‎ W	*err*

CHAPTER NINE

TEXT AND CONTEXT

Manuscripts may be related to general areas and specific
localities, and so be considered 'local texts'. The standard text
is related to a specific monastery, so suggesting its role as
authoritative from the time of Timothy I; aspects of Syriac
church history give further support to this argument.

1. *Texts and their provenance*

Previous chapters have discussed the Peshiṭta of Leviticus as
part of a version of the Hebrew scriptures, touching upon its
characteristics and the shaping of its text traditions. The
obscurity of its origins is a reflection of the obscurities and
complexities of Christian origins and the variety of thought
and practice found within Judaism in the eastern provinces
of the Roman empire and the western areas of Parthian,
later Sassanian, authority. In "*Pervenimus Edessam*" the
present writer drew attention to the nature of a Christianity
in which the names Bardaisan and Tatian were held great,
and the Ebionite idiom referred to by Winter in "The origins
of Ben Sira in Syriac", pp. 251-253, was not unknown. A
term such as "Jewish Christianity" is hardly helpful, for a
concept is a point of reference rather than a definition. The
Peshiṭta may, however, be taken as an illustration of a
pattern of exegesis when a reservoir of acceptable
interpretations was at hand for use. It may be regretted that
previous studies on the Peshiṭta were given their impetus by
text critics concerned with MT, and were circumscribed by
convictions that a written version was constructed as it were

mechanically from a written text; but interest is now
turning to methods of translation, and more, to the
circumstances of the promulgation of texts. Jenner, in his
Leiden Symposium paper on 8a1, linked the revision of that
manuscript with Timothy I and relations with Islamic
authority. Timothy I was in good standing with the Muslim
governor of Baghdad, was installed as Catholicos in 780, and
in a rule of over 40 years extended his authority over the
bishops of Persia. Dirksen in his article "East and west, old
and young, in the text tradition of the Old Testament
Peshiṭta" comments on the withdrawal from circulation of
the older manuscripts as a consequence of being collected
for use in the Syrian monastery in the Nitrian desert of
Egypt. It is more likely that cause and effect were related
differently: when "Nestorianism" prevailed, and
"monophysitism" was displaced, the older manuscripts found
a natural home in that Syrian monastery in Egypt so strongly
supported by "monophysite" Takrit.

The present writer has said in such papers as "A Turtle
Dove or Two Young Priests" that a link should be
established between the manuscripts and their places of
origin or use; these connections between manuscript
traditions and church traditions were further discussed in
"Text, Scholar and Church". Talmon in "The Textual Study
of the Bible" commented on a similar phenomenon: the
societal aspect of texts, and the socially integrating force of a
"Gruppentext". Text families were not, he said, to be
regarded as recensions, but the product of natural growth. It
might be said that this is a textual equivalent of the political
and theological concept of solidarity and subsidiarity.

There is little satisfactory evidence concerning the
provenance of manuscripts. It is not often that there is such
a notice as the one discovered by Jenner, and discussed by
Van Koningsveld in "The monastery of Bâqûqâ in Iraq and

an old owner's entry in MS Syr 341 of the Bibliothèque
Nationale in Paris" which made it possible for him to link
the manuscripts with a notable scriptorium in that
monastery. Iconography enabled Hunt, in "The Syriac
Buchanan Bible in Cambridge", to suggest the scribes Šimun
and Išo for 12a1, and to link Edessa and Tur 'Abdin as
homes of related scribal activity. Sadly, not all catalogues
are as complete as Wright's for the British Museum, (now
British Library), and guesswork is necessary. Some results
can, however, be elicited by a combination of internal and
external evidence. The manuscripts for Leviticus have been
grouped in the Introduction to the Edition; but not all
manuscripts need to be discussed in detail now.

For present purposes four groups need to be identified.
The first group contains the manuscripts which are witnesses
to the standard text: 9b1, 10b1 and those which resemble
them. The second group contains the comparatively late
manuscripts of 12a1*fam* which, perhaps regrettably, provide
the base for the printed editions. The third group is formed
from the earlier "ancient" texts 6b1 and 9a1; and the fourth
group is that of the median manuscript 7a1 together with
those resembling it, 8a1 and 8b1.

12a1, the Buchanan Bible, is known more for its progeny
than for its ancestry. Until the recent article of Hunt there
was little known of its ancestry, other than the comment of
Burkitt quoted earlier, based on the surmise that the script
was that of Tur 'Abdin, and the recognition that it came
from the last part of the twelfth century. The most that can
be established is some near-contemporaneity to the
thirteenth-century flowering of Jacobite culture associated
with Bar Hebraeus, and a connection with the monastic
centre of Tur 'Abdin, the Mount Athos of Syriac Christians.
Philoxenos spent part of his youth there. Whether a link can
be established between this centre of Tur 'Abdin and that

other great centre of Jacobite monasticism and episcopacy,
Gabal Maqlub, "Le Mont des Milliers", near Mosul, and also
with the monastery of Mar Matta can be shown only as
probability and not as certainty. The present writer's view
on the matter has support in Hunt's opinion that there was a
network of support between monasteries in the area
dominated at some time by Roman (Byzantine) control.
Hence the link between Edessa, Tur 'Abdin, Mar Matta, and
Takrit.

Palmer, in *Monk and Mason on the Tigris,* speaks of the
flight of the non-Nestorians to the monasteries, and
especially to Mar Matta. Mar Matta was itself founded by a
monk from Tur 'Abdin. Such a link, backwards to the
Edessa of early years, and forward to Mar Matta and Takrit,
would be in keeping with the internal evidence that 12a1
supplies a text which diverges from ancient tradition in a
way which is distinct from 9b1, 10b1 and the standard text;
yet both it and 12b2 (from Tur 'Abdin) show resemblances
with the median text of 7a1 and its companions 8a1, 8b1.

As the term "median" has been chosen for 7a1, and to a
degree might be used, by association, for the similar texts of
8a1 and 8b1, this group may be discussed next. By 8a1 is
meant the unrevised text, that which comes from the first
hand. The manuscript is linked with Bâqûqâ, described by
Fiey in *Assyrie Chrétienne* II, p. 130 as "certainement
priviligié parmi les couvents du Nord de l'Iraq". It was
founded on the site of an older monastery in the seventh
century, but was destroyed about 800, and thereafter
suffered much of the revival and disaster to which the area
was liable up to the seventeenth century. But of the origin
and making of this manuscript there is no evidence. Yet, as
the Introduction to the edition shows, textually it is like 7a1,
of whose history likewise only the later years may be
guessed. 7a1 was, as the note at the beginning says, bought

from the monastery of St Mary in the Nitrian desert. Wright's catalogue describes the acquisition of material from that source for the British Museum, and comments on the Jacobite character of that collection of material: works by Theodore of Mopsuestia and Jeshua bar Nun were cut up to provide binding for works by those considered more orthodox. But it is the link with Takrit that is the most significant aspect for the present discussion. Takrit became a Jacobite fief: its importance is that it was the centre for Roman (Byzantine) governors in the seventh century. Consequently its civil importance made it suitable to be the chief Jacobite seat, whose holder gained the title of Maphrian. Previous to that, the main episcopal centre, as well as the monastic, had been at Mar Matta. "Fittingly", said Nestorian wit, "so that they should lodge in the very nest of Satan". Yet, for the Jacobites, it was their southern counterpart to Tur 'Abdin, the "Mount of Worshippers", and suitable for the seat of authority from 540 to 629 (Fiey, *Assyrie Chrétienne* II, pp. 756-784).

In the interest of simplicity it is best to consider next 10b1. This has the advantage of a provenance: written by the monk Elia in the monastery of Mar Elia near Mosul. Some clarity now comes into the matter, both with respect to the present writer's urging of Mosul and Takrit as the home of manuscript traditions, and also with respect to a specific link with the change in dominance of text types, commented upon by others. For example, Koster, on p. 89 of his *Exodus,* speaks of a process from which a manuscript tradition emerges; Gelston on p. 87 of his *Twelve Prophets* writes of the almost universal diffusion of the standard text from the ninth century onwards; Jenner in his Leiden Symposium article on 8a1 writes of the consolidating activity of Timothy I.

Timothy I certainly had the chance of consolidating the

position of the "orthodox", that is of the Nestorians. The foundation of Baghdad in 762 and the beginning of the Abbasid dynasty saw a great emphasis on study, some idea of which may be gained from Mingana, *Job of Edessa's Book of Treasures*, which gives an account of the syllabus in the Academy of Baghdad at that time. Timothy moved the seat of his church authority from Seleucia Ctesiphon when the secular authority made the same move. But the interesting question remains, that if the consolidation of the Nestorians included an imposition of an agreed text, whence came that text?

The canons of the East Syrian church, as in Chabot's *Synodicon Orientale*, are silent on the subject of scriptural text. It is clear that the definition of this church and its character came through the authority and credal integrity of bishops; through the habits of life of priests and religious; through the forms of canon law; and above all through the liturgy. But the canon of scripture seemed taken for granted, and the text of scripture a matter of acceptance. But some remarks of Albrektson in "Reflections on the emergence of a standard text of the Hebrew Bible" seem to apply here, that is to the Syriac church from the time of Timothy I. Albrektson says, p. 49, that when diversity of text is replaced by unity of text, a conscious and controlled process is commonly held to be the cause. A standard text, rather than a critical text, is the basis of this: for a standard text is a pre-condition of exegesis. It might be added that that would still hold true, were it shown that the standard text itself, the result of translation and transmission, showed signs of exegesis within itself.

2. *Monastery, patriarch, and manuscript collector*

10b1 is an example of this standard text; and the monastery of Mar Elia is its provenance. Some account of this monastery is to be found in Fiey, *Assyrie Chrétienne* II, pp. 639-659. Often called Dair Sa'id, it was founded in the sixth century by Mar Elia, who had previously been at the Great Monastery of Mt Izla, and had left probably because of incompatibility with Babai the Great, protagonist of the prosopic union Christology, and theologically the founding father of Nestorianism. In the late eighth and early ninth century this monastery of Mar Elia was to be home, for 30 years, to Išo' bar Nun, who was later to be Patriarch, and who declared it to be subject only to patriarchal jurisdiction. In 985 it provided its superior Mari to be Patriarch, and in 1028 another superior, Abu Sa'id, was an unsuccessful candidate for that responsibility. The monastery was one of those in a ruinous state visited in 1821 by Claude James Rich, collector of manuscripts from the Mosul area which are now in the British Library.

However, two further monasteries come into the picture: one nearby, and one further away. The more distant one is on the prairie land between the Hazir and Great Zab rivers, on the rising ground that borders the territory, Marga, to the north. (Fiey, *Assyrie Chrétienne* I, pp. 257-260). There, at Sos, (sometimes Bâ Sos) Rabban Bawai the Musician founded a School of Liturgy and Ecclesiology, in which one of the teachers was Mar Abraham bar Dasandad, who numbered among his pupils both the later Patriarch Timothy I and his successor Išo' bar Nun, sometime resident at Mar Elia. There was at Sos a Jewish colony, and Mar Abraham wrote a Disputation on their account. Later in his life Abraham moved to Mosul, to the Upper Convent. In later years his name became attached to it, and it was thereafter known as the Convent of Mar Gabriel and Mar Abraham.

This Upper Convent is mentioned by Fiey in his *Mossoul Chrétienne*, pp. 128, 9. This Convent, too, had its association with the Patriarchate, in the person of 'Abdišo, 963-986; and at its period of greatest significance in the ninth and tenth centuries it had associated with it Rabban Sarkis, concerned with both Old and New Testament, and the production of 30 volumes of Theodore of Mopsuestia The monastery set up the liturgical norms of books and objects used in worship; some of its manuscripts are in the Rich collection in the British Library: Additional Manuscripts 7174; 7177; 7178; 7199.

The manuscripts 9b1, and 12b1.2 do not themselves provide evidence other than of a textual kind, whereas 10b1 testifies by its association with Mar Elia. 9b1 is one of those collected by Rich, in fact from a Jacobite monastery, but by its pointing and general tenor of text, stands within the tendency towards the standard text. 12b1 is also within this tendency, written by John, Bishop of R'ban: it was one of those consulted by Thorndike for vol VI of Walton's Polyglot. 12b2 was written in Mosul by Thomas bar Joseph, but was one of the four Gloster Ridley manuscripts sent from Amid. Although it is of the same pattern as the Mosul text, and therefore falling within the ambit of Timothy I's "orthodoxy", it is noted as having been written in the year 589 of the Hegira, in the time of Michael the Patriarch of Antioch and Syria, John of Alexandria and Egypt, and Gregory, Maphrian of Takrit. This is a monophysite, rather than a Nestorian, synchronism which would authenticate the text for use in Amid. But it is an interesting piece of corroborative evidence that the provenance of manuscripts has to do with place. The standard text is that of Mosul and its monasteries: there is a probability that the Mosul text had its origins in Sos.

The two manuscripts of most interest for Leviticus, in that they provide a different textual pattern, are 6b1 and 9a1. But they, too, provide little other than textual evidence. 6b1 came to London in the second group of manuscripts collected by Tattam from Nitria, and so can reasonably be supposed to have gone there on the transfer of manuscripts from Takrit and its environs. 9a1, that *ci-devant* among manuscripts, seems inexplicable. It represents a text found in such earlier manuscripts as 6b1, but comes so much later. One can surmise that it had its origins with such manuscripts as 6b1, and that it was in the Nitrian collection, whence it was taken either by Gabriel Eva or Elias Assemani on such expeditions as they made there, see *Bibliotheca Orientalia* I, pp. 561, 606; also Preface p. xi. It is regrettable that 5b1 does not give the text of Leviticus, as part of that manuscript provides the earliest dated biblical text: written in the year 463/4 by the deacon John at Mar Mara in Amid. 5b1 also came from Nitria in Tattam's second collection Its script reminded Koster of that of 7a1 (*Exodus*, p. 10). Pinkerton, on p. 17 of "The Origin and Early History of the Syriac Pentateuch", noted a resemblance between the script of 7a1, 7h3 and 8h3. This led him to surmise that all three had an origin in the area of Mardin and Ras'ain.

A likely explanation of the relationship of the textual traditions would be the following. Early translation took place in the centres where Jews and Christians were in some kind of symbiosis, certainly having in common a sense of the priority of scripture and its interpretation as a basis for religious and social practice. This is congruent with Talmon's comments in "The Textual Study of the Bible" on the connection between local texts and local life. The subsequent history of the regions to the east of Antioch and the west of the Tigris and the character of the Syriac church led to the localisation of church government, religious

thinking, and monastic life in a few centres. Scriptural and
textual study did not have equal priority in each of these
places. Among those places where, however, such studies
did predominate were the northern area of Tur 'Abdin, and
the southern areas of Mar Matta and its environs and Mosul
with its environs also. (It is to be noted that these areas are
clear of the disputed frontier territory in which Nisibis fell).
In these places local families of manuscripts grew up, neither
consciously independent nor yet officially controlled. Those
in Mar Matta had their origins in Amid; those in the
monasteries near Mosul had their origins in Sos. 12a1 is an
independent growth having some antecedents in Tur 'Abdin.
Such a theory might be dismissed as too thinly supported by
evidence, yet it does have some congruence with the history
of the Syriac church. Something must now said of that
history, though an impressionistic account only.

3. *Four elements in Syriac church history*

The difficulty of the problem lies in the interaction of four
different elements. The first is geographical. The area of
Syriac Christianity is large: extending from Antioch to the
east, following the silk road. Not only are there the better
known areas of Osrhoene (to the east of the higher reaches
of the Euphrates) and Adiabene (to the east of the Tigris and
to the north of the Greater Zab), but the territory lying on,
or reached by, the roads to the east from Seleucia Ctesiphon
to Hamadan, whence south to Isfahan and Persia, north to
Azerbaijan or east to Teheran. From Teheran the road
strikes still east to Herat, whence there is again a choice of
striking south and east, and then south-west to the Indus
valley, or north to Merv and Bokhara before once more
turning east for the high passes and so into China. It should
not be forgotten that the Tibetan alphabet is the Syriac
alphabet, written vertically. Possibly more significant than

the Syriac expansion along these roads and the association
with Jewish communities is the nature of the territory.
Mesopotamia is a land of city-states, on or near the
Euphrates and the Tigris, or, like Edessa, on the high ground
which dominates the lower levels. Persia is a salt plateau,
with its chief cities, like the present Teheran, Isfahan and
Qum, separated by great distances. To the east, such cities as
Herat and Merv are at river-crossings or crossroads, In Iraq,
the pattern of settlements has not changed: Takrit, Baghdad,
Kirkuk still dominate the centre and the north. As a further
point, there are no natural boundaries: so there is no natural
compact territorial self-definition. All lies open to outsiders'
claims, whether these outsiders come from Rome to the
west, Arabs from the south, the White Huns from the north
or the east. From the time of Ibn Khaldun to Tamerlane it
was dominated alternately by Turks or Mongols. Hence,
geographically, there was no natural cohesion, such as there
was round the "frog-pond" world of the Mediterranean.

The second element is that of the government of the
territory, briefly held together by Alexander of Macedon,
conqueror of the Persians. The first century of the Christian
era witnessed Parthian domination and Roman spheres of
influence; the second century saw Roman expansion and
withdrawal; the third century the replacement of the
Arsacides by the Sassanians and the confrontation between
them and Rome, including the defeat of Valentinus and then
the exile of Patriarch Demetrianus from Antioch. This last,
the exile of Demetrianus, led to linguistic and jurisdictional
dilemmas, for there was an uneasy amalgam of indiginous
and displaced Christians. Ultimately there came the
divergence between the non-Chalcedonian Persian Christians,
or "Nestorians", and the para-Chalcedonian independents, or
"monophysites". The fourth Christian century saw the
established Roman frontier provinces of Mesopotamia,

Osrhoene, Augusta Euphratensis, Syria Coele, Augusta Libanensis and Arabia, with the final settlement of the frontier to include Edessa, but not Nisibis. It is not as though this settlement (following the death of Julian in battle against the Sassanians) led to stability, as the fifth century saw incursions by White Huns, and the death of Peroz at their hands in 484; and the early seventh century saw Sassanian instability, temporarily moderated first by Byzantine aid and then by Sassanian expansion into Mesopotamia and into Egypt. To this the Byzantine response was the capture of Ctesiphon in 628. Yet the greatest change was to come, with the Arab invasions of Palestine, Syria, and Iraq in 633, of Iran in 637, and the establishment first of all of Ummayid rule, subsuming all to Mecca; then from 749 the Abbassid triumph resulting in the establishment of a capital at Baghdad and the consequence, which might be termed *Drang nach dem Osten.*

The third influence is that of imperial concern, whether Roman/Byzantine, Sassanian, or Islamic, with religion. The fortunes of Christians varied with the location of their community. The oldest communities, clustered in the territory of the Arab kingdom of Edessa, in the area bounded by the Euphrates on the north and west and by the Bialik to the east, and by mountain ranges to the north. Other settlements were more scattered, in Adiabene to the north of the Great Zab and bounded on the west by the Tigris; and at such garrison towns as Singara and Dura Europos and Ctesiphon. The exiled Antiochenes seem to have been settled in Fars, to the south. But of the formal establishment of the churches there is little firm evidence. The ethos of habit and mind may be summarised, as Murray has done in *Symbols of Church and Kingdom,* as exegetical and symbolic. That is to say, its early memorials are such as the Gospel of Thomas and the Odes of Solomon, followed by the hymnody and commentaries of Ephrem and the *Demonstrations* of Aphrahat. Organisational writings stem from the fifth century onwards, with the series of conciliar documents such as can be found in Chabot's *Synodicon Orientale*, demonstrating that centralising of secular government at Seleucia Ctesiphon was matched by a centralised ecclesiastical jurisdiction at the same place. There could thus be a fifth patriarchate at Selecuica Ctesiphon as counterpart to the academic excellence of Edessa and Nisibis each in their turn, and as an equal to the other four patriarchates.

The consequence of all this is that Syriac Christianity was never in the position that Christianity was in the west, where first the conversion of Constantine and then the conversion of the Empire ended persecution and made consolidation possible. To the east, Christianity suffered from the consequences of Sassanian - Roman conflict as well as Sassanian policy. For example, Trajan's attempt to expand towards the Persian Gulf was a physical threat in the second century; the Christianisation of the Roman Empire and its coincidence with the Christianisation of Armenia led to a sense of encirclement on the part of the Sassanians. The debatable territory in the north led to incursions by both parties, with the resettlement of some of the local population being the result. Furthermore, under the Sassanians there were five, possibly six, persecutions, with the result that Christianity was never able to find a hold in official or Court circles: royal blood made death more certainly the consequence of conversion. This fact, more possible than any of the other three, suggests why the number of surviving manuscripts is so small, and the character of Syriac Christianity as societal and exegetical, hymnal and canonical rather than organisational and textual.

The fourth element is that of religious tradition, with the two components of monasticism and theology. These combine, and meet in the concept of personal loyalty. Yet they divide, because of the double nature of the Syriac church, part indigenous and part refugee. The indigenous element is inward-facing, conscious of an origin which is ancient, and finding survival in staying loyal to its local customs and remembered traditions, Cappadocian in theology. A clear demonstration of steadfastness in thought is found in a classical expression of Syriac theology, Šubḥalmaran's ܐܬܘܒܝܢܕ ܐܒܬܟ , on which see the present writer's "A Nestorian Creed: the Creed of Šubḥalmaran". It should be recalled that the Syriac disenchantment with Chalcedon had as much to do with that Council's magnification of Constantinople as with other matters. Partly as a result of persecution and external forces, partly because of the internal emphasis, the early Christian centres seemed to be in the mountains rather than in the river basins: Mardin and Amid (Diyarbakir); and otherwise, except for the schools of Edessa and Nisibis, village rather than city. But it will be realised that the main urban centres were within Osrhoene and Adiabene. It is interesting that some of the early manuscripts are associated with Amid and other places in the province of Mesopotamia. There are grounds for thinking that the old manuscript tradition comes from such places, notably Mardin, Amid, and Zapharan. It is in later years that the name of the Great Monastery is mentioned, at a time when the consolidation of Abbassid control was matched by the re-affirmation of ecclesial authority by Timothy I and his successors, notably Išodad. But no more can be said in what can only be, as suggested, an impressionistic account.

But the source of the Peshiṭta traditions can only be sought in such places as had Jewish communities, with

Christian ones coming into existence as impoverished neighbours - as at Dura Europos. The "divagations mégalomanes" of Syriac church history writing, to which Fiey refers, p. 1, in *Jalons pour une Histoire de lÉglise en Iraq* are attempts to embody convictions that Christianity whatever its shadowy origins, was of a piece with apostolic origin and consonant with the church in Antioch and the west. Yet it is autocephalous: Syriac Christianity regards Chalcedon as an irrelevance theologically as well as politically. It is no concern to Seleucia Ctesiphon that Byzantium should have patriarchal status, nor does it impress that Persian see when the simple language and practicality of the Cappadocians give way to conceptual speculations concerning the nature of Christ. Nor was it in their own interests of survival to make too much common cause with the traditional enemies of the Sassanians The existence of Syriac Christianity under the Sassanians, as later under Islam, could be precarious. The number and the severity of early persecutions ensured that much of its early literature was martyrology: Tisserant wrote in his article for *DTC*, "Nestorienne, L'Eglise", that Christianity had a history only if the local governor chose it to have one.

The last chapter has been, inevitably, of a speculative nature. Some idea may have been conveyed of the Peshitta's origin within an old Arab kingdom, its later dissemination through a network of monasteries; its divergence between the Roman influenced and the Persian dominated areas, its stabilising in the centres of monophysite and Nestorian episcopacy and monasticism, and the finally dominant authority's imposition or acceptance of what proved to be the dominant textual tradition. This chapter has attempted to weave into a synthesis elements from the manuscripts themselves, an outline history of the church in Iraq and Iran, elements of theology and of Roman and Islamic history in

order to provide some background for the text traditions
that are the concern of others as well as of text critics. The
relations between church and synagogue, the character of
each, the history of textual exegesis as well as transmision
are the basis of studies which are interdependent. Both
Targum and Peshiṭta are monuments of their communities.
And if Peshiṭta is a term of monophysite colour, used by
Michael the Syrian, whose predilection was for the Greek-
based Syro-Hexaplar, it is one final point to indicate the
symbiosis of church and text. Without further study of
context, the study of text alone is a barren endeavour. The
final words of a monograph on the Peshiṭta text of Leviticus
can most appropriately be some words, in a French
translation of the Chaldean poet Eliya de Šaqlawa, (1860-
1943) taken from p. 755 of Fiey's *Assyrie Chrétienne* II:

> *Qui donc a eu le bonheur   du Couvent Supérieur*
> *de connaître 'Emmanuel,   ou de Mossoul Gawriel?*
> *le couvent de Sawrišo',   du Zab baigné par les eaux?*

ENVOI

1. *Retrospect*

The monograph, whose purpose and plan were set out in the Introduction, has been completed. By way of an afterword, the results of this brief study of Syriac Leviticus are summarised, and an indication given of the directions that some further research might take. This afterword is also by way of retrospect, as the writer has been involved in the Leiden edition since the late 1960's, and as a participant in the project, has been aware of changes of editorial policy and their consequences. The conclusions follow the order of the chapters.

1. The choice of 7a1 as the basic text gives the advantage of a median text, from which it may be seen how earlier texts developed, and to recognise the kind of changes which took place in later years. Something can be said, therefore, about the kinds of changes which a manuscript may show, and the history of the changes as different patterns of manuscript grouping may be identified. The two, methodologically different, goals of demonstrating both the earliest text and the developing text make it imperative that apparatus be regarded as more important even than the text when making use of the Leiden edition for such purposes.

2. The emendation of 7a1 has resulted in a mixed text, in which the fortuitous nature and number of extant pre-tenth-century manuscripts has determined whether a reading is placed in the text or in the apparatus. It is by no means clear that any manuscript now surviving has the purity that

is desired by text critics; but it must be admitted that the
Leiden text printed represents a text which could have
existed, rather than one which did exist. To suggest that it is
a text which should have existed would serve only to
emphasise the subjective nature of textual criticism.

3. The examination of places where 7a1 has been
emended, despite support from older or from later
manuscripts, shows that the importance of variants lies more
in their kind than in their number. More than may appear
on the surface can lie in apparently insignificant detail.

4. The consideration of ancient manuscript tradition raises
rather than settles questions of relationship with MT. The
relation with MT is not one of mechanical equivalents but of
penetration to its presumed meaning. The matter of a
rendering's fidelity to the presumed original is more complex
than it seems at first sight to be. Nor is it the prerogative
either of age or of youth in manuscripts to be right in this
matter.

5. Attempts to reconstruct a Hebrew text from the Syriac
are subjective and hypothetical. Translation is the art of
rhetoric, and a study of language as well as text is important
if the purpose and origins of the version are to be grasped.

6. The unit of translation is larger than the word or even
the phrase. Larger units of sense must be considered, and an
attempt be made to discover what the Syriac and its
neighbour versions had in common as the task of translation
was approached. It must also be recognised that translations
for public use might be the result of public trial and error
and discussion, and so reflect more than one mind. It is
clear that there is not in the Syriac Leviticus a literary
dependence upon LXX or upon Targum material, but that
there is a shared universe of discourse: the Hebrew text and
a common cultural background.

7. The editors of printed editions were caught on the horns of a dilemma. There was a need for a text which was complete and representative, correct as far as knowledge of texts and their transmission allowed. But the editions were sponsored by, or intended for use by, communities of faith rather than independent scholarly study. Hence there were constraints on the degree of textual work that could be done, or admitted to being done.

8. Comparisons of the editions shows that their difference lies chiefly in their attitude to Le Jay and his adaptors, and secondly in presuppositions concerning age (or unfamiliarity) as criteria for assessing the value of a manuscript or a printed edition.

9. The divorce between text studies and studies of church and eastern history has given text studies an unreality. Recent moves have seen a bridging of the gap between disciplines, with the result that the history of the transmission of text takes its place within the history of the communities which used the texts. It is possible to see a defensible theory of local texts and the association of individuals and movements which explains the solidarity and the subsidiarity in the Peshiṭta version: the median text representing the movement from the old centres of Syriac Christianity in Osrhoene and Tur 'Abdin to Nitria through Mar Matta and Takrit; the standard version representing the movement from Sos to Mar Elia.

2. *Prospect*

A retrospect suggests a prospect. Further work should consider these points:

1. That a study of Peshiṭta be considered part of a study of the history and method of Jewish exegesis, rather than, as hitherto, the reverse.

2. That the Peshiṭta be seen as evidence for the history of language, and that biblical Syriac be viewed as biblical Aramaic is: a genre in its own right, resulting from the two pressures of the subject translated and the medium of its expression.

3. That Syriac Peshiṭta studies be related more to studies of Persian, Roman, Islamic, synagogue and church history, so that the version is more clearly seen equally as the product and the creator of Syriac Christianity.

4. That Peshiṭta studies be recognised as suggesting that while something like MT is the source of the version, there is not an over-hasty assumption that the Peshiṭta must fit within the pattern of MT, or LXX or the Samaritan. For Leviticus the material from Qumran caves 4 and 11 does not suggest that there is a connection to be found there: but further work is needed on these fragments before much can be said which alters present consensus.

5. That more study should be done of complete individual manuscripts. A strength of the Leiden method is that collaborators know the variants of a biblical book, but not the vagaries of a complete manuscript covering many books or indeed the whole of the Old Testament or complete bible.

This study has been brief. It is the writer's hope that it has been possible for the brevity to make for a comprehensible synthesis of different kinds of study, each with its own expertise; but that the result has not been so impressionistic that it fails to carry conviction. But engagement with the material has convinced the writer that the Peshiṭta is the product of a sensitivity to text and to the circumstances of those using it. Translation, like rhetoric, depends for its full effect upon the character of the speaker.

For, in Plato's words, an orator is

vir bonus dicendi peritus.

SELECT BIBLIOGRAPHY

Peshiṭta studies have been well served in Bibliography, and it is unnecessary to repeat information which is laid out in P. B. Dirksen, "The Old Testament Peshiṭta", in M.J. Mulder, ed. *Mikra: Text, Translation, Reading and Interpretation of the Hebrew Bible in Ancient Judaism and Christianity*, Assen/Maastricht - Philadelphia 1988; or in P.B. Dirksen, *An Annotated Bibliography of the Peshiṭta of the Old Testament*, Leiden 1989. Consequently only those works are listed which have been of significance in the preparation of this monograph and to which reference has been made in the text.

1. *Basic editions*

Syriac: *The Old Testament in Syriac according to the Peshitta Version*, edited on behalf of the International Organization for the Study of the Old Testament by the Peshitta Institute, Leiden. I, 2 + II, 1b *Leviticus* (D.J. Lane), *Numbers* (A.P. Hayman), *Deuteronomy* (W.M. van Vliet, based on material collected by J.H. Hospers and H.J.W. Drijvers), *Joshua* (J.E. Erbes), Leiden 1991.
MT: *Biblia Hebraica Stuttgartensia*, edd. K. Elliger and W. Rudolph, Stuttgart 1976/77.
LXX: *Septuaginta id est Vetus Testamentum Graece iuxta LXX Interpretes*, ed. Alfred Rahlfs, 6th ed., Stuttgart n.d.
Vetus Testamentum Graecum Auctoritate Academiae Scientiarum Gottingensis editum. Vol II,2 *Leviticus*, Wevers, J.W. with the assistance of Quast, U. (eds.) Göttingen 1986.
Targum: *Neofiti 1. Targum Palestinense MS de la Biblioteca Vaticana*, Tomo III, *Leviticus*, ed. A. Diez-Macho, Madrid 1971.
Targum Pseudo-Jonathan of the Pentateuch: Text and Concordance, ed. E.G. Clarke, Hoboken 1984.
The Bible in Aramaic, ed. A. Sperber, Leiden 1959-73.
The Targum Onkelos to Leviticus and Numbers (The Aramaic Bible, Vol 8), ed. B. Grossfeld, Edinburgh 1989

2. *Printed editions*

Biblia Hebraica, Samaritana, Chaldaica, Graeca, Syriaca, Latina, Arabica. Quibus textus originales totius Scripturae Sacrae etc; (Paris Polyglot) ed. G.M. le Jay *et al.* Syriac text of Pentateuch

        in vol. 6, ed. Gabriel Sionita, Paris 1645.
Biblia Sacra Polyglotta etc; (The London Polyglot), ed. BrianWalton,
        London 1657.
Vetus Testamentum Syriace, ed. Samuel Lee, London 1823.
Ketaba qaddiša ha(naw): de-diyatiqi 'attiqta surya'it, ed. Justin
        Perkins, Urmia 1852.
Pentateuchus Syriace post Samuelem Lee, ed. W.E. Barnes with the
        collaboration of C.W. Mitchell and J. Pinkerton, London 1914.
Biblia Sacra juxta Versionem Simplicem quae dicitur Pschitta, ed. C.J.
        David and G. Ebed-Jesus-Khayyat, Mosul 1887-1891.

                            3. *Other works*

Aejmelaeus, A. "Translation Technique and the Intention of the
        Translator", *VIIIth Congress of the International Organization
        for LXX and Cognate Studies*, ed. Claude Cox, Atlanta 1991.
Albert, M. "La Langue Syriaque. Remarques stylistiques", *Parole de
        l'Orient* XIII, 1986, pp. 225-248.
Albrektson, B. "Reflections on the emergence of a standard text of
        the Hebrew Bible", *VTS* 29, Leiden 1978, pp. 49-65.
----- *Studies in the Text and Theology of the Book of Lamentations*,
        Lund 1963.
Alexander, P.S. "The Targumim and the rabbinic rules for the
        delivery of the Targum", *VTS* 36, Leiden 1985, pp. 14-28.
Avinery, I. *Tahbîr ha-lašon ha-sûrît 'al pî targûm ha-pešittâ la-
        Hûmāš / Syntaxe de la Peshitta sur le Pentateuque*, (Hebrew
        with French summary), unpublished dissertation, Jerusalem
        1973.
Barnes, W.E. "A New Edition of the Pentateuch in Syriac", *JTS* 15,
        1913, pp. 41-44.
----- *An Apparatus Criticus to Chronicles in the Peshitta Version*,
        Cambridge 1897.
----- "The Printed Editions of the Peshitta of the Old Testament", *ET*
        9, 1897/98, pp. 560-562.
Bloch, J. "The Printed Editions of the Peshitta Old Testament", *AJSL*
        37, 1920/21, pp. 136-144.
Brock, S.P. "Aspects of Translation Technique in Antiquity", *Greek,
        Roman and Byzantine Studies* 20, 1979, pp. 69-87.
----- "Text History and Text Division in P-Isaiah", *The Peshitta: Its
        Early Text and History*, edd. P.B. Dirksen and M.J. Mulder,
        Leiden 1988, pp. 49-80.
----- "Towards a history of Syriac translation technique", *III
        Symposium Syriacum = OCA* 221, Rome 1983, pp. 1-14.
Cornill, C.H. *Das Buch des Propheten Ezechiel*, Leipzig 1886.
Chabot, J.B. *Synodicon Orientale*, Paris 1902.
Day, J. *Molech: A god of human sacrifice in the Old Testament*,
        Cambridge 1989.
De Boer, P.A.H. "Towards an edition of the Syriac version of the Old
        Testament", *PIC* 16 = *VT* 31, 1981, pp. 346-357.
Diez Macho, A. "The recently discovered Palestinian targum; its
        antiquity and relationship with the other targums", *VTS* 7,
        Leiden 1960, pp. 222-245.
Dirksen, P.B. "East and West, old and young, in the text tradition of
        the Old Testament Peshitta, *PIC* 19 = *VT* 35, 1985, pp. 468-484.
----- "The Ancient Peshitta MSS of Judges and their Variant
        Readings", *The Peshitta: Its Early Text and History*, edd. P.B.
        Dirksen and M.J. Mulder, Leiden 1988, pp. 127-146.
----- *The Transmission of the Text in the Peshitta Manuscripts of the
        Book of Judges*, Leiden 1971.
Drazin, I. *Targum Onkelos to Exodus. An English Translation of the
        Text with Analysis and Commentary*. New York, 1990.

Emerton, J.A. "The printed editions of the Song of Songs in the
    Peshitta version", *VT 17*, 1967, pp. 416-429.
----- "Unclean Birds and the Origin of the Peshitta", *JSS* 7, 1962, pp.
    204-211.
Fiey, J.M. *Assyrie Chrétienne*, 3 vols, Beirut 1986.
----- *Jalons pour une Histoire de l'Eglise en Iraq*, Louvain 1970.
----- *Mossoul Chrétienne*, Beyrouth 1959.
Fitzmyer, J.A. *The Dead Sea Scrolls: Major Publications and Tools
    for Study*, rev. ed., Atlanta 1990.
Freedman, D.N. "Variant Readings in the Leviticus Scroll, from
    Qumran Cave 11", *CBQ* 36, 1974, pp. 523-534.
Freedman, D.N. and Matthews, K.A., edd. with contributions by
    Hanson, R.S. *The Paleo-Hebrew Leviticus Scroll (11Qpaleolev)*.
    Winona Lake 1985.
Gelston, A. "Some Readings in the Peshitta of the Dodekapropheton",
    The Peshitta: Its Early Text and History, ed. P.B. Dirksen and
    M.J. Mulder, Leiden 1988, pp. 81-98.
----- *The Peshitta of the Twelve Prophets*, Oxford 1987.
Goodman, M. "Proselytising in Rabbinic Judaism", *JJS* 40, 1989, pp.
    175- 185.
Goshen-Gottstein, M.H. "Prolegomena to a Critical Edition of the
    Peshitta", *Studies in the Bible*, ScriptaHierosolymitana 8, ed. Ch.
    Rabin, Jerusalem 1961, pp. 26-67.
Grierson, H.J.C. *Rhetoric and English Composition*. London and
    Edinburgh, 2nd ed. 1945.
Gwilliam, G.H. "The Materials for the Criticism of the Peshitto New
    Testament, with Specimens of the Syriac Massorah", *Studia
    Biblica et Ecclesiastica* 3, ed. S.R. Driver, Oxford 1891, pp. 47-
    104.
Haefeli, L. *Die Peschitta des Alten Testamentes mit Rücksicht auf
    ihre textkritische Bearbeitung und Herausgabe*, Münster 1927.
Hayman, A.P. Review of M.D. Koster, *The Peshitta of Exodus*, *JSS*
    25, 1980, pp. 263-270.
Heinemann, J. "Early Halakhah in the Palestinian Targumim", *JJS* 25,
    1974, pp. 114-122.
Hospers, J.H. "Some Remarks with Regard to Text and Language of
    the Old Testament Peshitta", *Von Kanaan bis Kerala*, edd. W.C.
    Delsman *et al*, A.O.A.T. 211, Neukirchen-Vluyn 1983,   pp. 443-
    455.
Hunt, L-A. "The Syriac Buchanan Bibe in Cambridge: Book
    Illumination in Syria, Cilicia and Jerusalem of the later Twelfth
    Century", *OCP* 57, 1991, pp. 331-369.
Jenner, K.D. "Some Introductory Remarks Concerning the Study of
    8a1", *The Peshitta: Its Early Text and History*, edd. P.B. Dirksen
    and M.J. Mulder, Leiden 1988, pp. 235-240.
Kahle, P. *The Cairo Geniza*, 2nd ed., Oxford 1959.
Klein, M.L. *The Fragment Targums of the Pentateuch According to
    their Extant Sources*, Rome 1980.
Koster, M.D. *The Peshitta of Exodus: The Development of its Text in
    the Course of Fifteen Centuries*, Assen/Amsterdam 1977.
----- "Which came first: the Chicken or the Egg? The Development of
    the Text of the Peshitta of Genesis and Exodus in the Light of
    Recent Studies", pp. 99-126, *The Peshitta: Its Early Text and
    History*, edd. P.B. Dirksen and M.J. Mulder, Leiden 1988.
Lane, D.J. Review of Gelston's edition of *Dodekapropheton*, *JBL* 103,
    1984, pp. 107/10.
----- "A Nestorian Creed: the Creed of Šubhalmaran", *V Symposium
    Syriacum = OCA* 236, 1990, pp. 155-162.
----- "'A Turtle Dove or Two Young Priests' - A Note on the Peshitta
    Text of Leviticus", *II Symposium Syriacum = OCA* 205, 1975, pp.
    125-130.

----- "*Pervenimus Edessam*: The origins of a great Christian centre outside the familiar mediaeval world", *Florilegium* 3, 1981, pp. 104-117.

----- "Text, Scholar and Church: the place of the Leiden Peshitta within the context of scholastically and ecclesiastically definitive versions", *JSS* 38, 1993, pp. 33-47.

----- "'The best words in the best order': some comments on the 'Syriacing' of Leviticus", *PIC* 21 = *VT* 39, 1989, pp. 468-479.

Lund, S and Foster, J.A. *Variant Versions of Targumic Traditions within Codex Neofiti I*, Missoula 1977

Maori, Y. "Midrashic Influence on the Peshitta's Choice of Words", *Tarbiz* 46, 1977, pp. 212-230.

---- *The Peshitta Version of the Pentateuch in its Relation to the Sources of Jewish Exegesis*, Unpublished dissertation, Hebrew with English summary, Jerusalem 1975.

Matthews, K.A. "The Leviticus Scroll 11Qpaleo Lev and the text of the Hebrew Bible", *CBQ* 48, 1986, pp. 171-207.

Miles, J.R. *Retroversion and Text Criticism: The Predictability of Syntax in an Ancient Translation from Greek to Ethiopic*, LXX and Cognate Studies Series 17, Chico 1985.

Mingana, A. (ed) *The Book of Treasures by Job of Edessa*, Cambridge 1935.

Mulder, M.J. "Einige Beobachtungen zum Peschittatext von Ezechiel in seinen Beziehungen zum Masoretischen Text, zur Septuaginta und zum Targum", *Salvacion en la Palabra. Targum-Derash-Berith* (En memoria del professor Alejandro Diez Macho), ed. D. Muñoz Leon, Madrid 1986, pp. 463-470.

Murray, R. *Symbols of Church and Kingdom: A Study in Early Syriac Tradition*, 2nd. ed., Cambridge 1977.

Neusner, J. *History of the Jews in Babylon*, 5 vols, Studia Post Biblica 9, 11, 12, 14, 15, Leiden 1965-70.

----- *Sifra: An Analytical Translation*, 3 vols (Brown Judaic Studies 138-140), Atlanta 1988.

Nida, E.A. and Taber, C.R. *The Theory and Practice of Translation*, Leiden 1969.

Ohana, M. "Proselytisme et Targum palestinienne: Données nouvelles pour la datation de Neofiti I", *Biblica* 55, 1974, pp. 317-322.

Palmer, A. *Monk and Mason on the Tigris: The Early History of Tur 'Abdin*, Cambridge 1990.

Perles, J. *Meletemata Peschitthoniana*, Breslau 1859.

Peters, C. "Peschittha und Targumim des Pentaeuchs", *Mus* 48, 1935, pp. 1-54.

Pinkerton, J. "The Origin and Early History of the Syriac Pentateuch", *JTS* 15, 1914, pp. 14-41.

Puech, E. "Notes en marge de 11Q Paleo Levitique des fragments inédits et une jarre de la grotte 11", *RB* 96, 1989, pp. 161-183.

Rabbinowitz, J. *Mishnah Megillah Edited with Introduction, Translation, Commentary and Critical Notes*, Oxford 1931.

Rahlfs, A. "Beiträge zur Textkritik der Peschita", *ZAW* 9, 1889, pp. 161-210.

Rogers, J. *Reasons why a New Edition of the Peschito, or Ancient Syriac Version of the Old Testament, should be Published, with Variae Lectiones from Ancient MSS and Editions*, Oxford 1849.

----- "Professor Lee's Remarks on the Collation of Syriac MSS", *The Classical Journal* 46, 1821, pp. 245-249. (Under initials J.R.)

Rosen, F. and Forshall, J. *Catalogus codicum manuscriptorum orientalium qui in Museo Britannico asservantur. Pars prima, codices syriacos et carshunicos amplectens*, London 1838.

Rosenbaum, M and Silbermann, A.M. *Pentateuch with Targum Onkelos, Haphtaroth and Prayers for Sabbath and Rashi's Commentary*, London 1946.

Salvesen, A. *Symmachus in the Pentateuch*, *JSS* Monograph 15, Manchester 1991.

Samely, A. "The background of speech: some observations on the representation of Targumic Exegesis", *JJS* 39, 1988, pp. 251-260.

Schürer, E. *The History of the Jewish People in the Time of Jesus Christ*, Vol III, 1, rev. ed. Geza Vermes *et al*, Edinburgh 1986.

Sebök, T.A. (ed) *Current Trends in Linguistics*, The Hague 1970.

Talmon, S. "The Textual Study of the Bible", *Qumran and the History of the Biblical Text*, edd. F.M. Cross and S. Talmon, Cambridge (Mass) and London 1975, r.p. 1976.

Tisserant, E. Article, *Nestorienne, L'Église*, *DTC*, XI.1, 1931, cols. 157-323.

Tov, E. "Hebrew Biblical Manuscripts from the Judaean Desert: Their Contribution to Textual Criticism", *JJS* 39, 1988, pp. 5-31.

Van Koningsveld, P.S. "The Monastery of Bâqûqâ in Iraq and an old owner's entry in MS Syr. 341 of the Bibliothèque Nationale in Paris", *PIC* 20 = *VT* 36, 1986, pp. 236-240.

Vosté, J.-M. "La Pešitta de Mossoul et la révision catholique des anciennes versions orientales de la Bible", *Studi e Testi* 121, 1946, pp. 59-94.

Weitzman, M.P. "The Origin of the Peshitta Psalter", *Interpreting the Hebrew Bible*, ed. J.A. Emerton and S. C. Reif, Cambridge 1982.

----- "The Originality of Unique Readings in Peshitta MS 9a1", *The Peshitta: Its Early Text and History*, edd. P.B. Dirksen and M.J. Mulder, Leiden 1988.

Winter, M.M. "The origins of Ben Sira in Syriac, Part 1: *PIC* 12 = *VT* 27, 1977, pp. 237-253; Part 2: *PIC* 13 = *VT* 27, 1977, pp. 494-507.

Wright, W. *Catalogue of Syriac Manuscripts in the British Museum, acquired since the year 1838*, 3 vols, London 1870-1872.

York, A.D. "The Dating of Targumic Literature", *JSJ* 5, 1974, pp. 49-62.

----- "The Targum in the Synagogue and the School", *JSJ* 10, 1979, pp. 74-86.

SELECT INDEXES

1. READINGS DISCUSSED, MOSTLY IN CHAPTER SIX

Passages discussed in other chapters, especially Chapters 1 - 4 and Chapter 8, may be found in the normal verse order found under the heading of the appropriate discussion.

OTHER READINGS

Matt   23:15   114
Acts   2:10   114

2. AUTHORS QUOTED